Jan Helenus Ferguson

The Philosophy of Civilization

A Sociological Study

Jan Helenus Ferguson

The Philosophy of Civilization
A Sociological Study

ISBN/EAN: 9783337070816

Printed in Europe, USA, Canada, Australia, Japan

Cover: Foto ©Suzi / pixelio.de

More available books at **www.hansebooks.com**

THE PHILOSOPHY OF CIVILIZATION

A SOCIOLOGICAL STUDY

BY

JAN HELENUS FERGUSON

Author of "The Red-Cross Alliance at Sea," "Manual of International Law," *etc.*

THE HAGUE:
MARTINUS NYHOFF.

LONDON:
W. B. WHITTINGHAM & Co.

HONGKONG:
KELLY AND WALSH. (Lim.)

1889.

(All rights reserved by the Author.)

PRINTED AT THE PRESBYTERIAN MISSION PRESS, SHANGHAI, CHINA.

TO

JAMES LORIMER, LL.D.,

PROFESSOR OF LAW AND JURISPRUDENCE IN
THE UNIVERSITY OF EDINBURGH,
AUTHOR OF "THE INSTITUTES OF LAW,"

ETC., ETC.,

THIS STUDY IS DEDICATED,

AS AN HUMBLE MARK OF HOMAGE
TO HIGH INTELLECT AND ERUDITION THAT GUIDE,
THROUGH CONSCIENCE AND SYMPATHY,
TO THE GOAL OF RIGHTEOUSNESS.

PREFACE.

This essay is an attempt toward the organization of the general principles of sociology which are considered to constitute civilization in its broadest sense.

What the author aimed at was the construction of a system, to serve as a practical guide in the study of history, particularly with regard to the moral development of society, and, at the same time, to serve as a natural standard by which civilization could be tested.

The best method for judging civilization is to observe the natural development of the human mind in connection with the divers influences acting on this development. This method is followed in the present essay, which, in essence, is a dissertation on Moral-Mental Philosophy based on the theory of Evolution.

In the following Introductory Notes the necessary exposition is given with regard to the development of the subject-matter treated in the text. This latter has been condensed as much as clearness of statement would allow.

I embrace this opportunity to bring a special plea to the notice of my readers. Having been compelled, by official duty, to be constantly absent from the place where the printing of this work was going on, the correction of proof-sheets, which came to me, on my journeys in China, in an uncomfortably irregular manner, had to be done in a traveller's mood. I must therefore solicit the indulgence of my readers, with regard to the errors that have been overlooked at the proof-revisions.

China, 1889. J. H. F.

INTRODUCTORY NOTES.

The Introduction is the morphology of the subject, exhibiting its origin, growth and consummation. Here the notions which form the premises of the propositions, and their development to the end aimed at, are concentrated into one focus to establish a standpoint, from which all the statements and conclusions, propositions and theories can be passed in review. To this end it is necessary to give a summary of the subject-matter that is to be developed in the text. This we shall do now, part by part, as briefly as possible, and as explicitly as we can, referring, at the same time, to the text for further explanation.

Philosophy and Science.—Science deals with the principles and laws of phenomena. Each separate science points out beyond itself not merely to some other science, but also to some sphere where all sciences must meet if carried out to their utmost consequences. This sphere is the domain of Philosophy. As such, philosophy is the science of sciences.

There are two main methods of human inquiry in philosophy. 1.—We may start with the effects and proceed to find the causes, which is to take phenomena directly from experience and follow them up into their ultimate grounds, and thus—reasoning from a part to the whole, or from the particular to the general, from the concrete to the abstract, or from the senses to the ideas,—arrive at the conception of the necessary all-pervading *law*, through considering the entire empirical finite in the form of an intelligently jointed (*articulated*) system. This is called the *inductive* or *synthetical* method. 2.—We may postulate a speculative cause and make out a law by inference, and then proceed to test this law on some phenomena which have come under our experience, bringing down the general into the particular, reasoning from the abstract to the concrete, from the ideas to the senses, affirming of the latter the distinctive qualities of the former, and corroborating the former through the latter, thus arriving through deduction at the definition of the system of law or principles. This is called the *analytic* method. Truth must stand the test of both analysis and synthesis. By applying, *à priori*, a law, the ascertained result of former induction, to some new phenomenon, the law is tested at the same time as the phenomenon is empirically defined. This proves Sir William Hamilton's assertion that analysis and synthesis are two necessary parts of the same method of philosophy; each is the relative and correlative of the other.

From the foregoing follows, as Dr. Schwegler puts it, " that philosophy (as the thought totality of the empirical finite) stands to the empirical sciences in a relation of reciprocity, alternately conditioning and conditioned by them." * It is especially in connection with newly observed phenomena, which science has not yet quite succeeded in arranging into articulated systems, called laws of nature—*e.g.*, the theories of organic evolution, biology and sociology—that philosophical speculations must supply the missing links of empirical investigations,

---

* Dr. ALBERT SCHWEGLER : *Handbook of the History of Philosophy*.

to help science over the dead-points of its conclusions. It is, therefore, as idle to expect at any time the completion of philosophy, as to expect the completion of empirical science. Philosophy, exhibiting thought in various stages of development, has no other laws and principles than those according to which the mind thinks, and is thus the *natural* way to explain and test general scientific, social and political progress or retrogression,—for the laws and principles according to which the mind thinks are the same as those according to which the world is constituted. This is Hegel's fundamental philosophical principle, and in accordance with the saying of Pythagoras: "*Man is the measure of all things.*"

The Philosophy of Civilization.—The philosophy which reduces into systems of laws and principles the various phenomena of the social organism based on the biological organism of man, points out also how his mind becomes intellectually and morally developed, and is naturally the same indicator of the laws and principles by which all phenomena in which the human mind is concerned are to be explained. This is the philosophy of civilization, aiming at the systematizing of historical facts connected with the moral and intellectual development of the human mind, in relation to social organism

While the science of Sociology teaches the origin, growth and development of social organisms as concrete physiological phenomena, and the term Political Economy is applied to scientific inquiries into the material branch of social development, depending from the mere intellectual organism of the mind—*i.e.*, the physico-mental organism (§4)—the whole range of subjective activities of the mind, and the objective results of these activities, both moral and intellectual, **is embraced by** the Philosophy of Civilization.

The attempts which have been **made to** discover the laws of nature which regulate human affairs, *i.e.*, the laws **under** which social organism grow and develop, have not been in vain, as, among others, is proved **by the Philosophy of** History—which prepares the **way for the Philosophy of** Civilization—and its doctrine that the **mental and moral progress of the human race is measureable by a natural standard of civilization,** which is universally applicable (§42).

"That the reign of law," says Prof. Flint, "somehow extends over human affairs, that history has not been abandoned to caprice and chance, is not mere anarchy and chaos, but embraced within a system of order, more or less perfect, that amidst all its apparent confusion and incoherence there has been some sort of growth, some sort of development of the mind and spirit of the human race, that events are connected by some determinate relationships, and that one social state arises out of another to which it retains some correspondence in character—is a conviction which every man is likely to bring with him in the study of history."*

Men of cultivated mind must know well that the institutions and conditions of a nation are simply the application of the dominant morality of that nation, and that in every really sound political procedure this dominant morality—which is the *Spirit of* **Law** (described in §33)—should be constantly kept in view.

History is the record of facts, indicating the changes which the conditions of men are continually undergoing.

---
* Prof. ROBERT FLINT: *The Philosophy of History in Europe*, Introduction, p. 2.

The Philosophy of History is the interpretation of these facts—how they have come to be what they are, and what their relations are to the general development of other facts, the what, how, and why of changes, *i.e.*, the causes and effects of historical events; while the Philosophy of Civilization reduces these causes and effects of the events in the history of mankind, into a system of sociological phenomena and shows their connection with the moral and intellectual development of the human mind.

The Moral Law of Nature. The Moral Element in Nature.—"The intention of Moral Philosophy," says, Hutcheson, "is to direct men to that course of action which tends most effectually to promote their greatest happiness and perfection, as far as it can be done by observations and conclusions discoverable from the constitution of nature. These maxims or rules of conduct are therefore reputed as laws of nature, and the system or collection of them is called the *Law of Nature.*"* The constitution of nature, on which Moral Philosophy is based is the constitution of the human mind, and the name of Moral Law of Nature is applied to the order in nature in accordance with which the moral development of the human mind takes place. As such, it is the law determining the conditions of human co-existence and of progress towards the realization—so far as this is realizable—of perfect human co-existence, *i.e.*, of civilization. It is the same natural law *(Jus Naturale)* which Grotius and his followers defined as the law which is intrinsical and essential to all rational creatures. It represents the *Moral Element in Nature*, the ethical basis of Law *(Jus)* as stated in sections 32 and 40, constituting the

---
* HUTCHESON: *Moral Philosophy.* Vol. I., p. 1,

common ground of speculation, alike for the moral philosopher and the jurisprudent, while the task of the historico-philosopher is only possible when the Moral Element in Nature is the medium of connection of isolated facts of history, which the knowledge of the law governing the moral development of the human mind alone can explain.

The natural Evolution-process comprises the co-existent and co-extensive action of three factors, viz: heredity, variation and external action. These natural factors of evolution are continuous in moral-mental evolution, *i.e.*, in moral phenomena. But while in physical phenomena, the primordial factor of "natural selection" is the phisico-chemical medium of the organism,—in *moral selection* the medium of action is the Moral Element in Nature, while the moral senses are the primordial factors in the development of *moral varieties*. Like the physical structural variations in species, arising mostly from unknown combination of causes, generally comprized in the term "natural selection," so the varieties of the Moral-Mental organism of man differing one from another in moral advancement, are attributed to conditions collectively called in this sphere "moral selection."

The phenomenon of consciousness is the *Ego*. Professor Huxley holds that it is quite correct to call consciousness a phenomenon. He speaks of phenomena of consciousness and of "psychical phenomena," which is perfectly scientific, for the Ego of consciousness exists and does not require any demonstration, so that, in strict logic, it is an event of the natural evolution process in Nature.*

---
* *Science and Morals.*" Fortnightly Review. December, 1886. p. 790 and 797

In the same scientific proceedings the existence is proved of the Moral Senses, *Conscience* and *Sympathy*, and, through these, the Moral Element in Nature, of which Energy they are the effects and the manifestations in the evolution-process of the moral-mental organism of man (§5).

The chief factor of evolution of the social organism is the state of mind of the people. This state of mind is the effect of the moral senses, the agents through which the motives for outward action originates in the mind; but no attempt has been made as yet by evolutionists to bring this active agency scientifically into account. The study which we venture to submit for consideration in these pages, is the expounding of this law of the moral senses, called the Moral Law of Nature, under which all normal development of the social organism, of which the State is the evolved result, can be classed. This law represents the conditions under which the intellectual and moral development of human beings exist in their relations to each other, as the naturally evolved result of their biological organism.

Sociology based on Biology.—According to the theory of the modern scientific school of biologists, social phenomena, in spite of their much greater complexity, are essentially analogous with those of inferior cosmic life. Mr. Cattaneo, in his recent work *Le Colonie Lineari e la Morfologia del Molluschi*, distinguishes four degrees of animal individuality, viz., (1) *plastides*, *i.e.*, living cells or any other primordial elements, which consist of mere amorphous organic matter; (2) *merids*, *i.e.*, aggregates of plastides; the merids forming the living organic being called (3) *zoids*, *i.e.*, autonomous individuals, uniting, like the other superior animals, with individuals of their own series for preservation of species. Colonies of zoids, in couples or pairs, families, tribes, societies, are called by him (4) *dems*. Social life thus begins with the individuals of the series *zoids*, and this is the natural starting point of the science of sociology. The aim of sociology is the investigation of the natural connections between individuals and the social organism formed by them.

Thus the science of sociology is based on that of biology, both having the same philosophical theory in common, viz., the theory of organic evolution.

There is, however, one essential difference between these two branches of general physiological science; that is, the difference of the sphere in which the factors or agents of evolution are working in the one and in the other. Though Biology, and its crowning development Sociology, may have the same object in contemplation, viz., the human being, yet, while the data of biology are discernible by direct empirical investigation (though these data may be sometimes merely the effects of undemonstrated causation, as *e.g.*, in most cases of organic evolution), sociological data, composed of motives formed in the human mind, require a subjective synthetic process to prove their objective truths, which have to pass the dangerous and often fatal crucible of subjective exercises, before being brought by the purifying process of philosophical speculation into connection with logical facts. The consequence of this is that the dialectics of sociological philosophy differ in the essential data of mental agencies from that of biology, while the greater complexity of social phenomena necessitates hypotheses and postulates which take more frequent and ample function in the speculations of Sociology than in those of Biology.

Spirit of Creation. **Life,** in organisms of all forms and definitions, appears as continuous minute changes in the units of the organism,—whether these units be atoms, **cells or** individuals,—to bring internal co-existences in correspondence with external co-existences,—or, as Mr. Herbert Spencer puts it,* " **the** continuous adjustment **of internal relations to** external **relations,**"— *i.e.*, the adjustment of means to ends. Here we have, in this effect of the evolution process, the indication of the **Cosmic** Power which is treated in this study **under the** name of Spirit of Creation *(Werdekraft der Natur).*

If we cannot discover truth by **direct investigation,** it is better to learn it by **inference** than not to find it at all; postulates and hypotheses **are** admissible on this assumption. Now, "biologists **in general,"** says Mr. Herbert Spencer,† " agree that in the present state of the **world no such** thing happens **as** the **rise of** a **living creature out of** non-living **matter,"** and, **it not** being in **any way** proved how, **at a remote period in** the past, **life has been** originated on the earth's surface, we have no other choice, scientifically speaking, then to postulate an energy, **through** which inorganic matter was **transformed** into organic matter, in other words **a** power as the originator **of life.** And *life* being irrefragably the absolute motive factor **of** organic evolution **in** all its branches, the primordial energy which originated life, through successive transformations and complications of inorganic **matter** into organic, is thus not only the motor of growing development of organic matter, but also of all motions of transformations, in inorganic **as well as** in organic matter.

* " The *Data of* **Ethics."** Chapt II.; §7.
† " The Factors **of Organic Evolution,"** *Nineteenth Century,* May, 1886, p. 769.

This universal power is postulated under the name *Spirit of Creation*, as defined in §2 of this study, and represents physically the persistency of force, in all its bearings; it is, in fact, the indestructible Force.

The breach in the continuous chain of Evolution being unaccounted for by Science, for reason of the essential distinction between organic and inorganic matter,—a special act of Creation is thus postulated, as taking place through the outside action of an independent constructive agent, which,—in a mode as yet unexplainable by human investigation,—quickens certain modes of collocation of matter into *life*. This energy of life is latent in *matter*, pregnant of the primordial energy bestowed on it by the creative Motor of the cosmic nebula.

Creation does, by no means, imply an abrupt appearance of an isolated capricious fact, but an unavoidable phenomenon, although its place in the chain of events may not always be perceivable or comprehensible to our present state of consciousness. Whether the phenomenon has come into existence, through visible transformation of energy, or through invisible gradual changes in the process of evolution, the result is, in either case, the manifestation of the same Ultimate Cause, postulated under the name of Spirit of Creation.

It is obvious, through physical science, that surrounding influences of gravitation, heat, light and the mechanical and chemical actions of water, moisture, air and other media, would act organically on individual plastides and their aggregates—(which now depend on these media for the continuation of their existence)—in the reverse of a growing development, and would cause their immediate decomposition, were it not for the counteracting of these otherwise destructive processes, by the—scientifically speaking—yet unknown **vital condition,** commonly called *vital energy,*—which represents the Spirit of Creation,—the cause of concrete existences and the motor of growing developments.

Thus the term Spirit of Creation is a postulate necessary for the support of reason, which can neither think of these series of effects held in equilibrium by life as interminable nor as terminable. It is also a purely scientific hypothesis, representing that beginning of *motion,* producing motions, agitation or alteration, working on the physical senses and on the brain;—which Hobbes called "*endeavor,*" and which he, from his standpoint, sustained as proved by scientific researches, to be the basis of all our knowledge of the external and internal world. "We do not even know what it is that moves; we only know that when some modes of motion pass into other modes, we perceive what we understand by matter," says Mr. G. Romanes* with regard to our knowledge of the external world.

As such, the expression Spirit of Creation stands good as a postulate for the genesis of both inner and outward stimuli, and represents, as a universal natural force or power, the ultimate cause not only of organic evolution, but also of all the interdependent actions and reactions of motions and their results of agitation and alteration in the cosmos. The term Spirit of Creation is thus proposed to include in its agency all morphological phenomena which are scientifically ascribed to various, as yet, hypothetical causes, producing concrete actions, inner and outer, direct and indirect, and whether these actions are produced in conformity with Mr. Spencer's theories of

---

* "Mind and Motion," *Contemporary Review,* July, 1885, p. 76.

"survival of the fittest" and "outer influence of media as primordial factor," by the Darwinian theory of "natural selection," or by the theory of Prof. George Romanes called "physiological selection." * While, on the evidence of these great thinkers of our century, scientific inquiries with regard to the causes of organic evolution, from the physical standpoint, are yet far from being conclusive, from the moral or so-called spiritual point of view, examinations into these causes are not even attempted as yet. We may therefore safely legalize the term Spirit of Creation, as a scientific postulate,—especially in Sociology, where the human mind is the principal factor—to represent the ultimate cause of social evolution, which works by inner as well as by outer actions—*i.e.*, by the inherent mental agency of Intuition, as well as by the outside or non-ego agency of environment.

Intuition.—The condition of the Ego which is called Intuition is defined in §10 as the "reflex-action" of consciousness. Like as the neuro-muscular system is affected by mechanical movements, called reflex-actions, in response to physical stimuli, evoked by external objects through a sensory nerve to the nerve-centre, so do intuitive ideas exist in the mind as an instinctive reflex-action of our consciousness. The intuitive ideas are produced by the inherited effects of evolved experiences, through the evolution-process of the human mind (§5), and serve—through the thus inherited feelings,—as motors or internal stimuli for subsequent ideas or thoughts, which determine the motives of the will to set forth volition, as described in sections 18 and 29. Through Intuition the mind

---

* HERBERT SPENCER: "The Factors of Organic Evolution," *Nineteenth Century*, April and May, 1886. GEORGE J. ROMANES: "Physiological Selection," *Nineteenth Century*, January, 1887.

arrives at the conception of *Primary Truths* or *First Principles* which form the basis of all sciences (§13).

The *Theory of the Moral Senses* is based on that of Intuition. This theory is not transcendentalism; it does not transcend the fundamental principles of human knowledge, for no state of consciousness has been better experienced than that of Conscience and of Sympathy and nothing more reasonable than Justice and Benevolence combined.

Moral **Mental Organism.** *Moral Senses.* *Spirit of Law.*—Professor Huxley said in his speech at the unveiling of the statue of Darwin in the South Kensington Museum, while denying that the ceremony was a scientifical sanction of the Darwinian theory of evolution exclusively, that "science commits suicide when it adopts a creed." Philosophy also, and especially moral philosophy, proclaims its impotence when admitting as its premises any scientific theory which does not cover the whole ground.

"It is imperative," says J. S. Mill in his Logic,* "to determine exactly the attributes which a name is to express, if it is to be used as an instrument of thinking or as a means of communicating the results of thought." Thus far we have accounted for the introduction, as hypotheses, of the terms "Moral Law of Nature," "Moral Element in Nature," "Spirit of Creation" and "Intuition," and the ideas they have to convey in Sociology. For the explanation of other terms, viz., "Moral Mental Organism," "Moral Senses," "Public Consciousness," "Spirit of Law"—which is commonly called the "Spirit of the Time" or "Spirit of the Age" (*Zeitgeist*)—and

---
* Book IV., Chapter iv.

Common Sense—all verifiable realities—we refer our readers to the respective sections in the text where these expressions are defined (§§5, 15, 32, 33, 34, and 36). In case their actuality as elements of the human mind may not already be sufficiently proved by the conviction of consciousness, we cherish the hope that their usefulness, as connecting links in the chain of thought, may justify their introduction into sociology, at all events, as necessary postulates.

Common Sense, as described in section 34 of this essay, is not the culture of intellect but of the moral senses. It is the human instinct of righteousness,—*i.e*, of what is just and benevolent combined,—the spontaneous working of the moral senses, Conscience and Sympathy, which combined originate the impulses of the Good (§15).

Common Sense is that consolidated comprehension of truth (the basis of Faith) which unites, in compact meaning, all that could be said to complete consciousness and conviction. What cannot be told short and convincible is doubtful. Truth does not require the long spinning out of arguments, neither elaborate preparation of premises; it comes out boldly and unprepared, and is at once recognized as truth by *genuine* common sense.

Common sense is *impartial but not neutral*,—that is, it gives full value to the arguments on both sides, but it has the courage of its opinion, and does not withhold its decision, to whatever side the truth may lead. Its test lies in the conception of the Good.

Here we have an instance of the influence that the Moral Element in Nature exercises on the progressive social evolution of the human race.

Laws of Nature.—With regard to actions attributed

to "Laws of Nature" in this study, we must state that, by suggesting the general primordial agent, termed Spirit of Creation, we have for brevity's sake combined the forces of this general source of action in Creation with the idea *Laws of Nature*. The motive for so doing we trace to unimpeachable scientific sources. The regular and persistent recurrence of surrounding conditions can certainly, by the definition given by Mr. Darwin and Mr. Herbert Spencer, be called a law of nature, and styled (*e.g.*) the *law of surrounding conditions*, just as the systematized ascertained persistency of the agency of evolution styled "*direct action of surrounding conditions*," is regarded by Darwin as the cause or inducement to variations in organisms. Now, if this truly realistic expression—"direct action of surrounding conditions"—is allowed to convey scientifically the idea of an active agency in organic evolution—which surely it is—why should it be less scientific to speak in a hypothetical way, of the "influence of the Moral Law of Nature" on men's actions—thereby meaning the influence of the conditions of consciousness, called Conscience and Sympathy, on the will. The agency which produces these mental conditions is not yet empirically proved, any more than the force which originates the "direct actions of the surrounding" knowable and unknowable or undemonstrated "conditions" in the science, or rather, philosophy of organic evolution. In this sense we ventured to postulate a *Standard of Civilization* (§42) as the outcome of mental conditions brought on through the moral senses conscience and sympathy, for brevity's sake called the Moral Law of Nature.

In his work, "Animals and Plants under Domestication," (from which different passages are quoted by Mr. Herbert Spencer in his recent papers, "The Factors of

Organic Evolution," *Nineteenth Century,* April and May, 1886), **Mr.** Darwin speaks of "condition" as an active power capable of direct action, viz., "*There are good evidences that the power of changed conditions accumulates,*"...further, "*some variations are induced by the direct action of the surrounding conditions on the whole organization*" (Vol. II., p. 270). To speak of the "power" or "direct action" of certain "conditions" as active agencies in organic evolution, is not more scientific than the postulating of the influences of surrounding "moral conditions" in the evolution of social organism. What we contend is that it is not personating the cause, or in any sense unscientific, to admit in sociology, as inducing agents of the evolution of social organism, certain conditions of mind, ascertained and corroborated as existent and persistent, over and over again, by similar states of consciousness of different individual minds in the same series or stage of evolution (§5), and to postulate the "power" and "direct action" of these "conditions" as effectively influencing the human will, and, through this, man's outward actions. In this sense, the power and direct action of the conditions of the mind, called conscience and sympathy, are set forth under the term Moral Law of Nature, as the inner "stimuli" to outward activity.

In the introduction of the work which has just been quoted, (p. 6) Mr. Darwin says: "For brevity's sake I sometimes speak of natural selection as an intelligent power...I have also often personified the word Nature, for I have found it difficult to avoid this ambiguity; but I mean by nature only the aggregate action and product of many natural laws, and by laws only the ascertained sequences of events." In the same sense the **expression** "laws of nature" is used in this work, though for the sake of brevity and for easier comprehension, laws of nature are spoken of as intelligent powers, in the same manner as we speak of "the force of circumstances," of the "rising" and "setting" of the sun, the "course" of the stars, etc., using subjective appearances to arrive at the objective reality.

The Dialectics. With regard to the forms used in the process of thought in this work, the dialectics will perhaps be found wanting in distinctness. But all systems of philosophy suffer more or less on this score; this is the natural consequence of human language. An original idea is a concrete image, when well formed in the mind, but also a living image, which cannot be completely portrayed in the language in which it finds expression. To express abstract ideas we have only concrete symbols; hence the synthesis in which the idea is put forward is often imperfect. The natural cause is to be looked for in the mechanical construction of human intellect, which can only be helped through its dead points by the impulses of intuition. Indeed, without the stimulating vitality of intuition the mechanism of reason would stop just at the point where its action is most wanted for the conception of primary truths, which, as said before, form the basis of all sciences (§§9 and 10).

Design in Nature. Investigations into natural causation show that events are not fortuitous; chance is unthinkable, every event has a cause, and, for the same reason, an end. Causation is not definable by Empirical Science. The perceptible efficient "motions" toward that which happens are called Agents. With regard to phenomena, causation could be called the Free Will of Nature and what are called Laws of Nature, her Volition.

Design in Nature manifests itself as Motor of Evolution and as the individual free will of organisms. This latter could be called *subjective* or *individual* design; imparted to matter, in the primordial germ of energy emanating from the Creative Cosmic Power, in the form of Motion, it is manifested in the inclinations (also called "habits") of Plants, the instincts of Animals and the free will of Man.* From the highest known development to the lowest perceptible organism or cell,—all quickened by the Spirit of Creation,—strive and struggle for existence and development in the universal evolution process. But it is obvious that *all* will not reach the end, or, with other words, comply with the progressive impulse of the evolution-process; many apparent "blunders" and "failures" are to be seen in this perpetual transformation of energy. For one case of successful adaptation of means to ends in the organic world there are a hundred deviations which we call "failures,"—not alone in the lower but also in the higher orders of organism.

When we cannot comprehend the *objective design* of the Motor of Evolution we call it "chance"; when we see any *subjective* or *individual* design of an organism unaccomplished, we call it "waste." And yet, we know that chance is not thinkable in the theory of Evolution and that matter and force are indestructible; so that it is unscientific to speak of *waste* in Nature, and where there is no waste there is no *failure*. That not every form of organism or variation needs to reach its utmost development in evolution, is comprehensive in this theory.

---

* Darwin's remarkable observations with regard to the habits of climbing plants, and animals under domestication, are so many expositions of the subjective design existing in Plants and Animals. (CHARLES DARWIN "On the movements and habits of Climbing Plants." IDEM "The variation of Animals and Plants under Domestication").

The Motor of Evolution is the energy which underlies the factors of organic evolution, for these "factors," whatever be their nature or conditions, could not be *factors*, without the transmutation of energy,—the origin of which we call the Spirit of Creation,—into mechanical or other forces. From this it is obvious, that all factors of organic evolution, which perform the individual or subjective design of evolving organisms, are the results of the objective design of the Spirit of Creation.

Here we can trace the basis of human subjective design, called *free will* (§18, p. 24).

The world of physical science is but a part of Nature and as Nature finds its consummation in the moral-mental organism of man, it is only when contemplating Nature with all the faculties of our mind that we can conceive the work of the absolutely wise and all-powerful Creator as a whole. And these broader views we owe to the progress of the Science that investigates not only and exclusively physical phenomena, but advances our knowledge in conformity with the development of the human moral-mental organism. Thus came the theory of organic evolution as a real revelation to Science, being unfolded to the human common-sense, in conformity as our knowledge of Nature advances; and as the vast field of Creation displays itself before our cleared vision, a deeper insight in biology enables us to observe "the wisest and most exquisite ends" of the Creator's design in Nature.

Physical Science cannot determine the laws of causation; but science is not a mere record of isolated discoveries; it insists that each fact is an offspring of some preceding fact, and the parent of some subsequent fact,—and thus impresses the conviction of the final unity of all causes into one Ultimate Cause.

This is the teleological view of *Design*, which, as demonstrated in this work (§80, pp. 200-213) is conspicuously manifested through all Creation on Earth,—from the searching tendrils of the vine and the instinct of animals to the moral motives of man in defining the course of Civilization.

What is Civilization? On pages 34, §28, and 226, §80, we have said that there are two sorts of *Evil*, viz : the subjective and the objective evil. There are also two sorts of *Good*, the subjective good which counteracts the subjective evil in the human mind and the objective good which constitutes the **Laws** of Society, as the practical results of Civilization, to ameliorate **objective evil.** Hence the definition of civilization,—as given in §§ 41 and 42,—is the actual state of Society in the process of transforming the subjective conception of the Good into objective practical Good, which simply means that Civilization is the amelioration of Evil in social life.

This is the thesis of the Philosophy of Civilization expounded in these pages.

After this brief **summary** in demonstration of **our** subject, we cherish the hope, that our reader, in appreciation of the end proposed by **our** task, **may** be persuaded to go through this new field of researches and expositious we offer him here for consideration.

When doing this patiently and with **the** sensibility of the vastness of the task, we may **rely** also on his indulgence with regard to the manifold shortcomings in this essay, of which nobody is more convinced than the author himself.

Chapter I.

THE MORAL LAW OF NATURE.

§1. The Universal Law of Nature.—§2. The Spirit of Creation. Its agency the Motor of Evolution. Is the manifestation of the Soul.—§3. Hypotheses in general.—§4. Hypothetical demonstration of the Universal Law of Nature in its course of Evolution.—§5. The Moral-Mental Organism of Man. Consciousness of the Good. The struggle for existence between the moral and the material element in the human mental organism.—§6. Origin of Species —§7. The Links of Evolution.—§8. The impossibility of demonstrating the primary motor of Evolution.—§9. Intellect.—§10. Hypothesis regarding Intuition. Feeling. Spiritual Feeling. Inspiration.—§11. The Soul.—§12. The Ego of Consciousness.—§13. The Conception of Primary Truths.—§14. The Good.—§15. The Moral Senses Conscience and Sympathy. Righteousness.—§16. Evolution of the Moral Senses.—§17. Virtue. Happiness.—§18. Moral Actions. Free Will. Volition. Motive.—§19. The Standard of the Good.—§20. Origin of Evil and its control.—§21. Love. Friendship.—§22. Vice.—§23. Attention on the Good controls Evil in the Mind —§24. Religion.—§25. Moral Doubt —§26. Christianity.—§27. The Creator.—§28. The Occasions of Stumbling.

§1. Social life is the natural consequence of the human organism, and, as such, necessarily develops itself in conformity with the Universal Law of Nature.

Nature is the word used to express the aggregate comprehension of all phenomena in the universe, and of their causes and effects, with the laws derived therefrom, and whether we are conscious of them through our moral senses or conceive them through our physical senses.

The Universal Law of Nature is the composite effect of the various natural conditions which are at work in the Universe, and which are called Laws of Nature in consequence of the persistency and regularity with which they appear to our consciousness.

§2. As laws are the uniform modes in which forces are manifested, and effects always indicate causes, we are accustomed to call the causes of these natural conditions the forces or powers of Nature. For the same reason the Universal Law of Nature, which is the constructing unity of the systems formed by the Laws of Nature, is correlative to the idea of a Universal Cause, Force or Power, and as this First Cause is made known to us by irrefragable induction as the absolute motor, force or life of all that we are conscious of in Nature, it may be represented, by way of a hypothesis which is based on natural phenomena, by the term Spirit of Creation.

By this term we intend to represent the causes of creation and development or evolution, combined in one and the same power, in order to express the simultaneous actions of producing and sustaining, coming into existence and expanding through growth, all in conformity with those sequences of events and causations which are called the Laws of Nature.

The term Spirit of Creation is the scientific equivalent for the theological expressions *Creator* and *Providence* combined, as well as for the philosophical appellation *Ultimate* **Cause** or *Ultimate Scientific Ideas* (§8).

The Spirit of Creation is manifested in all phenomena of Nature, from the forces in inorganic matter up to the highest development of the human mind by its innate **working** agency through the whole series of Nature's evolution.

The theory of *evolution* in its broadest sense, is based on the assumption of an absolute, general and **persistent** active force, permeating all inorganic and organic **nature, and** which, uniting all concrete phenomena in nature, can be regarded as establishing **the unification of matter with** organism, in which it is the originating cause of *life*, carrying it to its highest development on earth, which is the human *moral-mental organism*, and where it is called *soul*. This ever dominant and inherent working force of Nature is what we postulate here as the Spirit of Creation.

We would further state that, while the expression Spirit of Creation is intended to convey the idea of the Universal Ultimate Cause, as innate working effect of forces on matter and organism in general, the term Motor of Evolution, is used to represent the inherent causation of organic life. Perhaps these and other expressions used in this work might appear not quite suitably chosen, but, while we must regret the necessary limitation of the dialectic, we are confident that the reader will arrive at a sufficiently clear conception of the forces indicated, to speculate with logical conclusions on their manifestions, when contemplating their effects in Nature as objects of empirical science.

Concluding on the foregoing propositions we find that in inorganic and organic evolution, the Spirit of Creation is presented to our senses by the forces in matter and by the vital element in organisms. In the evolution of the mind, on the other hand, the Spirit of Creation is presented to our senses by that consciousness of its influence which is called the *Soul*, that is to say, the highest expression of the motive agency of the Spirit of Creation. The subject of the soul will be treated hereafter (§11).

§3. It is to Matter and Force, which constitute the primary manifestations of the Absolute, that independent phenomena must be traced.* But the inductive philosophy of external facts, called Science, is not yet able to trace all natural influences, by consistent induction from *external* facts only, to their primordial causes, nor has Science reached as yet " that highest

---

* "A further inference was, that Philosophy, as we understand it, must not unify separate concrete phenomena only; and must not stop short with unifying separate classes of concrete phenomena, but must unify all concrete phenomena. If the law of operation of each factor holds true throughout the Cosmos, so too, must the law of their co-operation. And hence in comprehending the cosmos as conforming to this law of co-operation, must consist that highest unification which Philosophy seeks."—HERBERT SPENCER. First Principles. § 186.

unification which Philosophy seeks." We are often hardly aware of the data of the Laws of Nature, which in scientific language are called *phenomena*. Therefore philosophical or speculative reasoning, based on *internal* facts, *i.e.*, *consciousness*, must often supply the place of Science, and has, under the name of *hypothesis* to be slipped into some scientific formula, to pave the way to comprehension by the mind of any inductive structure, based on the simplest truth. Such is the case with all methods adopted for the purpose of explaining the course of the development of the Laws of Nature. Thus it is also with the interpretation of developing phenomena in the description of organic evolution, through reproduction, perpetuation and modifications of the forms of living beings,— in the manner described by Professor Darwin in his famous books entitled "The Origin of Species" (the term Species being the scientific equivalent of forms of organisms) and "The descent of Man." Darwin's theories regarding the causes of the developmental changes in the structural forms and physiological functions and properties of organisms, called variation, adaptation, survival of the fittest, etc., are hypothetical statements of causation, which (whatever may be the controversial nature of philosophical assumptions, when taken up in scientific propositions) go far towards forming a development hypothesis explanatory of vegetable and animal organisms, which are the manifestations of the Spirit of Creation. Thus hypotheses may aid the human mind to infer, with the nearest possible accuracy and with a prestige of scientific plausibility, the existence of causes which it could not arrive at through direct demonstration.* These hypothetical propositions are at

---

* Evolution, whether by the process of successive changes of conditions "through multiplication of effects," as Mr. Herbert Spencer described it before Darwin, or by natural selection, which is the Darwinian theory, or whether both combined, (as Mr. Herbert Spencer accepts it, in the Fourth Edition [1880] of his "First Principles"), is as good as an established fact of history, but the cause or causes of these effects are yet a hypothesis, and it is with truth that Professor Huxley said on the evidence of palaeontology: "the evolution of many existing forms of animal life from their predecessors is no longer an hypothesis but an historical fact; it is only the nature of the physiological factors to which that evolution is due which is still open to discussion." (Encyclopaedia Britannica, 1878).

present indispensable to natural science in general, but particularly to physiology and psychology, in order to supply the want of sufficient data to fill up the gaps yet remaining in the corroboration of facts, as well as to make up for the imperfection or inadequacy of our *physico-mental organism*, which comprehends man's physical and intellectual faculties. The latter are called *reason*. "The privilege," says Professor Oscar Schmidt, "on which the progress of Science generally relies, is that of investigating, according to determined points of view, and accepting probabilities as truth in the **garb of scientific** conjecture or hypothesis."* "Do not allow yourselves," says Professor Huxley, "to be misled by the common notion that a hypothesis is untrustworthy simply because it is a hypothesis. It is often urged in respect to some scientific conclusion that, after all, it is only a hypothesis. But what more have we to guide us in nine tenths of the most important affairs of daily life than hypotheses, and often very ill-based ones? So that in Science, where the evidence of a hypothesis is subjected to the most rigid examination we may rightly pursue the same course." Further on he says: "There is a wide gulf between the thing you cannot explain and the thing that upsets you altogether. There is hardly any hypothesis in this world which has not some fact in connection with it which has not been explained; but that is a very different affair to a fact that entirely opposes your hypothesis. In this case all you can say is that your hypothesis is in the same position as a good many others."†

Hypotheses are, with regard to the nature of the evidence required for their verification, of three distinct classes, viz: *physical, mental,* and *moral,* and must accordingly be tested by evidence answering to the correlative Laws of Nature. A hypothesis based on physical causes must be verified through demonstration of the working of the forces inherent in matter.

---

* Prof. Oscar Schmidt. The Doctrine of Descent and Darwinism. Chapter on the Pedigree of Vertebrate Animals. (Henry S. King & Co., London, 1875.) p.248.
† Prof. Thomas H. Huxley. Lectures on "Origin of Species." Humboldt Library of Popular Science Literature, vol. i., pages 518 and 529.

It is to be tested by the Physical or Chemical **Laws**. A hypothesis built on purely logical bases is to be verified through abstract mathematical or logical reasoning. It is to be tested by **the** Mental Law. Finally, a purely moral hypothesis requires verification by inward conviction of what is morally right or **wrong**. Its test lies in the Moral Law. The latter is the most subtile of all, **as being the** youngest Law of Nature, that is, the latest ascertained sequence in the chain of natural evolution **in** which the human mind shares; a law whose abstruse subtilty necessitates our pushing our investigations into tenuous and recondite truths, based on reason and feeling combined. Though differing in modes of verification, hypotheses of all classes have this criterion in common, that they must be based on the assumption of factors competent to produce all phenomena **forming the** respective Law of Nature, of which the *verae causae* are undemonstrated or inconceivable to our mind. This is the standard **rule** in all attempts to determine Laws of Nature, whether physical, mental, or moral, and on this principle **the** following hypothesis of the general development of the Universal Law of Nature is proposed.

§4. A general observation of the Universal Law of Nature, as it appears on our globe, indicates that the development **of** Nature has taken **place** gradually, as by stages, which may **be** called Stages of Creation, while the influence of the Spirit of Creation, which is the originative cause of the forces operative in Nature, is manifested through all these stages, admitting of no line of demarcation between the different stages,—**for** science may divide and classify, but nature remains a whole;—so that by **the** term stage we mean **merely** a generalization **of** groups of bodies or objects in which a particular force **or law** of nature becomes more conspicuous to our observation.

Submitting six **of** these stages to a general review, and including what we think to be the *beginning* **of** the evolution of matter (that is to say the *first* **stage**) **up** to the stage in which we exist at present (that is to say the *sixth* stage), we find that the evolution of the **Universal Law** of Nature, that is the gradual development of **the** different forces of Nature, is manifested as follows.

When Matter,—which **term** is but a symbolic name to designate that simple substance, which could as **well be** called *consolidated* or *latent force*, or centres of forces, constituting the original groundwork of creation as the permanent cause of phenomena, whether physical or spiritual,—is formed into aggregate or compound substance, through the operation of forces, **whose** influences are perceivable in the Physical or Chemical **Law, the first** stage in Creation is accomplished. This law includes all isomeric and isomorphous transformations of inorganic matter, and all decomposite combinations of compound substances. The forces affecting matter **are called** electric, magnetic, galvanic, cohesive, **capillary,** endosmose, exosmose, adhesive, gravitation, equilibrium, etc.

The vital power which emanates from the Spirit of Creation, **already** manifested as a combination of forces through the Physical **Laws in** the chemical metamorphoses and other phenomena **of matter** and forces, appears, through the special action of light, **more developed in the second stage,** which is the reign of the **Law of** Vegetable Organism.

Lo**wer animal** life belongs to the groups that may be styled the third **stage, that** is **to say the sphere of the** Law of Animal Organism, **while the fourth** stage is the province of the Law of developed Animal Organism **or** Instinct, and represents the highest stage **in Creation** in which animals not endowed with **reason** are found.

The appearance of **the** human mind on earth constitutes the fifth **stage** of Creation, that **is to** say, the reign of the Law of Physico-Mental Organisms, or, otherwise, the reign of Rational Life. This **stage** includes the intellectual as well as the physical faculties of man;—that is, man considered as the species, such as he generally appears all over the earth, developed from the first principles of matter to a complete, erect and stalwart form of being, retaining his material nature and animal propensities, but now endowed with that higher physiological development of animal instinct and mental faculties which in the case of man are called Reason. This species is the perfect man of the materialist.

§5. But man's development, or strictly speaking the development of his mind, does not stop here, for by degrees corresponding with his social progress, and in the same proportion as the surrounding conditions were more or less favorable to the adaptations of his moral organism, he has entered the sixth stage, which is called the sphere of the Moral Law, comprehending the highest order of Creation at present known on the Earth, viz., our *Moral-Mental Organism*,—the reign of Spiritual as well as Rational Life; in other words, he has now attained the moral development, through which *Consciousness of the Good*, which is the perfect harmony of justice and benevolence, is created in the mind, through the moral senses *Con-cience* and *Sympathy*, the elements of this higher moral organism. The process of evolution of the Moral-Mental Organism is analogous to that of the Physical, but, with the development of the moral senses just named, under the influence of the Moral Consciousness, a new phase in the universal struggle for existence has set in for the moral being. Here the struggle for material existence is encountered by limitations caused by the moral senses conscience and sympathy (§15) and often neutralized by this fiercer strife of the moral element of Nature, in its struggle to maintain its existence in opposition to the surrounding animal propensities (§76); a battle which follows the line of evolution from the lower to the higher mental organism, through development and adaptation of the higher moral and mental organs, and leads up, in gradual progression, to that harmonious combination of justice and benevolence in the human mind, which constitutes the Good, and is the manifestation of the Soul (§32).

This progress through evolution of the human mind may be called the survival of the Moral Element of Nature, in contradistinction from retrogression, through degeneration of the moral-mental organism, and sometimes total suppression of the same, caused by want of application or through disuse of the moral senses conscience and sympathy; in which cases the mind remains within the range of a lower stage of moral development, or gradually sinks back to that state of soulless materialism, unguided and unchecked by the moral senses, and in which only the instinctive egoism of the material animal propensities has claim and influence on the will.*

With regard to the mind and its moulding of Society, as the aggregate of human beings, the evolution theory holds good, and struggle for existence takes place, but in the sphere of the Moral-Mental activities. Evolution here means struggle between the Moral Element and the material animal nature of man (§14).

It is thus with constant strengthening of his moral senses, Conscience and Sympathy, through the discipline of Religion (§24) and through the inherent impulses of his soul, that man can succeed in keeping up to the natural moral standard, so necessary, not alone to guide him individually, but indispensable for the existence of family life and society (§76).

---

* "If the process of continuously adapting organisms to their environment takes place in Nature at all, there is no reason why we should set any limits on the extent to which it is able to go, up to the point at which a complete and perfect adaptation is achieved." GEORGE J. ROMANES, M.A., LL.D., F.R.S. "*The Scientific Evidences of Organic Evolution*," Nature Series (Ed. 1882, page 5). "Now, not only is it rational to infer that changes like those which have been going on during civilization will continue to go on, but it is irrational to do otherwise. Not he who believes that adaptation will increase is absurd, but he who doubts that it will increase is absurd. Lack of faith in such further evolution of humanity as shall harmonize its nature with its conditions, adds but another to the countless illustrations of inadequate consciousness of causation. One who leaving behind both primitive dogmas and primitive ways of looking at things, has, while accepting scientific conclusions, acquired those habits of thought which science generates, will regard the conclusion above drawn as inevitable. He will find it impossible to believe that the processes which have heretofore so moulded all beings to the requirements of their lives that they get satisfaction in fulfilling them, will not hereafter continue so moulding them." HERBERT SPENCER, *The Data of Ethics*, chapter x., §67.

The mind will be treated in connection with the theory of Law (*Jus*) in §29. Further we must state, that by action of the Moral Law of Nature is meant the influence of the Moral Element in Nature on the moral-mental organism of man.

§6. Thus the different forces or powers of Nature constitute in their successive combinations, as united by the motive element of the Spirit of Creation, the different Stages of Creation, in which the Universal Law of Nature represents itself to human consciousness in the form of groups, as stated above. Each group has its own peculiar classes of bodies or objects, embracing countless developed forms and varieties of forms, called *Species*, and coming on the scene in the course of each stage at the point at which the respective power, or the Law which is the manifestation of that power, predominates in Creation. The various objects and classes of objects of organic nature have each its own inherent constituent qualities, and find their respective places in Creation through development in conformity with the Universal Law of Nature; and having sprung up through the Law of Nature governing the particular condition of the substances of which they are respectively constituted, they appear as distinct offshoots of the main trunk, which, gradually growing, throws out higher branches, each giving origin, in its respective line, to countless shoots of its own, whilst the same source feeds all, and each derives its organic life from the same Motive Power and Universal Cause.

§7. The links of Evolution cannot be looked for amongst the Species. We are obliged to reduce these vast masses of observations to general laws, to find some main solution for the development of Nature through evolution, for, by searching in the by-paths of Creation, we are apt to lose the main track, while looking in vain for many a missing link.

By the foregoing hypothesis the development of the Universal Law of Nature or of Creation on Earth, or, in other words, the evolution of Nature on Earth, is represented as a chain of continued progress, with links of which each is necessary as a base for the continuation of the next, forming a system of mutual dependencies, for each serves, in its special sphere and to its full extent and capacity, for the development of the other. These links are the combined results of the different powers of Nature, and that these powers are all subject to the influence of one Universal Cause is manifested by the systematic development of Nature, called *Evolution*, the factors of which are Matter, Force and Life, which, as stated before, are combined by the Spirit of Creation as Motor of Evolution (§2).

§8. But neither the nature of these forces, nor what is called Matter, nor the origin of Life or the Motor of evolution in organic nature, are explicable by science or by any system of logic in the description of evolution, that is, by any evidences from the Physical or Mental Law. No better exhibition of the inadequacy of science could possibly be given than by quoting the words of Mr. Herbert Spencer with which he concludes his chapter on Ultimate Scientific Ideas. "Ultimate Scientific Ideas, then, are all representative of realities that cannot be comprehended. After no matter how great a progress in the colligation of facts and the establishment of generalizations ever wider and wider—after the merging of limited and derivative truths in truths that are larger and deeper has been carried no matter how far; the fundamental truth remains as much beyond reach as ever. The explanation of that which is explicable, does but bring out into greater clearness the inexplicableness of that which remains behind. Alike in the external and the internal worlds, the man of science sees himself in the midst of perpetual changes of which he can discover neither the beginning nor the end. If, tracing back the evolution of things, he allows himself to entertain the hypothesis that the Universe once existed in a diffused form, he finds it utterly impossible to conceive how this came to be so; and equally, if he speculates on the future, he can assign no limit to the grand succession of phenomena ever unfolding themselves before him. In like manner if he looks inward, he perceives that both ends of the thread of consciousness are beyond his grasp; nay, even beyond his power to think of as having existed or as existing in time to come. When, again, he turns from the succession of phenomena external or internal, to their intrinsic nature, he is just as much at fault. Supposing him in every case able to resolve the appearances, properties, and movements of things, into manifestations of Force in Space and Time, he still finds that Force, Space and Time pass all understanding. Similarly, though the analysis of mental actions may finally bring him down to sensations, as the original materials out of which all thought is woven, yet he is little forwarder; for he can give no account either of sensations themselves or of that something which is conscious of sensations. Objective and subjective things he thus ascertains to be alike inscrutable in their substance and genesis. In all directions his investigations eventually bring him face to face with an insoluble enigma; and he ever more clearly perceives it to be an insoluble enigma. He learns at once the greatness and the littleness of the human intellect—its power in dealing with all that comes within the range of experience; its impotence in dealing with all that transcends experience. He realizes with a special vividness the utter incomprehensibleness of the simplest fact, considered in itself. He, more than any other, truly *knows* that in its ultimate essence nothing can be known.*

This proves the inability or inadequacy of our physical and intellectual faculties, and explains the reason why the Spirit of Creation, the Absolute Cause of all, and its influence on the human mind are indemonstrable by Science, or, in other words, incomprehensible to the mind through reason, unaided by the prevision of that herald of a higher conception, called Intuition (§10), which quickens the physico-intellectual functions into the higher development of the moral-mental organism, in the sphere of which it is called the soul (§11).

---

* FIRST PRINCIPLES, Chapter iii. *Ultimate Scientific Ideas.* §21.

§9. Reason is the evolved result of different impressions of experience as adapted to actual physiological conditions. Those impressions vivified by Intuition and brought into relationship with each other by the evolution process, have gradually developed from Instinct into what is called Intellect, the basis of the higher mental development.

§10. With the foregoing propositions we couple the following hypothesis regarding Intuition.

Intuition is the association of ideas in the mind, instinctively, as it were by "reflex-action" of consciousness. It is the response, of the Ego as the moral "nerve-centre" to the stimuli of the moral senses, analogous to the reflex actions of the physical nerve-centre which follow mechanically on the stimuli of the physical senses. This essential substratum of the *Ego* constitutes a law of the conscious mind, and forms the condition under which we think when the mind, having entered into its full intellectual and moral development is unbiassed, pure and unshackled by *à priori* theories. In the intellectual growth of the mind where it is manifested as the motor of a nascent development, Intuition is foreshadowed through that spontaneous lucidity of Instinct, bordering on Reason, which we are so often astonished to observe in animals. Forecasting the adaptations of Intellect, it becomes permanently conspicuous at the first dawn of Reason, of which it is ever a concomitant in the human mind, whose continued evolution and adaptation to a higher stage of moral and intellectual progress it presages. Intuition underlies all our scientific speculations, and helps them through the dead-points of the mechanism of Reason; indeed, without its stimulating and subtile vitality, this mechanism would stop just at the point where its forces are most wanted for the conception of Primary Truths, which form the bases of all sciences (§13).

Intuition awakens in the mind a degree of consciousness, distinct from the intellectual perception of Reason, which is called Feeling, Spiritual Feeling or Inspiration. This Feeling and

Reason, when combined, form the popular understanding, that spontaneous perception of all normal minds, called *Common Sense* (treated in §34). Hence truth is *felt* where science cannot procure any evidence or demonstration, while we speak of *feeling* the truth of a proposition or the force of an argument; of feeling our obligation to do this **or** that. The more the human mind advances in its course of development, the more Intuition is **pre-eminent**, and the more extensively and consistently will **it be** listened to. Genuine Intuition will then be kept free from **the** delusive influence of *Imagination*, which latter is often mistaken for the former. But Imagination is the faculty or combination of faculties by which certain ideas are evolved in the mind, whilst Intuition is the criterion by which these ideas, created by Imagination, are tested, when Reason, overpowered by Imagination, is not to be trusted or is inadequate for its functions. Imagination is thus merely the effervescence of Reason, **which** sometimes produces ebullitions dangerous to the stability of **the** mind, whilst Intuition, constant and constructive as all the forces of Nature, is the regulating principle of Reason (§20). Being concomitant with Reason it connects human consciousness with the Unknowable, **with** that Inscrutable Cause which manifests itself as the Universal Law of Nature, by causing us to feel intuitively what is indemonstrable to Reason, and thus to exercise, as nearly as possible, the same kind of control over the unknowable world as that which we already possess in respect of the phenomena of the material world. As such, it is recognizable as the Soul, which unites the human creature with its Creator.

§11. The Soul is represented in the Ego of our consciousness through that power of nascency in the evolution of mental organism described in the preceding section as Intuition. The **influence of** the Spirit of Creation, as noted above, is manifested in the process of evolution, *i.e.*, the process of forces in matter, in organism, and in the impulses to the respective processes of devel-

---
* First Principles, §14.

opment and growth, in conformity with the general progress of the Universal Law of Nature, of which it is the Power. "The Power which the Universe manifests to us," says Mr. Herbert Spencer, "is utterly inscrutable."* This First Cause, or absolute, this fountain-head of all laws, physical and moral, with their all-pervading principles, which we call *the Spirit of Creation*, transcends human knowledge, and is indemonstrable to the human mind, which can only perceive its effects in Matter, when it is called Force; in Organism when it is called Life; and be conscious of it through that special innate state of the conscious Ego, called Intuition, where its impulses and inspirations are the manifestations of the Soul.

§12. Thus **Intuition** and the *Ego* of consciousness are manifestations of the **Soul**. The idea of the good and the evil, as derived from the moral **senses** Conscience and Sympathy, is contemplated by our Ego of Consciousness and compared and contrasted with our own action and that of others,—with our perception (through our physical senses) of external objects and conditions, and finally judged. Thus the soul is represented through **Intuition by the Moral Element** (§5) in the Ego of Consciousness **which is** the centre of the moral senses, and of the free will; the **power "which** summons, suspends, or dismisses," and which sits as supreme judge over our moral conceptions and the will (§18).*

As the Ego, the self conscious subject, is the power of impulsion and of inhibition, of acting and of restraining, is the centre of free will and of the moral senses, this centre is seldom at rest and in unity in face of the many complex and adverse tendencies and conflicts of activity between volition, conscience and sympathy. This makes the Ego often appear divided between action and resisting, which constitutes the state of mind called Moral Doubt, **to be noted in** §25. But in **the** morally and intellectually well developed **and** disciplined normal mind (§24), the Ego, in spite of all adverse chances, will retain its moral mastery and rational activity.

* RENOUVIER. *Essai de Critique Générale.* 2nd Edit. Vol. i., p. 395 et seq.

The influence of the Spirit of Creation in the evolution of the Mind not being perceivable through Sense, as in the inorganic and organic evolutions, this influence is made cognizable to the Mind through the Soul, which is then presented to our consciousness as the relation which exists between our moral-mental organism and the Spirit of Creation; in other words, the soul is the representative of the Spirit of Creation in the process of the higher evolution of the human mind (§29). If the mind is in an abnormal or unsound state, through complete moral depravity or physical unfitness for moral or rational conception, then the current of communication between the Soul and the Mind is suspended, the rays of Intuition which enkindle the moral senses, conscience and sympathy, are excluded, the spiritual life is suppressed, and the body is *morally* dead, being then only animated by the common animal instinct, or by those shreds of intelligence which sometimes cling to the human mind after Reason has become extinct. In this morbid state of the mind the Ego is dislocated and the will not being under control of the moral senses, the individual is not accountable for his deeds. When derangement or decomposition of the physical organs obstructs the circulation of the blood, physical life is impossible; thus it is with spiritual life, when the mind is unfit to retain the impulses of the Soul.*

§13. Primary Truths or First Principles are brought under the cognizance of the mind through Intuition as stated previously (§10). These Truths are ideas which are fundamental to and presupposed in the operation of the understanding; they are, however, not furnished by sense awakened in the mind on occasions of material experience, nor are they produced by sensuous experience, for they spring up in the mind intuitively whenever the fitting occasion is presented; whence it may be inferred that

---

* "Then shall the dust return to the earth as it was, and the spirit shall return unto God who gave it."—Ecclesiastes xii. 7. "There is a spirit in man, and the inspiration of the Almighty giveth them understanding. Who teacheth us more than the beasts of the earth and maketh us wiser than the fowls of Heaven."—Job xxxii. 8, and xxxv. 10 and 11.

they are conceived in the mind through the special power of Intuition, operating under appropriate circumstances.*

These Truths are of two distinct classes, viz., *Physical Truths*, the principles of the physical laws of nature; and *Moral Truths*, the primary ideas of right and wrong, which are the First Principles of Justice. (Comp. §30).

We must note here, that the terms Intuition and Soul are of one and the same meaning to express the manifestation to our consciousness of that unexplainable power which we postulated under the name of Moral Element of Nature (§§5 and 32). The term **Soul** is used in preference in the description of the moral-mental development.

§14. The source of moral development, from which mankind derives the impulse for the continuation of the strife in the progress of civilization in its purest nature, is the Soul. Emanating from the Spirit of Creation,—the absolute Cause of the Universal Law of Nature, and the fountain head of Perfect Good,—the Soul imparts to the human mind, through its moral senses, the nature of the *Good* (§5). The Good is not what is agreeable or disagreeable to the senses, nor any concept of speculation based on the principle of utility, though it is intimately connected with general welfare. It is the perfect harmony of Justice and Benevolence, the parent of all virtues, which constitutes the rules of action of the moral senses called the Moral Law of Nature.

The Good is not a utilitarian theory. Deeds are right not *because* we approve of them, but we feel happy when approving of them *because they are right*. They are right not *because* they are commanded; on the contrary, they are commanded *because they are right*.†

This is the subjective Good, which becomes objective in customary and written laws, through the Spirit of Law, described hereafter (§33).

---

* JOSEPH HAVEN, *Mental Philosophy*, Ed. 1878, p. 34-229.
† IDEM, *Moral Philosophy*, p. 47.

§15. The two elements of the Good, Justice and Benevolence, as revealed to us through impulses of the Soul, are presented to our consciousness through the moral senses Conscience and Sympathy. These moral senses are the special senses of the mind whose office it is to take cognizance of moral distinctions, as the eye distinguishes colors and the ear sounds. The basis of the moral senses is Intuition, described above (§§5 and 10).

Conscience impresses on the mind the distinction between right and wrong, and the principles of Justice, which constitute the Law of Conscience. Sympathy, on the other hand, is the moral sense through which the emotions, which engender the disinterested affections called Benevolence, are awakened in the mind.

The conception of the one is not necessarily preceded or followed by the emotion of the other. They are co-existent in the sound and pure mind, and, though distinct, stand in equal counterpoise in the balance of *Righteousness*, which is the state of mind when the will is in perfect harmony with the Moral Senses. Justice is the rule of right conduct and duty, as dictated by Conscience, which keeps alive the awful sense of right and wrong. But Benevolence, which is the reflection in the pure mind of the Creator's love for His creatures, allows no rules to be imposed upon human nature except such as the frail human powers are able to bear, and such as are beneficial to the progress of mankind, without overtasking its strength. For Justice, apart from the moderating control of Mercy, degenerates into despotism, and from despotism into tyranny. But to keep Benevolence free from any bias to laxity or excessive lenity in procedure, which might encourage lawlessness in the human mind, Conscience, which approves of and commands just actions, can forbid the will to contribute to the gratification of Sympathy whenever affections, excited by Imagination, become dangerous to that genuine Benevolence which is in perpetual agreement with the principle of Righteousness. There is no justice without mercy. Justice and mercy combined constitute righteousness, and righteousness is *peace of mind*.*

Thus the **Good** is presented to the conscious mind, as a state of perfect harmony between Conscience and Sympathy. Hence, the **more these** Moral Senses **are** developed, the stronger **is** the conception of the Good in the Mind.

§16. Akin to their common source, viz., Intuition, both Conscience and Sympathy likewise derive their origin from Life itself, and pass, with the latter, through all stages of evolution. Both Conscience and Sympathy are sometimes, to a certain degree, manifested in animals, especially when those powers are awakened by training; but their harmonious combination, effected through the Soul, is only developed in the higher stage of mental evolution, which is called the moral-mental organism. This harmony is the manifestation of the Moral Element in Nature, and reveals the influence of the Soul in the human Mind. The Moral Law of Nature, *i.e.*, the rules of action of the Moral Senses, through which the natural distinction between virtue and vice is cognizable, is as essential for the interpretation of Nature in her consummation of the evolution of the human race, as the Physical Laws are with regard to material and organic development.†

As Justice is the right Reason, so is Benevolence the right Sentiment in man. Both are impulses of the Soul, proceeding from the divine elements of Justice and Mercy, which, when

---

* "Justice and Mercy are **met together;** righteousness **and** peace have kissed each other."—Psalm lxxxv. 10.

† **As** it is with the physical, **so** it is with the ethical. "A belief, as yet fitful and partial, is beginning to spread amongst men, that here also there is an indissoluble bond between cause and consequence, an inexorable destiny, a law **which** altereth not. Confounded by the multiplied and ever new aspects of human affairs, it is not perhaps surprising that men should fail duly to **recognize** the systematic character of the divine rule. Yet, in the moral as **in the** material world, accumulated evidence is gradually generating the conviction that events are not at bottom fortuitous; but that they are wrought out in **a certain** inevitable way by unchanging forces. In all ages there has been some glimmering perception of this truth; and experience is ever giving to that perception increased distinctness. Indeed even now all men do in one mode or **other,** testify of such a faith. Every known creed is an assertion of it."—**HERBERT** SPENCER, *Social Statics*, Edit. 1883, p. 54.

combined, produce the disinterested affections or virtues called piety, humanity, love, integrity, modesty, chastity, faithfulness, temperance, self-control, patience, self-sacrifice, manliness, self-respect, and the noble passions of courage, indignation or unselfish aversion to wrong, and all further impulsive ardour towards the good, the true and the beautiful.

§17. Virtue is the inherent quality of the moral-mental organism of man; "the natural instinct of the Soul which demands and strives for the good, and which approves and is satisfied with that only which is right in human conduct and endeavor."* When governed by the Moral Element in Nature, the normal condition of man's moral-mental organism is the perfect equilibrium between its moral senses Conscience and Sympathy, from which harmony emanates the Good, when these moral senses completely possess the mind. This makes a good man act rightly on the simple ground that it is natural to do so.

As such, virtue can never be conceived as a speculation on reward or as dread of punishment; neither is the Good a utilitarian principle, for Righteousness being the perfect harmony of Conscience and Sympathy, a mind with fully developed moral senses in perfect equilibrium cannot contain any evil thought but with an acute sense of pain which brings his whole nature into revolt, struggling to regain its moral gravity. To the mind in which the moral senses are dumb through depravity it is an equally difficult task to become virtuous. The will in the righteous mind is more easily subjected to the moral senses, for in such minds these senses are predominant, while, in the mind without developed moral senses, the will is at the mercy of the animal propensities. When the mind is abandoned to a vicious imagination, and Conscience and Sympathy are silenced, man is left a wretched prey to animal passions and vices, and, if by education or surroundings he being conscious of his state, yet persists, he is morally below his species and worse than the brute, whose

---
*ARISTOTLE. JOSEPH HAVEN, *Moral Philosophy*, p. 73.

organism does not include consciousness, which in the human mind is the moral Ego (§12).

As any condition of the mind is the final result of man's *free will* (described in the next section), it is obvious that Virtue, though being the natural outcome of the state of mind wherein the moral senses are predominant, is merit to man, and thus leads to human happiness, even to *true* happiness. Not the gratification of the senses, surely; for in this respect, man would be in no way superior to the brute. The true happiness for man is the highest activity of his intelligent and his moral nature, in harmony with free will, the unrestrained energy of *knowledge* and *goodness*, which satisfies all the conditions of his mental and moral nature. It is the perfect activity of a perfect life.*

§18. As the state of perfection, *i.e.*, the pure unpollutable mind, in complete possession of the moral senses and unable to harbour evil thoughts, is not attainable in the present state of human nature, man must ever strive and unflinchingly adhere to the Good. On the other hand, as the moral senses can never be completely crushed out from any moral-mental organism, man, in a normal condition, is ever accountable for his moral actions; and on the same ground, the regeneration of a criminal is to be expected. This natural result of free will is the basis of Penal Law.

Moral actions are those to which the quality of virtue or guilt, of praise or blame, can be attached and pertain only to the normal state of the conscious mind of rational beings, and only to the *voluntary* actions of such beings. This refers to the various forms of mental activity, not merely the putting forth of physical power. An external bodily act is moral only so far as it involves and proceeds from some activity of the mind, the body being the instrument of the mind.† It is obvious that in this psycho-physiological definition of moral actions the physical views concerning the human activities are not included. The descriptions of

---

* ARISTOTLE. JOSEPH HAVEN, *Moral Philosophy*, p. 74.
† IDEM, *Moral Philosophy*, p. 60.

the mechanism of the different *kinds* of movements and their respective centers, viz., those which imply consciousness (and which are called voluntary in the strict sense of the word) and those which are noted as automatic, instinctive, responsive or reflective (including the instinctive expression of the emotions and other motor-adaptations) which are more or less perfectly organized in the centers underlying the cortex, belong to physico-physiological researches into the nervous system of the human body, *i.e.*, of the mechanism of the instrument through which the soul inspires human consciousness and brings the body into action through the will.

The *Will* is the executive power of the Ego; that power which our consciousness has of deciding or determining that it will do certain actions or will restrain from acting in certain directions. Willing is the exercise of that power. When the determination of the will is put forth in actual deeds, the execution thereof is called *Volition*.

The basis of the will is the *Motive*, that which incites the normal mind to action, the reason why it acts, and acts as it does; that is, with regard to the intelligent and voluntary action which we called above Moral action, and which alone is here in question. There may be many inducements to action, but only one final motive; the prevailing inducement, that which actually moves the will to put forth volition, is designated by the term Motive* (§29).

Motives are of two classes, viz., the *Desire*, which springs from self-love, and is more or less in contradiction with righteousness, in conformity with the subject's notions of material happiness,—and *Duty*, the moral motives, that spring from that sense of obligation which corroborates with the Moral Senses Conscience and Sympathy (§§15 & 20). Motives of duty are not resolvable into motives of interest, but when desire and duty coincide, peace of mind is secured. Then man no longer views as agreeable that which is not in pure harmony with his moral senses,

---

* JOSEPH HAVEN, *Mental Philosophy*.

and he realizes "the peace of God which passes all understanding" (§§14 and 17). But, says the utilitarian, this very approval of the moral senses which procures the peace of mind that constitutes happiness is, after all, self-love, the desire of happiness, the *only motive* to act righteously. Such assumption proves the utilitarian logic exhausted, for consciousness contradicts it. That there is such a thing as the distinction between doing right for righteousness' sake, in opposition to the motive of conduct which prompts us to secure our own interest, every man is conscious of, the egoist not the least, and the history of the human race gives ample and irreproachable proofs of genuine self-sacrifice.

From the above will be noticed that the will is free, but that volition can be physically and even morally diverted from executing the decision of the will. Physiology shows that in every voluntary act there are two distinct elements, viz., the independent free power of decision, centering in the Ego of consciousness (§12);—the will, and the practical result of this power—volition—the execution of the fiat of the free will on the motive for action or inhibition, which takes place through the complex physico-physiological mechanism, consisting of muscles and sinews and vital forces. Thus the will is the cause, but volition the physiological power of acting or inhibiting.* But, as said above, the harmonious working of these two elements, in the voluntary activity of the mind can be disturbed. This is often the case not alone in consequence of pathological paralysis of the physiological mechanism, through which the volition takes place,—the physical constraint,—but also morally caused by the struggle between the two classes of motives described above. Hence the difference between *willing* and *doing*, good intentions and good acts, the knowing what is right and the practising of it, the condemning of an unlawful passion and the withstanding of the same, in fact, the struggle between the moral senses and the animal propensities of the human nature (§76).

Thus the Will is the power of voluntary moral action, which

---
* Schneider, *Der Menschliche Wille*, etc. Th. Ribot, *The Diseases of the Will*, etc.

constitutes the basis of human accountability and lies therefore at the foundation of ethics. As such, it is the active moral power of man, and duty pertains first and chiefly not to the external conduct, but to the responsible normal mind, whose *free will* finds its expression in the outward conduct called moral actions. This brings us to the problem: What is Free Will, and is a *free will* compatible with a settled order of Nature?

For the solution of this, like any other problems regarding the human mind, which is a concrete phenomenon, we must search the Book of the direct Divine Revelation, which is the open book of creation where the laws of Nature are inscribed by the Creator's own hand without any intervening medium.

With regard to individual free will, we learn from the theory of natural evolution the following definition.

Human individual free will is the moral faculty evolved from the organic germ of that innate instinctive power of spontaneous variation which is observable in individual members of animal species, in their selection and adaptation of appropriate specific characters, for their physical development, or adapted to fit their material nature to actually surrounding influences. This is the manifestation of a design in the Motor of Evolution, noted above (pp. 3 and 11).

The accumulated development of these adaptations leads to amelioration or degeneration of the subject, according to the nature of the affecting circumstances. Together they constitute the physiological cause, which with the aid of the physical conditions, called "factors of organic evolution,"* produce those particular variations from which new species are evolved. This natural evolution process is called "natural selection" or "physiological selection"†.

With the development of the human moral-mental organism

---

* Herbert Spencer, "Factors of Organic Evolution," *Nineteenth Century*, May, 1886, p. 748.

† George J. Romanes, "Physiological Selection," *Nineteenth Century*, January, 1887, p. 59.

from the lower organic forms (§5), this animal instinctive power of variation and adaptation, to fit material surroundings, has gradually developed into the moral faculty of *free will*, which now operates through the moral senses (§16) and by means of the activities, called moral actions, as described above (p. 21). It strives henceforth to fit the now more complex organism not alone to material surroundings, but, as a necessity of the gradually developed moral as well as material nature of the subject, also to satisfy the altruistic injunctions of the social organism (§48).

This is the individual free will. Man's will, following any spontaneous wish or desire to arrive at some definite condition or position, or to perform some act for any purpose, is *free*, but the result of any voluntary act comes immediately with the execution of his free will in the order of the respective law of Nature, which, with regard to man's moral volition, is the Moral Law of Nature (§§5 and 29).* The arbitrary will has normal effect. The will once executed, man stands powerless before the natural effect of this voluntary causation, but nevertheless completely accountable for all the consequences of his volition, for whatever evil he has brought by his *free will* into the world. He who brings evil into the world is responsible for all the results of his evil. To the doer belongs his deed. *Causa causæ est causa effectus* is a true principle of Justice.

---

* Laws of Nature, as stated on page 2, are conditions formed by sequences of events and causations which appear with persistency and regularity to our consciousness. They are the "rules of action" of perceptible agents and the "modes" in which not perceptible forces are manifested. Thus the rules of action of our cognizable Moral Senses are called the *Moral Law of Nature* (§14). "We call these rules laws of nature," says Prof. Huxley, "not because anybody knows whether they bind nature or not, but because we find it is obligatory on us to take them into account both as actors under nature, and as interpreters of nature."—("Scientific and Pseudo-Scientific Realism," *Nineteenth Century*, February, 1887, p. 201). As "actors under nature" these "rules" are the uniform modes in which the Ultimate Cause, called Spirit of Creation, is manifested (page 2), while Nature's design, i.e., the spontaneous variabilities in organic evolution, does not admit of persistent invariability in "sequences of events."

On the other hand, for the same reason, he who, by moral act or conduct, produces virtuous results has also all the merit of his free will in moral sphere. The results of human free will are analogous to the variations in physical nature; the first are classed under the Moral Law and the latter under the Physical Laws of Nature. A moral variation may cause an amelioration or deterioration of the human mind in conformity with its effect as tending towards a higher or a lower moral standard, just as a physical variation affects the species in its structure and utility for the better or for the worse. Thus it is that man's free will causes the appearance of *Virtue* or *Vice*.

§19. All manners of conduct which are styled *Virtues*, are marked by an intrinsic similarity of character through having a common source. This source is the Moral Element of Nature, the Motor of the Good, which is manifested to the human mind through the moral senses Conscience and Sympathy. Good and evil, or right and wrong, are by no means variable or merely relative qualities, changing with temporary circumstances of civilization. The value of man's ethical judgment, the susceptibility of his Moral Senses, naturally varies in conformity with the degree of development to which his moral-mental organism attains. Hence it comes that certain acts are in some particular stage of the evolution of this organism, through deficient development of the moral senses, regarded as indifferent, as matters with which morality has no concern; that certain acts are in conformity with the relative state of ethical valuation, deemed expedient, which in the respective stage of moral development is tantamount to good; whilst the very same acts are, in another more highly developed stage of civilization, condemned as actually vicious. When we clear away from the path, which this development has gradually traversed in the history of the human race, all desultory human acts prompted by special motives of expediency, or caused by the contending propensities of mankind in its struggle for moral existence, we cannot fail to acknowledge that the working of the Moral Element in Nature is plainly manifested through the mist of ages and in the midst of what, at first sight, we should think hopeless barbarism. Side by side with grievous deviations from morality, caused by the lower animal propensities of the human mind, the history of mankind shows often the most lucid appreciation of the Good, which is the manifestation of that universal motor of the Good, the Moral Element of Nature, that mysterious power which guides the human mind. The Good is ever the same. The appearance of differences in the valuation depends upon the standard of ethical judgment, that is to say upon the state of the *Popular Conscience* and the development of the *Spirit of Law* (§33) in the respective stage of civilization, which is the exponent of the relative state of development of the moral-mental organism of man. The Moral Element of Nature, in the natural course of evolution, grows into that state of preponderance, in the human mind, which forms what we termed above the sixth stage of creation on earth (§5), but its progress is often checked by the animal propensities of the lower stages, though its development is undeniably traceable in the history of mankind as a whole, when viewed from the stand-point of the Philosophy of Civilization.

§20. Against this influence of the Moral Element in Nature there is constant war waged by Egotism, through Imagination,—that active agency of evil thoughts in the mind when wrongly excited,—on the part of the rapacious, selfish inclinations of man's animal nature.

It is impossible to estimate the mischief to which a wrongly excited imagination may lead the human mind, with its tendency to believe what it desires to think, for "the wish is father to the thought."

The supremacy of Egotism, in this war between its agent Imagination and the moral senses Conscience and Sympathy, is marked by the vices, which are caused by love of power, by feelings of ambition, envy, jealousy, love of wealth, lewdness and by other animal appetites. Unless checked by Conscience and right Sentiment, those vices produce a habit of malignity, which, as the reverse of Righteousness, is the state of depravity of the human mind when not under the ennobling influence of the Soul.*

§21. The deceitful Imagination, that parent source of evil thoughts, which arouses our animal propensities by exciting the material nature of man, creates by its hallucinations false virtues. What is only covetousness based on rapacity is represented by Imagination as a noble ambition striving to reach the Great and the Good. What is only vanity based on brutish propensities, is held up by Imagination as courage, as a noble passion of disinterested self-sacrifice, which in reality can only originate from sympathy with the welfare of our fellow-creatures. Finally, alas! lewdness, that vilest of animal inclinations, is represented by Imagination in the pure and unguarded virgin mind, as real unpolluted sympathy, as the noblest conception of which the human mind is capable—as love.

But the baneful influence of Imagination on Reason is here easily detected, if the will is but strong enough. Trace Love from its noblest character as ardent, active sympathy, when in perfect harmony with Conscience, down to that sordid sensual feeling of the libertine,—which is wrongly called "love,"—and you have run down the scale of retrogression of the mental organism of man from its lofty Spiritual Feeling to its lowest animal propensities. At this stage the passion thus wrongly called "love" is but the animal propensities swept up by Imagination. Its source is not sympathy nor is its basis friendship, for it springs from that spurious compound of base desires which is the product of Imagination and does not listen to Reason. Pure love is reconcilable with duty and can stand the test of the Moral Law of Nature, because the Good is manifested in the

---

* "I delight in the law of God after the inward man: but I see a different law in my members, warring against the law of my mind and bringing me into captivity under the law of sin, which is in my members."—Romans vii. 22 and 23; and Romans viii. 1.

perfect harmony of our **moral** senses which arises when Conscience and Heart, Reason and Feeling agree.

Such Love is sympathy in its active form concentrated on a special object. When love is combined with reason, pure and free from sexual bias, it is called *Friendship*.

§22. When fanciful Imagination is **inflamed** by the passions of selfishness, and, unfettered by **judgment**, reasoning, knowledge, truth or facts, takes entire possession of the mind's field, she becomes then the active agent through which malignity is instilled into the human mind. Imagination, the **creative power of the** ideal so beautiful and sublime in her pure state, **so useful an** agent and so indispensable for success in **poetry, music, and** in the plastic arts and sciences, to minds **of a high order, in the** discovery of new combinations, through happy conjecture, supposition or invention,—is the fiend of the human race whenever she becomes the servant of malignant passions. As Conscience is the moral faculty of Justice, and Sympathy that of Benevolence, thus also is a vitiated Imagination the parent of Vice.*

§23. But, fortunately for man, his mind is so constituted that the evil engendered by his animal nature **can** be neutralized in the **mind,** and **the power of a vicious** Imagination counteracted, **in its own** sphere, by another faculty of the mind called Attention. **This is** the power the mind has to direct its thoughts towards any **given object to the exclusion of** others. As both of those faculties are **under the control** of the will, it only requires strength of will **and** discipline of the mind, and the growth of evil, which is **engendered by** a corrupting Imagination, will be checked by fixing Attention on the Good to the exclusion of all

---

* Imagination—cette superbe puissance, ennemie de la raison, qui se plaît à la contrôler et à la dominer pour montrer combien elle peut, en toutes choses, à établir dans l'homme une seconde nature. Elle a ses heureux, ses malheureux, ses sains, ses malades, ses riches, ses pauvres ; elle fait croire, douter, nier la raison, elle suspend les sens, elle les fait sentir ; elle a ses fous et ses sages : et rien ne nous dépite d'avantage que de voir qu'elle remplit ses hôtes d'une satisfaction bien autrement pleine et entière que la raison."—PASCAL. Pensées. Art. iii. 53.

evil thoughts. If you have the good luck to possess any bright conception of that state called *peace of mind*, which is the harmony between your actions and the Good, bring that up in your mind and fix attention on it, and, by contrasting it with actions which have disturbed the harmony of this peace of mind, this attention on the Good will save you. When discontentment is the cause of evil thoughts, compare your better lot with some worse state of unrelenting misery, let your sympathy place yourself in such a position of greater pain and worse state of mind, and let your conscience give the verdict; hope and faith will return, and, through this exercise of your moral senses, peace of mind is regained. Thus the harmony between conscience and sympathy gives pleasure, and shews that *there exists no happiness outside the Good*, while it predicts the pains of the reverse.* This anchor is safe, for it is cast in good holding ground, provided that the cable of your attention on the Good does not part, but succeeds in arousing the determined resistance of the mind to all aggressions of the awakened selfish passions and desires of the animal nature, which are so fatal to purity of mind, a requisite indispensable for the maintenance of harmony with the Soul. But strength of will and discipline of mind cannot be attained except by earnest effort, by resolute purpose and diligent training, for "the spirit truly is willing but the flesh is weak."

§24. This moral training of the mind is essential for the completion of our moral organization and for the maintenance of strength sufficient to guard us from the evil of our own nature, by preserving us from those temptations which are engendered through evil thoughts, by means of keeping the mind in constant communion with the Good. Now this moral training of the

---

* "Oh what a glory doth this world put on
To him who, with a fervent heart goes forth
Under the bright and glorious sky, and looks
On duties well performed and days well spent!"
      LONGFELLOW.

mind is the province of the religion, which teaches how to keep the mind sound and pure, and in perfect harmony with the soul. We mean that religion which teaches Divine Love, and shows how Eternal Justice is mitigated by Mercy for the gradual elevation of mankind, the Christian Religion, in fact, the only religion operating through Divine Love in perfect harmony with our moral-mental organism;—provided we do not wilfully spoil this most sublime result of evolution, the work of creation on earth, which forms the corresponding medium between soul and mind, by damping the strings of moral sense and thus untuning the harp on which the soul would bring forth those harmonious vibrations, which are to our inward ear the voice of our Creator.

§25. Another instance of the inadequacy of Reason to supply, unaided by the Soul, all the wants of our moral-mental organism, consists in the fact that, where Reason is not supplemented by Moral Sense, there remains a void, a darkness in the human mind, which may be called *Moral Doubt*. The more Sympathy is suppressed and timid Conscience kept aloof, the greater becomes the Doubt, which is the disturbance of equilibrium between the moral senses and the will. But when Reason is in harmony with the Moral Senses, so that Conscience and Sympathy regain their sway, controlling the will, there is no place for doubt in the mind, which is then in a state of harmony between the moral senses and the will. Then the Ego is in unity and in its rational undivided state of conciousness as the centre of the moral senses and the will (§12).

§26. The two elements of the Good, viz., Justice, whose agent is Conscience, and Benevolence, which is represented by Sympathy in the human mind, constitute in their combination the Moral Law of Nature, and are conceived in the mind through the mind's moral faculties just named, by the inspiration of the Soul.

From this proposition we draw the conclusion, that through

the conception of the Good, the Soul, the active agent of the Spirit of Creation, is manifested in the human Mind.

But this is not all. The Christian Religion, as noted above (§24), is the natural discipline of the mind, for it is the fosterer of our moral senses, Conscience and Sympathy, through its teachings of Justice and Mercy. The conviction of the necessity of the moral senses we receive through logical induction, when tracing the natural evolution from matter and force up to the moral-mental organism of man. Faith in the Creator and in Christianity, as imposed on our consciousness through our moral senses, is thus strengthened by Natural Science, and Science is thus the agent of Religion, through which the unbeliever is brought to conviction, if he only give his consciousness fair chance for unbiased conception.

When we thus contemplate the evolution of the human mind, we cannot help feeling conscious of the fact that the condition of progress towards perfection, which we call the moral-mental organism, when developed in the highest degree through the Moral Element of Nature, represents the physiological condition of the most perfect being this earth ever beheld in the shape of man; we refer to Him who came, by the will of God, to impress on mankind the fact of their being connected, through the Soul, with the Eternal Creator; to foreshadow the future nature of human beings, by throwing light on the goal to which the Moral Law of Nature is leading. It might be possible to reach, by scientific induction, the conception of the nature of Christ, as such, when on earth. Indeed, if the history of mankind did not already possess this ever living example, the philosophy of evolution, if consistent in its search for the goal of the development theory,—for the final link which unites man, in his highest development, with his Creator, would postulate such a being, as this final link, as the utmost result of evolution.

Thus is Christianity corroborated by Nature, and if religious institutions of Christian denominations, called churches, shrink from the alliance of science, they give up with this efficient agent for the conviction of the human mind, the test of *real faith*; for faith is consolidated conviction, and conviction is the settled harmony between Reason and Feeling, when Conscience and Sympathy agree (§34). Faith without conviction is superstition, which is caused by imagination, and has full sway of the mind where Science is obscured. By science is not meant here that curbed incomplete investigation of Nature, which we called above (p. 3) the philosophy of external facts, and which, though based on primary truths, awakened in the mind through intuition, ignores intuition and the state of consciousness it creates (§13). This incomplete science leads often to mistaken views of natural causation where the physical senses cannot reach. The testimony of that consciousness awakened by intuition, which is the basis of Reason and called Feeling,—an essential element of common sense (p. 13),—being rejected, scepticism, which is inadequate conception of causation, is created in the mind, with the tendency to restrain the development of the mind within the limits of the physico-mental organism (§4). The outcome of this coercing of the natural faculties is the grossest of all superstitions, called *atheism*,—the false assumption of a superficial and inadequate investigation of causation, which accounts for natural phenomena, but through external facts only, so far as the physical senses are able to go. Deprecating consciousness established through the moral senses, it disjoins the Ego, and, instead of leading to the natural goal of evolution, wanders away into pyrrhonism, the universal doubt which is the abortive fruit of this incomplete science. But there is a real science which in its investigation of causation includes the entire Nature, all we are conscious of, whether through our moral senses or through our physical senses (p. 1), the ego as well as the non-ego, employing all the faculties of the human mind, in its full moral as well as physical development. This complete science leads to the convinced consciousness of a primordial causation, emanating from an intelligent Ultimate Cause and acting as Motor of Evolution, through factors and agents perceivable through the physical senses. It thus excludes superstition as well as scepticism, by establishing, through scientific conviction, our faith in the Creator, for there is no law of nature, physical, mental or moral, of which the discovery has not all the character of a Divine revelation through intuition. It is by intuitive revelations that all phenomena become explicable (comp. §§35 and 38).

§27. From the foregoing propositions, which are connected with our hypothesis regarding intuition (§10) as the manifestation of the Primary Cause or the Absolute in the evolution of the mental organism, we draw this final conclusion, based on the broad principle of evolution in its utmost consequence, viz., that through the conception of the Good the soul is manifested in the human mind, and that by cultivating our moral senses and maintaining their harmony (which is the Good) we find the medium of communication with our *Creator*, which will carry us safely to our destination, if we sincerely adhere to the Good (§§14, 15 and 24).

§28. There are two sorts of evil, viz., material or physical evil, which, when properly viewed, gives impulses to the Good by stimulating the moral sense of the well-ordered individual mind; and moral evil, which is called Sin. The one unforeseen and unavoidable in life is necessary in the world for the development of moral sense in man; the other can and must be prevented, for its appearance is not simply a misfortune to ourselves and others, but baneful to the Good in all its aspects, a woe to man. Hence the originator of evil is cursed, while the evil produced by him is brought under control, by the Moral Element of Nature.* *Sin* is the evil which disturbs the equilibrium between the elements of the human mind, in altering the proportion of its parts and powers, in introducing the rebellion of the lower

---

* "Woe unto the world because of occasions of stumbling! for it must needs be that the occasions come; but woe to that man through whom the occasion cometh!"—St. Matthew xviii. 7.

animal propensities against the higher moral element. The evil which comes to us from without, the accidental misfortunes which meet us on our way, are calculated, in whatever form they may arrive, to awaken our Conscience and Sympathy, to strengthen the relation between Soul and Mind,—in fact, this struggle for improvement serves to bring us nearer to our Creator. "To be in constant conflict with evil, in some shape or other, is the condition appointed by Providence for men and nations, and the moment the struggles for improvement cease, corruption and decay commence."* But the evil which originates from our own animal nature, which pollutes not only our own mind and makes it unfit to receive and develop the impulses of the Soul, but generates also evil in others, is the evil we pray to be guarded against and from whose temptation we desire to be delivered. "Watch and pray, lest ye enter into temptation" is the Divine commandment. The purest mind stands the nearest to God.†

---

* Earl Grey, *Parliamentary Government*, p. 113.

† St. Matthew vi. 13. "La Vertu a son germe dans l'âme humaine c'est une conséquence de son origine. Particule émanée de la Divinité, elle tend d'elle même à l'initiative du principe de son émanation; ce principe la meut, la pousse et l'inspire. Cette particule détachée de la grande âme, spécifiée par son union à tel ou tel corps, est le génie de chaque homme, ce génie le porte au beau, au bon, à la félicité. Sa souveraine félicité consiste à l'écouter; alors on choisit ce qui convient à la nature générale, à Dieu, et l'on rejette ce qui contredit son harmonie, sa loi." ZENO.

Chapter II.

THE INSTITUTES OF LAW.

§29. The Human Mind. Development of Law *(Jus, Droit, Recht.)*—§30. Moral Truths and Physical Truths.—§31. Conscience. The Law of Conscience.—§32. The Moral Law of Nature manifested through social evolution as the standard of the Good. Is the origin of International Law. Grotius.—§33. The Spirit of the Age. *(Zeitgeist.)* The Popular Consciousness. The concentrated *sensorium* of the social organism. The Ego of the social organism. The National Spirit of Law. Free State Education. Public Opinion. Free Press.—§34. Common Sense.—§35. The Scholastic Philosophy and Positivism.—§36. The International Spirit of Law.—§37. International Law is the manifestation of the influence of the Moral Element of Nature on Social Organisms.—§38. The Philosophy of Law and the Historical School.—§39. The Moral Element in Nature is the motor of Civilization, *i.e.*, of Material as well as Moral progress. The Aesthetic. Moral progress comes through the individual to the Race.—§40. The subjective and the objective form of Law *(Jus, Droit, Recht.)*

§29. The expression Human Mind, so often used in the foregoing pages, is the term by which is designated the individual subject of thought in general, as the result of consciousness. Here the Ego, when in sound normal condition and activity, exercises its natural powers and susceptibilities in various mental operations. These powers and susceptibilities are called Faculties, to distinguish the different functions or modes of activity of the mind. The conditions under which these various activities of the mind operate constitute the *Mental Law*, so far as these conditions regard the connection of the mind with objects outside itself, *i.e.*, with the Non-Ego; this is the sphere of *objective* activity of mind. The same conditions of activity constitute the *Moral Law* when regard is had to the relation of the mind with the moral senses Conscience and Sympathy; which is the *subjective* activity of the mind in connection with the Ego of our consciousness (§12). Such is the condition of mental activity when the Moral Principles or Moral Truths, described in the next section, are conceived in the mind through the moral senses just named. As such the Mind can be defined as the workshop of the Soul, where the impressions of the Moral Senses are formed into Motives (§18).

Moral Truths are the principles of Ethics which form the rules of man's conduct, *i.e.*, the rules of life, individual as well as social, in the language of jurisprudence called *Customs*.

Thus by the operation of the human mind, through the Moral Senses (§§15 and 29), aided by suitable surroundings of social conditions, the subjective moral obligations, which constitute the main guidance of men's acts, are developed into objective Customs, controlling the individual moral conduct of man as well as regulating his relations with his fellow-creatures. These objective ethico-legal obligations form the basis of the rules which, regulating the conditions of the social relations of men, are called LAW *(Jus, Droit, Recht.)* They give us the natural test by which the condition of Society called civilization is gauged. Hence the natural conditions under which the development of the human mind, *i.e.*, the moral development of man, takes place constitute the Moral Law of Nature.

§30. Primary Truths or First Principles, the consciousness of which is described above (§13), may be divided into two distinct classes, viz., *Moral Truths* and *Physical Truths;* which differ from each other in regard to the modes in which Truth develops itself in the mind. As the capabilities of the mental powers often differ in their application, so the development of Primary Truths in individual minds really differs in proportion to the capacity and relative freedom of the mind.

This variety gives prominence to the differences which mark the process of development in the mind of Moral and

Physical Truths respectively. Moral Truths are less dependent on the physico-mental development of the mind's functions than Physical Truths, for the development of Moral Truths does not depend upon the degree of cultivation of the different faculties of knowledge, collectively called Intelligence, but upon the measure of purity and soundness possessed by the mind; that is, upon its moral as well as upon its physical aptitude to receive the intuition of the truth. The development of Physical Truths, on the other hand, is independent of any state of purity or perversion of the mind, and of any moral conception of Conscience and Sympathy, being performed through the power of Reason, which differs in each individual; so that those Truths are more or less discernible in accordance with the degree of development to which these faculties have attained. Hence arises the distinction which is observed between the nature of the development in the human mind of Moral Truths and Physical or Scientific Truths. The former, as principles of Justice, develop, through the moral senses, into those laws of ethics, of human conduct and duty, by which we perceive and follow the Good. The development of Physical Truths, on the other hand, depends on the more or less completeness of our conception of physical causation, when arived at with or without consciousness created by intuition. This proves the connection which exists between the two stages of mental evolution we styled above the *physico*-mental and the *moral*-mental organism.

Moral and Physical Truths are both constituent principles of the Universal Law of Nature, which indicate the general order of Creation, but Moral Truths form the basis of human responsibility, the law of human conduct and duty, and give certain directions *to* Reason, while Physical Truths, finding their development *in* Reason, through the Mental Law (§29), and thus brought forward by the strength of reasoning, are dependent on the degree of development to which the individual faculties of knowledge have attained, and seem to have Reason for their source.

The same moral obligations, which in the present generation extend their sway over all mankind, were acknowledged by human Consicence as Moral Truths long before human Intelligence conceived the simplest Physical or Scientific Truth. And the simplest Scientific Truths, with or without the co-operation of scientific education, teaching, or experience, may be forgotten, or they may be displaced by the knowledge of other Physical Truths, with their correlative sciences. Whereas the spiritual impulses of Justice and Love, which are in their tender germs already discernible in the spontaneous action and inclinations of the child, at the first dawn of reason, when yet free from all bias of human training or worldly experience, cannot be effaced from the pure Mind, whose natural inclination when in a normal state, ever was and is to follow the impulses of the Soul. Now, as Reason is the reflective power whose office it is to disclose the right and the wrong, as well as the true and the false, the beautiful and the reverse, it is one and the same faculty of our organization through which the synthetic process of induction both of Moral and of Physical Truths takes place. The consequence is that the differences which mark the process of their respective development in the mind are often disregarded, as the same test applies to both, viz., the reliability of our mental faculties and the correctness of their operations.

This is what leads the sceptical materialist, who can see nothing beyond his narrow horizon, to ignore the moral element in Nature and to deny to the human mind the moral organism with its power of prescient or intuitive conception. He banishes all this from creation, as not being comprehended in his philosophy, which does not admit of any progress of evolution beyond the physico-mental organism. But the inadequacy of Reason is fully demonstrated by the fact that, if our faculties were limited to the physico-mental organism, *i.e.*, the mind without the help of Intuition (§10), our rational knowledge of simple material experience would be the limit of our consciousness; but this is not the case, for who does not readily apprehend, without any attempt to define them, the meaning of the terms truth, ought, right, conscience, sympathy? Can reason alone or logic define them? No more than they can define space and time, or matter and force. But these ideas do not require any analytical definition to be understood, for if we cannot circumscribe them by logical definition, we can surely feel them through intuition and be perfectly cognizant of all the emotions they engender.

§31. Thus is manifested the inadequacy of Reason to constitute, when left alone and without the help of a higher faculty of intuition, the criterion of human accountability. It indicates also the existence of a moral sense in the human mind, which immediately approves or disapproves without reference to any further consideration of logical utility, and serves as an inspiring agent to Reason, tending to develop in the mind the principles of Justice. Yet, though the nature and constituent principles of this moral sense called Conscience, may be beyond the sphere of logical definition, it has real existence, for its infallible hold on the human mind, its dominion over Reason and Intelligence, and its powerful influence on the dealings of mankind, are manifested in all periods of human life, in all states of Intellectual development and in all stages of civilization. This is likewise the case with regard to the other moral sense, viz., Sympathy, which imparts to the mind the element of Righteousness called Benevolence.

But Conscience is timid and speaks tenderly to Reason, while Egoism, through dazzling Imagination, overpowers it. Hence Conscience appears a coward when it has to wrestle in the mind with malignant passions or with shrewd selfishness, operating under the disguise of "general utility" or "reasons of state," and shrinks alike from the burning fury of the one as from the other's cold grip of treacherous arguments, which, owing to their false colors, are often mistaken for common sense,—and yet this timid Conscience, though bullied out of countenance, for the moment, is the agent of immortal truth, for the power of remorse, the strength of an accusing conscience, can never be overawed by passions nor lulled into inactivity by reasoning. Can Conscience err? Conscience is the connecting link of Justice between the Soul and the Mind, and, as such, the messenger of truth, but its promptings are perceived through the faculties of the mind, and the human mind is not and cannot be infallible. The reasoning power as well as the judgment may fail. This is the consequence of the frailty of the human organization, with which the mental faculties keep equal pace, but this does not and cannot dispense a rational man, endowed with a sound mind, from the moral obligation (when not prevented by forces beyond the control of free will) to act as he sincerely believes to be right, that is, to follow the dictates of his Conscience, which will not mislead when listened to with sincerity, *i.e.*, with purity of mind free from any bias of interest and emotions. But when conscience casts its full light on an impure mind, depraved by rapacious selfishness or moved by angry passions, its image is distorted like the gentle moon reflected in stormy waters; yet, the voice of this faithful messenger of eternal truth keeps ever sounding in our moral ear, until fully acknowledged, though, alas! often too late, and this is the cause of all human misery.

At the most solemn period of human history the question was asked: What is Truth? But, as we perceive the true nature and power of moral truth when we are ourselves the actors, and the decision of Conscience concerns our own good or evil deeds, so the heathen philosopher, who put that question, gave the answer himself when he made an effort to appease his accusing conscience by formally washing his hands of the guilt of shedding innocent blood.

From the Soul, which is the originator of the principle of Good in the human mind, and which distinguishes the intuitively rational man from the brute acting by instinct, proceeds the intuition, which through the moral sense of Conscience awakens in the mind certain elementary ideas and impulses, whereby the mind retains its impressions in the form of necessary and immutable obligations, which come so natural to our reason that not to follow them seems contrary to our nature and thus wrong, while to obey them, seems natural and right. The fact is, the Ego of our consciousness, the centre of our moral senses and free will (§12), is then pervaded, adjusted and agitated by **an innate criterion through which our judgment pronounces the spontaneous verdict of right and wrong,—the ought or ought not of moral obligation.** This takes place through the same natural judgment by which we perceive the distinction between simple truth and direct falsehood, or between two contradictory propositions, whenever the voluntary act of any responsible rational being—in our own case or in that of others, and irrespective of the question whether it be an act already performed, or one only proposed or designed—is made an object of contemplation. The verdict, which is always in harmony with Reason, is the expression of approval or disapproval pronounced on the part of Conscience with reference to the act contemplated. The will based on this verdict is *good faith*, and the action resulting therefrom *honesty*.

This harmony of Conscience and Reason, the test of right judgment, which is the basis of all individual and social intercourse between man and man and state and state, is the *Law of Conscience*, the Law of right and wrong, of the immutable natural justice, the manifestation of the Moral Element of Nature, discribed in the next section. (*)

---

* Conscience is also represented as the moral ego, i.e., "the phase in which our consciousness appears when manifesting itself ethically." This theory is ably sustained by Professor LORIMER, in his work "*The Institutes of Law.*" 2 Edit. p. 181, et seq. But, since, in §12, we have represented the Ego as **the intuitive** power of Consciousness and the manifestation of the Soul, as the power of **impulsion** and of inhibition, **of acting** and of restraining, in fact, as the **centre** of the moral senses (conscience and sympathy) and of the Will,—I may venture to hope that my system of the *moral senses* does not essentially differ, in its outcome, from that of my venerable and highly esteemed friend, as it does not sin against the "law of integrity," but maintains the fact of a state of moral consciousness in the mind, centered in the Ego.

§32. The Moral Element of Nature is the agency through which the force of moral actions (§18), the moral *vis-viva*, is developed in the human mind. Its effects are perceptible in the moral-mental activities of man, but its nature is as undemonstrable through empirical science as that of the (so-called) physical forces or forms of energy, **viz.**, gravitation, electricity, etc. The idea of the absolute nature of forces is beyond the power of experimental science, whose definition of force, based on experience, can say nothing of its nature, and **must** confine itself to effects which are regarded to be due to force.

Newton said (in the third **letter** to Bentley) with regard to gravitation—and **it is the almost** universal opinion of physicists that this is applicable **to all forms of energy** generally,—"It is inconceivable that inanimate matter **should**, without the mediation of something else which is not material, operate on and affect other matter without mutual contact . . . . Gravity must **be caused by** an agent acting constantly according to certain **laws; but** whether this **agent be material** or immaterial, I have **left to the** consideration of my readers."

As now forces, power or energy,—or whatever we may call those, scientifically, as yet unexplained effects or actions which matter has **on** matter without mutual contact,—cannot be accounted for without the hypothesis of the existence of some medium or agent unlike ordinary matter, a so-called *imponderable*, we may fairly regard forces as the manifestations of a universal agency, acting constantly and persistently according to certain laws. Of what this medium or agent consists,—whether it is material (ponderable) or immaterial (spiritual), and whether **it is non-**continuous or continuous (*i.e.*, working with or without **the help of** separate atoms)—is simply impossible to demonstrate before we know what matter itself is. That this agent or medium of energy must be regarded as persistent throughout the entire evolution process of Nature is the natural consequence of the evolution theory. This universal agent we called above (§2) Spirit of Creation or Motor of Evolution, and in the moral organism, more particular, the Moral Element of Nature. It manifests itself though the organic evolution process as instinct in the lower, and as intuition (p.17) in the higher mental organism.

In mental philosophy the Moral Element of Nature is a necessary postulate. If we deny the existence of that stimulus through which the ascertained activities of our Moral-Mental organism (§5)—the highest stage of creation on earth, reserved to mankind—take place, we could not realize the ethical conditions of the human mind called Justice and Benevolence, and must make good and evil dependent upon the ever-varying subjective stand-point of egoism. Such a view brings mankind back to the level of the brute endowed with reason,—to what we called the perfect man of the materialist,—with only the Physico-Mental organism (§4), in its struggle for merely material existence, under the animal instinctive rule of "might is right." Without a natural standard of the Good which is indicated by the moral senses, by the ethical instinct of the Moral-Mental Organism, Society is impossible, for the basis of Society is not animal selfishness but the mutual practice of justice and benevolence, or, as Herbert Spencer puts it, "the marching towards a state of identification of altruism with egoism, in the sense that personal gratification will come from the gratification of others." And when he says further, that "we are shown undeniably that it is a perfectly possible thing for organisms to become so adjusted to the requirements of their lives, that energy expended for the general welfare may not only be adequate to check energy expended for the individual welfare, but may come to subordinate it so far as to leave individual welfare no greater part than is necessary for the maintenance of individual life,"—he simply indicated the condition of the Good, the moral condition of the human mind which answers to the full development of the Moral Senses, in that state of perfect harmony which we call the Moral

Law of Nature.* This state of perfection is only arrived at by the survival of the fittest through the struggle for existence between the moral senses and the egoism of the animal nature of man,—when the moral element has gained the battle (§5).

But, furthermore, this inspiration of the soul, this longing toward the Good, as the natural consequence of our moral-mental organism (§14) is corroborated by history in all its stages, and is most conspicuous in the process of development of societies or states, in Europe as elsewhere. This is a plain indication of the influence which the Moral Element has on the growth of civilization, and which is exhibited by the general craving after some positive rules of conduct calculated to bring the moral principles of Nature, which in the inwardly conscientious man is universally felt to exist, into practical or visible shape, for the regulation of the mutual rights and obligations of men, and for the peaceful intercourse between nations.

Mr. Hall, in his recent great work, gives the following historical account of the way in which the conception of International Law arose. The state of things which presented itself in Europe for a considerable time before International Law came into existence, is described by him as follows:—

"1. Such material restraint as was supplied at an earlier period over the greater part of civilized Europe by the feudal relations, and over much of it by the superiority of the Empire, had disappeared, and such moderating influences as had been exercised by the church had also disappeared; influences, in other words, which, whatever their material power, had at one time deeply affected the imagination, had died away.

"2. No means existed of setting up any authority of a like external nature, competent to maintain international order; and no habit of reference to a formulated moral standard, independently of external authority, had grown up.

"3. Rules of conduct were becoming daily more necessary,

---

* *Data of Ethics*, 3rd edit., Appendix.

through the increasing intercourse between both States themselves and the subjects of States, and through the wider area over which the relations of States were continually spreading.

"Under such circumstances it was natural that a craving should be felt for the discovery of a rule of international conduct, capable of impressing itself on the mind with something of the force of Law That such a craving was generally felt, there are many indications, and, in fact without its existence as a powerful motive among the European peoples at large, international law could obviously not have obtained recognition. The only distinct attempts to satisfy it were, however, made by legal writers, and it was by them, as the medium through which the ideas found expression which were latent in the general mind, that International Law was placed upon its original speculative basis. To understand how that basis came to be adopted, therefore, it is only necessary to examine the works of the writers by whom the advent of Law was prepared."*

What, then, was the cause of this general craving, of this universal and urgent demand for law which was the advent of International Law in Europe? It was the general sense of the necessity of establishing some rules of conduct between nations. When the thinking minds of Europe, after the fall of the feudal system, of the superiority of the Empire and of the international influence of the Church of Rome, being freed from material restraint and blind obedience, were, with their degenerated consciences, cast adrift in a sea of boundless doubts as to what was right or wrong in their mutual dealings, they were brought to the sense of justice by the regenerating, self-acting *vis-viva* of the Moral Element of Nature, the source of the moral sense of Justice, that powerful motive which gave birth to the ideas that were latent in the popular Conscience, but found expression through the leading minds of the time, by men like Franciscus à Victoria, Covarruvias, Soto, Saurez, Melancthon, Olendorp,

---

* W. E. HALL, *International Law*, Edit. 1880, p. 657.

Hemming, Albericus Gentilis. Their arguments were finally summed up conclusively by Hugo Grotius before the grand jury of civilized humanity, and the verdict was thereupon given which saved modern civilization from drifting back into the chaos of the dark ages of European barbarism.

Hugo de Groot, more generally known as Grotius, the acknowledged founder of the science of International Law, the blessed reformer who stemmed the current of moral corruption caused by the policy of dissimulation, injustice and crime, as taught by Machiavelli and his school in that dark period of European society, in which criminal frauds and treacherous artifices made up the policy called Reasons of State, maintained in his famous work, "The Laws of War and Peace"* the existence of a fixed standard of right, and thus of a real distinction between right and wrong. He also taught that the rule of conduct imposed by our conscience, which enjoins certain actions while it condemns others, a rule which is indispensable for the maintenance of any society of rational human beings, constitutes the Law of Nature *(Jus Naturale)*.†

§33. This craving after Justice, which has been defined as "a constant and perpetual disposition to render every man his due," is the result of the working of the Moral Element of Nature in the individual minds of the thinking and leading members of Society, by which process, rendered more or less perfect, according to the degree of susceptibility possessed by those minds as to the influence of the moral element, the *Popular Conscience* is formed.

Scarcely two individual members of any society will be found to think exactly alike or to have the same perception of data, in right or wrong, for it is seldom that individual minds are in such

---

* DE JURE BELLI AC PACIS, of which the last Latin edition, corrected by the Author, appeared at Amsterdam in 1642, has been repeatedly translated. The best French translation is that of Mr. Pradier Fodéré, published in 1867.

† DE JURE BELLI AC PACIS, Lib. I., Cap. 1., §10.

a like condition of soundness and purity as would enable them to develop the intuitions of the Soul into identical conclusions, though as regards the main principles many leading minds of the society may agree, and form on this agreement a common conclusion.

This common conclusion, generally called the "Spirit of the Time" "or Spirit of the Age" *(Zeitgeist)*—the outcome of the principles on which all agree, is the manifestation of the Popular Consciousness, the concentrated *sensorium* of the social organism, formed by *Public Opinion*, as tested and consolidated by the intellectual powers and moral senses of the people. This popular consciousness is based on *Common Sense*, as described in the next section, and as such applied as a standard or ultimate test of the Law *(Jus)* of that society, or in other words, as its lawgiver, to teach its jurisprudence and to explain the facts of its history; and it is then called the *Spirit of Law*. (*Comp.* §49).

Public opinion is the nebula formed by individual opinions and thoughts on particular subjects, from the generalizing of which the Spirit of Law is consolidated. The agents through whose influence on the mind Public Opinion is rectified and condensed into Popular Consciousness and Spirit of Law, are free State-Education and Free Press. By free State-Education—free from sectarian principles or prejudices—Common Sense (§34) is cultivated in the unbiased mind, while, through a Free Press—impartial but not neutral, and, above all, *moral*—individual utterances of subjective thoughts become active agents in the forming of that generally working power of the Spirit of Law, through whose agency these subjective thoughts become objective laws for the moulding of society into civilization. Hence it is the duty of each thinking member of the society to give utterance to what he judiciously thinks to be the highest truth in science and philosophy in all their branches. Freedom and facility for such utterances are essential requirements in the constitution of the State.

Thus the Spirit of Law represents the consciousness of the social organism, of the State as moral being, the concentration of the sensibilities of the intellectual faculties and the moral senses of divers individual members, and **forms**, through legislation, the **Will** of the respective social **organism**, of which the jurisprudence and the governmental **executive of the State** constitute the **Volition**. Thus, in analogy with the human mind, the will of the **state**, in making proper laws, is **not sufficient if the volition**, the **proper execution thereof, is lacking.** *(Comp.* §18).

Through legislation and jurisprudence the Spirit of Law is manifested as the indicator of **the progress made on the road to** civilization by the respective **Society, Nation or State**,—for which reason it is also called the *National Spirit of Law*,—and must naturally change its **aspect at every** stage on this road, made by the subject whose immanent phenomenon it is, *i.e.*, by the collective leading minds of the respective society. In the same proportion as civilization progresses, the Spirit of Law advances **in a rising scale** towards the standard of the Good, but likewise retrogression in that respect, caused **by general disturbances of the harmony of** the Moral Law within the individual state, must have a depressing effect on that scale. It represents the sum or balance **of the abstract** moral principles of the individuals **composing the Society or State, being formed and** modified by **these** individual minds on their road to moral excellence or deterioration. **As such, the** Spirit **of Law is** the medium through which the subjective good is formed **into objective Law** (§40).

The Spirit of Law having given birth to the usages of Society, these, gradually developing, become, through the expressed or tacit sanction of the faculty invested with sovereign power in the Society, consolidated into Positive Law, for the government of that Society as Body-Politic and for the definition of the reciprocal relations between individual members, and between these and the sovereign power of the Society or State formed by them. Thus the Spirit of Law of every State and every period manifests itself through the *Law* (Jus), with which it changes, correlatively and contemporaneously, on the road to civilization, by the influence of the Moral Element of Nature, which is beyond the caprices of the day. Every era in the history of a nation has its own Spirit of Law and its correlative usages and Positive Law. In consequence thereof the Positive Law of each individual State differs from that of another State, in proportion to its respective condition, history, tradition, morals, climate, nature of the soil and other inherent natural circumstances. It is not possible to make, *a priori*, one set of laws suitable for all nations, unless every individual mind had the same moral capability; nor can this be the province of the Moral Law of Nature, which, as the Law of the moral-mental organism, is evolved—like all Laws of Nature—by spontaneous gradual development. This gradual moral development of societies of human beings, called *Civilization*, operates, through the action of the moral senses of the individual mind, on the practical medium which we have described as Spirit of Law, and which explains itself to the popular mind through *Common Sense*, the intellectual element of civilization.

§34. Common Sense is plain, practical logic, the conviction generated through *intellect* and *feeling* combined. It is the sense of human beings generally as felt by common intelligence; the logic of the normal mind under the influence of moral development, and thus the language of Conscience and Sympathy in union, by the harmony of which its arguments are proved. As such it is the only sure foundation for the loftiest structures of human thought, the safe holding ground for the anchor of a sound mind, which, losing this, is cast adrift among the cliffs of inextricable doubts and destruction. It is the only logic comprehensible to the popular understanding, as it speaks to Feeling as well as to Reason, of which two co-existing elements the Popular Consciousness is formed (§10). Where the mechanism of Reason is inadequate, there Feeling, which is awakened by Intuition, supplies the want. Hence it is that the mind is able to feel as well as to reason, and its common sense partakes of both.

How often we find the most intellectually cultivated mind painfully destitute of Common Sense. If we cultivated our Feeling as we cultivate our Intellect, they would be in better harmony with each other, and our Common Sense would be good and complete; while now, in many cases, it is only half the faculty it should be. This makes man, the more he learns, become the more one-sided, selfish and sceptical, and at last it causes his mind to give way, through its not being properly balanced by those two inseparable elements of our moral-mental organism, Conscience and Sympathy. Such is Common Sense, which, as the natural test of logic, is impartial, though not neutral, taking over sound ideas from all systems indiscriminately, without sanctioning or criticizing any special doctrine, because it follows a course of its own. Only that which comes deliberately in its way is utterly demolished, for it is the power of popular conviction, the consciousness of the living generation heralded by its Spirit of Law on the high road of civilization. When the Moral Law of Nature is applied to common life, Common Sense is the logic by which its ethical rules are explained, to test the practicability of these rules in the actual circumstances of social life, and to co-ordinate the facts of Social Science, as it is through Common Sense that the isolated facts of history are brought into a comprehensive whole. Here we have an instance of the influence which the Moral Element in Nature exercises on the progressive Social Evolution of the human race.

§35. The pure dogmatism of the old Scholastic philosophy is not stranger to Common Sense than the Positive Empirical. Both fail to keep a firm hold on the free popular mind. The one might influence the human imagination and thus captivate Reason for a while, and the other might fascinate the masses by the false lore of a material liberty which is without spiritual freedom, or charm the imagination of unthinking youth into loyalty to the empire of Reason—the promised land of an animal materialism free from all moral restraints, where the mind stops short of the highest development allotted to it in creation. But neither the one nor the other can make man believe without thinking or make him think without feeling. If the one can make believers without faith, it cannot make non-thinkers void of reason; and if the other should succeed, through the attraction of a delusive simplicity of shallow arguments, under the disguise of Common Sense, in forming inexperienced minds, wanting in self-organization or purity, into sensuous unbelievers, it cannot complete its task by bringing the everliving inspiration of the unbiassed human mind under the positive mode of thought of Empirical Philosophy. The tyrannical shackles of all one-sided, narrow and exclusive philosophies will be cast off by the self-seeking and self-determining mind, when left free to follow its own inspirations, to regain its natural course of thought in Common Sense, to satisfy the convictions of Reason and the longings of Feeling. (*Comp.* §26, p. 33).

§36. In conformity with the Popular Consciousness, an *International Spirit of Law* is generated by the relations which naturally must spring up between individual states. This Spirit of Law displays the influence which it exercises on the external life and voluntary acts of nations towards nations, by producing those usages which form the basis of what is called the *Law of Nations* or *International Law*.

These usages of nations cannot be formed into written or Positive Law, for the reason that there is no Body-Politic endowed with legislative and executive power and having for its constituents nations or states. They have, however, inherent binding force, because international usages are, when generally acknowledged, a reflex of the best part of the various Positive Laws, that is to say of those parts which bear more conspicuously the mark of the influence of the Moral Element, for these usages must satisfy the Popular Conscience, in the case of each Nation individually. The ultimate common basis of the Popular Conscience, as it appears in the various nations or states, is the Moral Law of Nature. In this all agree. But starting from this common standard, the Popular Conscience of each nation or state is differentiated by the varying progress of civilization at every period in history. The indicator of these variations is the International Spirit of Law of each successive period, which, in harmony with the changes in the sentiments and external conditions of individual nations, is the reflex of the moral development of the international life of the body of states. These subtle elements of Law form the common source from which International Law, that brightest part of the history of nations, flows forth, as "bright effluence of bright essence increate." (*Comp.* §63).

§37. Thus it is that International Law, not being capable of being put into the form of Positive Law by any worldly authority, depends for its support entirely on the spontaneous development of civilization, as engendered in the moral-mental organism of man (§5) through the moral senses conscience and sympathy. Under this influence, which might be called the influence of the Moral Element in Nature, *i.e.*, the Soul, International Law has been gradually modified, in conformity with the progress of civilization. Instances of this process of modification are: laws enhancing respect of alien life, rights and property; law and treaties regarding slavery and the slave-trade; the definition of rights of nationality and domiciliation; liberty for the navigation of the seas; neutrality; the laws of war, and so forth. These are so many instances of international moral progress which is ever going on, indicating the International Spirit of Law of the present state of civilization in Europe and America;—for, " the life of Nations," says Savigny, "can be compared to the human life, which is never stationary, but represents a continuous succession of organical development."*

---

* Von Savigny, *System des Rom. Rechts.* Vol. i., ch. ii., §7.

From this devolpment has resulted the code which treats of the rights and duties of nations. It is not a written code, indeed, but one which does not the less subsist as an effect of the collective working of the Popular Conscience, operative in civilized nations at all stages of the history of mankind. It is founded on the mutual consent, tacit, expressed, or presumed, of the moral senses of mankind.

"Cette loi," says Heffter, "se rétrécit ou s'élargit avec le degré de culture des nations. Reposant d'abord sur une nécessité ou sur des besoins purements matériels, elle emprunte, dans ses développements, à la morale, son autorité, et son utilité, et s'affranchit successivement de ses éléments impurs." Who could fail to acknowledge here the clear manifestation of the effect of a moral element in Nature? This is what we ascribe to the ennobling influence of the soul, exhibited in this development of moral principles through the International Spirit of Law* (§63).

§38. By this devolpment of the moral principles, the intuition of the Soul is combined with the actions of the Mind and shows the relation in which the Soul, as the Moral Element in Nature, stands to Reason in the Mind, and thus to the motives of our actions. This may furnish the clue to the fountain-head of many causes, which are only discernible in their effects, but remain unexplained by the mute facts of history. When we attribute to this motive power the relation we feel *must* exist between these effects and the common origin of their causes, between the phenomenon and its inherent factor, or, to comprehend all in well-known terms, between historical and philosophical data, we should surely not expect to satisfy empirical science; but neither are we sinning against any of its demonstrations, by attributing this onward strife of Society, this incessant progressive evolution of civilization, which plainly shows an inherent action of the mind, to the influence of the

---

* HEFFTER, *Le Droit Intern. de l'Europe.* Edit. *Bergson*, §2.

soul, for the Moral Law of Nature, the Law of the Good, is also the Law of Society. This cannot be otherwise, for the Moral Law of Nature consists not only in the dictates of Justice, but in the perfect harmony of both elements of Rightousness, as imparted to our nature; of which Justice, as expressed by the Law of Conscience, is but one element, the other being Benevolence, which, as we have noted before, takes into account the frailty of human nature, tempering the stern sense of Justice in proportion to the actual tottering pace of Society, and promoting its gradual developement and the sure progress of the human race towards the Good, for virtue without charity does not exist.*

The omitting to take into account this mitigating element of the Moral Law of Nature, which makes Justice applicable to the natural state of Society, so that, of the two elements forming the popular Conscience, called the Spirit of Law, one always qualifies the other, or in other words, the mistaking of the fluctuating Spirit of Law for the immutable Moral Law, seems to be the cause of the difference which exists between the Philosophy of Law and the Historical School.

When contemplating history in the different aspects of that social evolution which civilization has undergone through the working of the soul on the individual mind, and which is exhibited in the written laws of the different epochs of civilization, we may well exclaim with a recent writer of the Historical School, "L'évolution progressive du Droit n'a jamais subi de temps d'arrêt et depuis sa première manifestion inconsciente sortie de l'instinct populaire, jusqu'a son riche épanouissement fécondé par les travaux des savants, le droit s'est développé comme la vie même, comme une force inhérente à l'humanité.

"Et quel spectacle grandiose que d'assister ainsi à la formation lente du Droit, de le voir émerger du travail latent de la

---

* Though I speak with the tongues of men and angels and have not charity, I am become as sounding brass or a tinkling cymbal."—St. Paul: I Cor. xiii. 1.

conscience populaire, surgissant pour répondre aux nécessités sociales et constituant peu à peu l'individualité nationale."*

This is the action of the Popular Conscience, which, as Spirit of Law, is permanently at work, in conformity with the Law of conscience,—which is the harmony of conscience and reason, the test of right judgment (§31)—to find the minimum sacrifice of individual right, which will produce the maximum of public welfare. This is the combined effect in the mind of both elements of the Moral Law of Nature, the perfect harmony of which constitutes the Good. But when this harmony is broken, the cheerful prospect is converted into the mournful contemplation of a retreat on the road to civilization, for then the moral congruity and strength of the individual mind are affected, and, the mind gradually becoming distorted and polluted by passions, by prejudices or selfish motives, personal morality is impaired. Where this is the case as regards the leading minds of a nation, there the national standard of morals is degenerating, civilization is coming to a standstill and civil liberty and national prosperity decline. When the moral principles of a nation are corrupt, its international conduct becomes untrustworthy and vile, and the nation, having sinned against itself, is ready for any act of injustice towards its neighbours, and in spite of temporary aggrandizement, effected through violation of the principles of justice and humanity towards its weaker neighbours, the decay of the unsound state is irrevocably decreed by the Moral Law of Nature, as proved by all recorded facts of history.

Thus the Moral Element in Nature, which has its agent in the *Popular Conscience* and its logic in *Common Sense*, manifests its influence not merely as regards the individual progress of the nation or state but also in the dealings of nation with nation; for it represents in the mind the elements of the law as laid down in

---

* "*La Philosophie du Droit et l'Ecole Historique.*" Leçon d'ouverture de cours de Droit Naturel, par Mr. ADOLPH PRINS, Professeur a l'Université de Bruxelles. *Révue de Droit International.* Tome xiv. 1882, No. 6, p. 565.

the divine commandment, "As ye would that men should do to you, do ye also to them likewise," which is the only true principle of utility, and the loyal rule for the combination of self-interest with general welfare.

§39. As stated before, it is through the moral senses conscience and sympathy that the ideas of righteousness are created in the mind of the individual man, and that rules for the guidance of his conduct and for the performance of his duties are laid down. These rules are, in turn, communicated through the individual man and through family life, to the general community or society, and exercise eventually an influence on its external as well as internal condition, moulding the political as well as the moral conduct of the nation, as an aggregate of rational beings.* Thus, progress in civilization emanates from the individual Moral-Mental Organism, through development of its moral senses conscience and sympathy, spreading from the individual over the whole race. Races and nations, like states of all forms of social organization, assume the nature of the individuals of which they are composed, for it is the nature of individuals, collectively taken, which defines the race (§42).

The influence of the Moral Element in Nature, as indicated by the ennoblement of the mind, can be traced also outside our moral nature, and, in fact, in all concerns of life in which the mind has actually a share, for when the mind is morally developed, habits and taste and judgment are refined. Hence it is that our ideas and our judgment, when contemplating scenes of nature or works of art or science, are moulded by the inspiration of the Good, when emotions run parallel with intellectual powers. Traces of this fact may be noticed in many productions of the mind within the spheres of art, science and literature. There are certain objects in nature and art which, so soon as perceived, strike the cultivated mind as beautiful or the reverse. Again, there are certain traits of character and courses of con-

---

* Sir James Mackintosh: Discourse on the Law of Nature and Nations.

duct which, so soon as observed, strike us as morally right or wrong. The ideas of the beautiful and the right are thus awakened in the mind by the perception of the corresponding objects, but they belong to two distinct classes of judgments, viz., *aesthetic* and *moral*.*

This progress in art and science, with the consequent refinement of habits and taste, is the outcome of the development of the Physical Truths in the mind. But although this progress bears the mark of the inspiration of the soul as the Moral Element in Nature, and thus shows the connection which exists between moral and physical truths (§30)—both of which being conceived through Intuition—it is progress only of the aesthetic element of civilization (§79); for taste is not more conscience than intelligence could be, nor can culture of the mind and refinement of manners constitute morality. All that is morally right is also inherently beautiful and great, but the civilization so-called, as exhibited by art and science, with the adherent refinement of taste and habits, does not always coincide in the history of mankind with a corresponding progress towards the Good. The latter is only attainable through the complete and harmonious development of the moral senses, which alone can engender clear consciousness of the good, the true and the beautiful.

The development of Society depends on those moral and material principles of individual progress, which lead nations gradually, through longer or shorter stages of development, from the original condition of barbarous races to the degree of excellence called civilization. The different types of these stages of moral and intellectual improvement and social and material advancement are exhibited to us by Ethnology, in the **savage**, the semi-barbarous, the less civilized and civilized tribes, hordes, peoples and nations of the earth.

From these types we learn what is meant by civilization and how the development of the moral element plays an essential

---
* JOSEPH HAVEN: *Mental Philosophy*, page 262.

part in the material progress of a nation, by leading it from its original condition, where brute force and narrow-minded egotism dominate all internal as well as external relations, into gradual acknowledgment of the principles of Justice and Humanity, in accordance with its internal moral progress and the ennoblement of its relations with other nations.*

§40. In the foregoing pages is explained how the **Soul, as** the Moral Element in Nature, must be **postulated as the motor of** progress in Civilization, by causing the development of the moral-mental orgamism **of man** through his moral senses Conscience **and** Sympathy; and how the Spirit of Law (§33) is **the medium through** which the subjective conceptions of the individual Conscience and Sympathy **are** brought into objective **rules, for the practical** conduct **of individuals and nations.**

The Moral Law of Nature, being the state of consciousness **when** complete development of the moral **senses, and thus perfect harmony** between Justice and Benevolence exist, **represents a mental condition which,** in objective form, constitutes the social **condition of perfection,** *i.e.*, **the state** towards which the natural **development of the social organism is** tending, provided the development of the moral senses is maintained by proper *discipline of the mind,* as described in §§23—26. Such a state of society, as what Mr. Herbert Spencer predicts, " when further identification of altruism with **egoism** will be made in the sense that personal gratification will come from the gratification of others " is the perfect civilization. But egoism does **not** give way to altruism without a fierce struggle **for** existence, the struggle for supremacy to be

---

* Les Sciences morales parviennent à mieux définir à l'homme sa nature spirituelle, à mieux lui tracer le cercle de ses devoirs, à mieux organiser les institutions. . . . . Admirable effet des grandes associations humaines: la marche incessante de l'homme vers le mieux. Car l'homme ne doit pas être séparé de ses œuvres, et l'experience nous montre que, réuni, comme exige sa nature, en Société avec ses semblables, ses œuvres, ses actes, ses principes, ses lois sont essentiellement prefectibles et s'avancent toujours, quoique irrégulièrement, quoique avec ses intervalles de recul ou de perturbations, dans cette voie de la perfectibilité."—ORTOLAN: *Règles Intern. et Dépl. de la Mer*, Edit. 1864, Vol. i., page 5.

carried on between by the moral senses and the selfish propensities of the animal nature of man (§5). And when this deepest of modern philosophers—as quoted before (§22)—says "that it is a perfectly possible thing for organisms to become so adjusted to the requirements of their lives that energy expended for the general welfare may not only be adequate to check energy expended for the individual welfare, but may come to subordinate it so far as to leave individual welfare no greater part than is necessary for maintenance of individual life,"—he surely does not mean to convey the idea of an evolved social condition of purely material altruism, of the communistic or anarchical types, but, as the natural consequence of evolution of the social organism, he predicts a state of perfect morality, the undisputed reign of Justice and Benevolence, in perfect harmony, which can alone be realized when the human mind is under complete control of Conscience and Sympathy in the highest development of these moral senses. To such a mind the subjective conception of Justice and Benevolence would be the objective Good, and if all the minds of a society were in this state of perfection, the Spirit of Law of that Society would be the Moral Law of Nature, *i.e.*, the subjective conception of the Good would be objectively applicable in practice, without any mitigation or amendment, in all the dealings of man with man.

That such a state of perfection is far from that in which the most civilized society exists at present on earth is obvious. The rules regulating the social relations of men, as shown above (§29), originate from the Moral Element of Nature, and being based on the moral obligations of man, as prompted by his moral senses, follow in the *actual* state of his mental evolution as nearly as possible the Moral Law of Nature, but represent a different standard from that law of complete harmony between Justice and Benevolence as conceived in the perfectly developed moral-mental organism. This standard or indicator of the actual moral condition of society is the standard of Law *(Jus)*, the Spirit of

Law as described above (§33), *i.e.*, the spirit of the Moral Law, indicating the influence of the Moral Element of Nature on the actual state of the civilization of a nation.

These rules are the objective forms in which the subjective conceptions of Justice and Benevolence are expressed in practical national customs,—the ethico-legal obligations, forming the rules of social life,—through the Spirit of Law, and, as stated before (§29), they form collectively the basis of Law *(Jus)*, regulating the social relations, the rights and duties of men towards men in the actual state of their moral-mental organism, forming the principles on which societies are constituted in the organized condition, termed State.

Chapter III.

THE DATA OF CIVILIZATION.

I. *What is Civilization?* §41. Definition of Civilization.—§42. The Standard of Civilization. The Theory of the Moral Senses.

II. *The Social Organism. State.*—§43. The Social Nature of man is the origin of States.—§44. Natural and Political Nationality.—§45. Conditions for the Political Individuality of States, as Persons of International Law.—§46. The basis of International Intercourse is the moral development of the human mind.—§47. States, as incorporate persons of International Law, have the same moral obligations as man, but modified by special prerogatives.—§48. Social Organism and Biological Organism.—§49. The Physiology of the State.—§50. The Physical and Moral faculties of States.—§51. The Natural-Constitutional form of the State's organization.—§52. The natural evolution of the Social Organism is opposed to Anarchy.—§53. The Government of the Natural-Constitutional State.—54. Forming the People into good Citizens.—§55. The Representatives of the People, and the basis of Representation.—§56. Public Opinion and the Representive Body.—§57. Political Parties.—§58. The Right of Veto is the result of the theory of Natural Equilibrium.—§59. The necessity of the hereditary head in the Monarchial-Constitutional form of Government.—§60. The Constitution.—§61. The two branches of Legislation.

III. *The Co-existence of Social Organisms. External Social Life. International Law.*—§62. International Rights and Duties of the State.—§63. International Morality.—§64. International Law. International Jurisprudence.—§65. The Moral Principles of International Intercourse.—§66. Interdependence of States.—§67. Right of Negotiation and Treaty.—§68. Moral Causes of the Imperfect Observance of Treaties. The durability of International Treaties is dependent upon the International Spirit of

Law.—§69. Material causes of the imperfect observance of Treaties.—§70. The Laws of Peace.—§71. Intermediate state between Peace and War. Confirmation of International Facts.—§72. The Law of War *(Jus belli.)* —§73. The principles of the Law of War considered in the light of Civilization. Effect **of War** on private individuals and private property. Enemy character. Enemy's private property on the high seas.—§74. Means of peaceable settlement of international disputes. Application of the Laws of Peace.—§75. **Measures** *via amicabili* and *via facta.*

IV. *Internal Social Life.. The Co-existence of Individuals.*—§76. The natural agency **of** internal development of Society.—§77. State-action is Justice **combined** with Benevolence.—§78. **State** or Scientific Socialism.

V. *The Intellectual and Moral Activities of Individual Co-existence.*—§79. **Culture,** Science, Art, Industry, Trade. The Æsthetic Element is the link between **the Material and** the Moral Element of **Civilization.—§80.** Morality and Religion. Natural Religion and Revealed **Religion.** The Christian Religion.

I. What is Civilization?

§41. In the two preceding chapters we have endeavoured to give a concise and clear account of the development—through the natural evolution-process—of the human mind, and its growth towards the highest stage of creation at present known on earth, which we called the Moral-Mental Organism (§5), and the further tendency of this development and growth toward the Good (§14), *i.e.*, the reign of perfect Justice and perfect Benevolence, in harmony combined—which, with regard to the Social Organism, is the state of perfect Civilization (§39). In other words, we have tried to show the origin of the motives of moral actions (§18) and the establishment, through those motives, of the moral obligations, as rules of life for men's practical guidance. This has been done, firstly, by describing the natural agency through which this moral development of the mind takes place and the system or law derived from the conditions created by this agency—the agency being called the Moral Senses (§15), and the system the Moral Law of Nature (§29),—and, secondly, by noting the *external* effect of the moral senses in the forming of the Spirit of Law (described in §33), through whose agency the subjective moral obligations are moulded into the Law *(Jus)* of societies, for the conservation and guidance of these aggregates of human beings (§40). We shall now proceed to investigate the evidences and manifestations of the Spirit of Law and its effect as a factor of the development of Society, in its organized and concrete expression, called State. Through this investigation we will arrive at the knowledge of those requirements of social forms and functions of the social organism which are indispensable to progress toward the state of Civilization. Concluding on this analysis of principles and facts, we shall try, finally, to arrive at some definite data, to formulate a natural Standard of Civilization.

First of all, however, we must define the conception of this state, by answering the question—What is Civilization?

Civilization is the term by which is generally understood a certain elevated state of physical, intellectual and moral development of man in society. Civilization is thus a social condition; a man out of society is analogous to being out of civilizing influences—"outside the pale of civilization."

The development of the individual mind, the amelioration of the social state, the carrying toward perfection of the relations between man and man, and between those aggregates of human beings termed Nations or States, are all data of civilization and, as we have seen before, all are dependent on the cultivation of man's moral-mental organism (§39).

Thus civilization consists in the full development of the individual mind, but as the stimulus of progress is brought on by the struggle of the *Moral Senses* of man's mind against the material propensities of his physical organism (§5), it is obvious that the motive power of civilization, the *quantula sapientia* that governs social life, is moral rather than intellectual or material, *i.e.*, that the moral element in nature is the basis of Civilization.

The rules regulating the social relations of men, as shown above (§§29, 39 and 40), are based on the moral obligations, which are prompted by the moral senses of the human mind and consolidated from subjective conceptions into the objective rules of Life called Law *(Jus)*, by the spirit of Law of the respective society (§33). As these ethico-legal rules permeate the whole social life, material as well as moral, they procure us the natural test by which civilization can be gauged.

Concluding on these premises, we can fairly define Civilization as the actual state of society in the process of transforming the subjective conception of the Good into objective practical Good (§29) and which state is indicated by the Spirit of Law of the respective society.

The marks of this prominent exponent of Civilization called Spirit of Law, by which the respective conditions of different civilizations can be compared, are the data of civilization, which we will try to formulate in the present chapter from the premises laid down in the two preceding chapters of this essay.

§42. A given state of society, whether as problem or phenomenon, is conceived and criticised by the actual standard of intellectual and moral-mental development of the subject under whose contemplation the object is brought; hence the different ways in which one and the same state of civilization is judged by different persons. Thus, to compare different conditions of moral and intellectual development, *i.e.*, civilization, we must first agree on a moral and intellectual standard, so that, to judge of any state of civilization an acknowledged gauge for society, a standard of Civilization, is indispensable. Such a standard test of human progress cannot be taken arbitrarily, nor artificially composed, but must be based on the natural evolution process of the human mind, the immediate source of civilization. The theory of the Moral Senses of man, as described in the first chapter, from which are derived the Statutes of Law noted in the second chapter, form the necessary basis for the data of a Philosophy of Civilization, from the speculations of which a standard of Civilization is arrived at.

The definition of civilization, as given in the last foregoing section, shows that by the development of a society or state is meant the attempt made, collectively, by the individual members composing the society, to bring the subjective good, engendered through the individual moral senses conscience and sympathy, into objective or practical form, for the maintenance and guidance of the social organism. The success attending such attempt is called *progress in civilization*. The test of the virtuality of any social condition and progress in civilization is whether this condition or progress be in accordance with the moral standard, *i.e.*, the Spirit of Law (§33) of the respective society or state, and whether, at the same time, it be conducive to the end of society, *viz.*, the real welfare of humanity.

In the theory of the moral senses above named, by which it is demonstrated that the human mind, as all natural phenomena, is subject to the natural evolution process, by which the moral senses are developed and through them conception of the Good engendered in the mind, we have the guidance of a principle, and a clue to that apparently tangled maze—the history of civilization, with the conflicting good and evil propensities of the human mind, its struggle for improvement against physical and moral evils, and its retrogression on the scale of civilization when that struggle ceases and corruption and decay set in (§28). And as to the future,—it is again this theory which will provide sure pilotage to clear the menacing cliffs of anarchy in its worst form; for, whatever tribulations may arrive through the enforcing of false doctrines on society, man cannot be flung out of the social organism as long as he retains his moral senses, and whatever disturbance the normal exercise of the functions of society may encounter, as history teaches, it is, over and again, the regenerating inspiration of the human mind in its moral development which is the rectifier of all disharmony in the elements of society, for the re-establishment of civilization.

II. THE SOCIAL ORGANISM.—STATE.

§43. In the preceding sections we have treated the proposition that civilization is the natural social condition, emanating from the development of the moral senses of the human beings composing the society or state, so that civilization can only be real when it is based on the moral development of the mind, and thus condusive to the progress, *i.e.*, amelioration, of the human race. Our next objects of investigation are now the nature and structure of the social organism, and the form best suited for a state to arrive at this desired end of social life. But to define the idea *State* as a concrete body-politic we must first take a view of the external condition of states, *i.e.*, their status as persons of International Law (§§44-48), and then proceed to the physiology of the state, *i.e.*, the description of a state as a social organism (§§49-61).

Social life, as stated at the beginning, is the natural consequence of the human organism; for man does not exist in an isolated state as long as natural causes have free play. By virtue of the intellectual faculties and the sensibility of his mind, man is essentially a social being, and he is always bound to be so, whatever may be the nature of his associations, which vary in conformity with the special circumstances affecting his development, and modify the degree of civilization to which he actually attains. Outside of social existence, man cannot develop his mind nor advance in civilization, physically or morally. He is then an abnormal unit, the disorganized particle, of a concrete phenomenon, which, left out of its normal sphere, cannot attain its natural destination, as not being influenced by the social evolution process of the Moral Law of Nature. Without any intercourse with his fellow-creatures, outside the pale of civilization, man must degenerate to a state of selfishness, void of conscience and sympathy, which brings him below the species to which he belongs. Thus the social nature of man is the natural origin of societies or aggregates of human beings, which are called *Nations* or *States*, the reciprocal moral and material or political relations of which form part of the subject matter of International Law.

§44. Groups of the same race, identical in origin, and having common usages, language, or idioms, and common moral aptitudes, are called *Peoples* or *Nations*, when designated from a natural historical or philological point of view, and constitute the *Ethnographical* or *Natural Nationality*.

When political individuality is ascribed to a people as subject to Law, it is called a *State;* which designation refers to the people as Body-Politic, possessing a common government, common laws, common internal and external powers, civil and political, and common interests, in all matters affecting the *Political Nationality*.

Different nations can, by their common consent, be united into one State; in which case all the individuals composing the State have the same political nationality, though they may vastly differ from an ethnographical point of view.

A nation can also be divided into several States, with as many different political nationalities; and different States may form a Union of States, in which all the individuals composing these States have one and the same political nationality defined by the Union.

§45. For the recognition of a State as such, that is, as a community having political individuality, certain conditions are indispensable. These are that the community claiming recognition as a State and all the rights and duties attached to such a status, viewed from the stand-point of International Law, must be an organized body-politic, which should consist of individuals who do not belong or owe allegiance to any other State, and which should not be incorporated by virtue of any outside authority, concession, grant, or charter, but definitively established on its own defined territory with its own government and legislation, possessing also the means and ability to maintain its integrity.

The fulfilment of these conditions constitutes the State, *de jure*, as a member of the family of States, whose mutual relations form the subject of International Law. Without these conditions, which make up the criterion of an independent State, no society or aggregate of human beings can be denominated a State, or admitted on equal terms into international relationship with existing **States**.

Thus, for instance, chartered Trading or Colonization Companies, though having their own government and administration, and uncontrolled management of their affairs on their own extended territorial property, cannot legally entertain international relations with any foreign government except through the government from whom their charter emanates, and under whose protection they are established or to whom they owe allegiance.*

Nomadic tribes, living in wandering groups without a permanent or defined territory, though they be closely united and organized **for** their internal government, cannot be regarded as States, because they do not comply with all the conditions above mentioned. They may, however, in some cases be admitted to the privileges of International Law and hold intercourse with civilized States, whenever such tribes are ready to reciprocate the international privileges accorded to them, to the extent of their ability or as far as their social conditions will permit. As a general rule, when privileges of International Law are extended to uncivilized nations, this is done, at the prompting of human**itarian** views, without requiring reciprocity on their side, unless as one of the methods made use of to gain them over to civilization.

Associations of pirates and other outlaws, though not belong-

---

* PHILLIMORE: *Comm. on International Law.*

ing to any nationality nor owing allegiance to any State, are disqualified to form States, as having themselves no right of **existence.***

"The marks of an independent State," says Mr. Hall, "are that the community constituting it is permanently established for a political end, that it possesses a defined territory, and that it is independent of external control. It is postulated of those independent States, which are dealt with by International Law, that they have a moral nature identical with that of individuals, **and that, with** respect to one another, they are in **the** same relation as that in which individuals stand to each other who are subject to Law. They are collective persons and as such they have certain rights and are under certain obligations."†

§46. The investigation and systematical arrangement of the rights and obligations of States in their outward relations, with **the** pratical modifications of these rights and duties, form the subject matter of International Law, as will be treated hereafter (§§62-75). But the clear understanding of the nature and structure of the Social Organism, as explained through the theory of moral senses, *i.e.*, the natural evolution process of the human mind (§42), is the indispensable light by which the various aspects and combinations, under which the reciprocal rights and obligations of States present themselves, must be viewed, to appear properly connected and formed into the system of rules called International Law. Hence the source of International intercourse must be sought in the moral development of the human mind (§63).

§47. In the work quoted above, Mr. Hall **says further:** "**The** capacity in a corporate person (State) to be subject **to Law** evidently depends upon the existence of a sense of right and a sense of **obligation to act in obedience** to it, either on the part of the community at large or, at least, of the man or body of men in

---
* PHILLIMORE: *Comm. on International Law.*
† W. E. HALL: *International Law*, Edit. 1880, §1.

whom the will governing the **acts** of the community resides."*
The cause of this sense of obligation to act in conformity with
Law as existing in the leading minds of those governing States,
having been investigated in the preceding chapters, we have
found it traceable to the working of the moral senses conscience
and sympathy on the individual mind, whose subjective conception of the **Good is** formed into objective Law by the Spirit of
Law, representing the ego of the respective community or State,
as described above (§33).

Considering that social life is the natural consequence of **the human** organism and, as such, subject to development in conformity with that organism, it is but natural that States, which are **the** outcome of social life, have, in their collective capacity **as** aggregates of moral beings, the same **moral** obligations assigned to them as man, but with a vaster and more complicated sphere of action, and consequently with some special prerogatives and rights.

§48. All social systems derive their origin from and are naturally connected with the development or evolution of the **human** mind. Social questions cannot be solved otherwise than by tracing them up to the conditions under **which the** society to which **they have** relation is developing **in its** moral as well as its physical aspects.

There are two main conditions **to** be considered, with regard to the social organism as well as the biological organism of man, *viz.*, the physical **and the** psychical nature of man. Professor Huxley says that modern science, taking into account all the phenomena of the universe **which are** brought to our knowledge by observation or experiment, admits that there are two worlds to be considered, the one physical and the other psychical; that their **phenomena** run not in one series but along two parallel lines, **and that,** though the bridge from one to the other has yet to be found, "there is a most intimate relation and interconnection between the two."*

---
* W. E. HALL: *International Law*, page 14.

Thus, to arrive at some sound conclusion with regard to the nature of any social phenomenon, we must invariably keep in view the intimate relation and interconnection which exist between the physical and moral aspects of Society, as the natural result of the biological relation which exists between the social organism and the organism of the individuals constituting the State. Without these conditions in view, it is impossible to arrive at any logical conclusion with regard to the theory of social evolution. Systems purporting **to explain** social conditions or theories with regard to pauperism, socialism, communism, anarchy, etc, must start from these natural premises as basis, or else they are simply speculations, the product of imagination, **if** not of one-sided party spirit, and their conclusions cannot be relied on to guide **political actions** of government.

It is obvious that social phenomena must be explained by the theory of biological evolution, but naturally taking into account **the** moral as well as the physical **aspects of** society.

Society has **not the perfect** concrete character of **direct adherence** which is exhibited by the embryological cells in animal organism, **as** biology teaches. The homogeneous units of which society is composed retain their respective physiological autonomy, but **their moral and** intellectual individualities are so interwoven and complicately united in conscious and voluntary harmony of moral and material co-operation, that society represents as well a concrete phenomenon, or a community aiming **at** an end which is not exclusively personal to any one of the homogeneous particulars. Neither is society a mere mechanical aggregation, for it represents itself in all phases as a growing, developing, and thus living concrete phenomenon, evolved from the sociological embryo, according to certain definite laws revealed by historical facts, analogous with the links of biological embryonic changes. This gives the most important clue to the origin of existing societies.

---

* Prof. Huxley: *Scientific and Pseudo-Scientific Realism*, "Ninteenth Century." February, 1887, p. 192.

The history of this growth, which is the province of ethnology, furnishes explanations for the relationships of various nations, at present apparently widely distinct in characteristics, and this in an analogous way with the history of the growth from the egg, which, in the study of animal embryology, furnishes the clue to the ancestral biological relationships of various distinct species.

In biological bodies, cells are regarded as the primordial elements, but these cells are not closely contiguous throughout; the connections are formed by the interstices between them being filled by the intercellular substance called the *medium*, a less perfectly organized matter, or, perhaps, matter in the process of being formed into organized substance, as, *e.g.*, the serum of the blood, etc. If, now, in biological organisms, the cells or *plastides* are connected by the intercellular medium, *i.e.*, the environing substance which supplies and perfects the organism,—in social organism the individual cells of society are brought into intellectual and moral adherence by the *active medium of mutual interdependence*. The moral senses conscience and sympathy establish the *inner* modifications, and material interest the *outer* modifications. These, in their mutual actions and counteractions, constitute the factors of sociological evolution. But besides these factors there exist manifold combinations of agencies of evolution in the environment of the social as well as the biological organism. These agencies are inorganic as well as organic, material, intellectual and moral. With regard to biological organism they are the *physical and chemical forces*, of which, however, we know only the effects, called gravitation, heat, light, electricity, etc. (§4), as so many phenomena in nature, but of their absolute nature we know so little as yet, that we are not even sure that they can be called "forces" in the sense of spontaneous activity. In the social organism, on the other hand, there are at work, besides these physical agents, the impulses caused by the *moral senses* of the human mind. Of these latter we know also only the effects on the social organism, their causes being to the same degree unexplained as those of the so-called physical and chemical forces (§32). Into all these it is consequently impossible to investigate in the sense of empirical science, and while science is trying to explain as yet only the effects produced by each of the several matters and forces, physical and moral—in scientific language collectively called "modifications of the environment,"—philosophy speculates on the causation, and postulates, as ultimate cause, a universally present primordial factor, the motor of organic life in the evolution process, in social as well as biological organism, under the term Spirit of Creation (§2).

Society is thus a growing, developing, concrete phenomenon, and as such a living organism. In this organism the individual *sensorium*, the concentration of sensibility in the Ego, is represented by the Spirit of Law described above (§33).

From the foregoing propositions the following conclusions arise. 1.—That society is not the product of a contract between parties, a mere creature of human agencies that can be made and unmade at will, and at any time, through dissolution of the primitive agreement, but that it consists of individuals, physiologically autonomous but yet closely interdependent upon each other, not only biologically for the procreation of the species, but intellectually and morally, for the development of their moral as well as their mental organisms. 2.—That society partakes of the biological character of the individuals of which it is composed, and that it is, consequently, a living concrete organism, vested with a special sensorium, having an end, aiming at the common well-being of the whole, individually as well as collectively. 3.—That the State, which is the organized expression for society, must be in nature, structure, and functions, analogous with the biological expression of man.

The application of these rules forms the subject matter of the next section.

§49. In foregoing sections (43—47) we have described the origin of states as social organisms and political bodies, with the natural and political nationality derived therefrom, and the conditions for the political individuality of states as persons of International Law; having, as such, the same moral obligations as man, but modified by special prerogatives. The sociological phenomenon state being thus defined in its outward expression, we have proceeded, in the last foregoing section, to trace the analogy which naturally must exist between the organism of States, as unions of homogeneous particulars, and the individual organisms of these particulars, *i.e.*, to compare social organism with biological organism. From these premises the natural structure and functions of the state must be traced, in order to establish what could be called the *Physiology of the State*.

As thus defined, it is obvious that the nature of the social organism does not admit of any theory based on preconceived legal conclusions or ideas, for the regulating of a partnership to carry on a social business association. The evolution of the social organism cannot depend upon an artificial *social compact*; it is the moral and social nature of man which forms the basis on which the organism of the state reposes.

"The growth of a thing," says Herbert Spencer, "is effected by the joint operation of certain forces on certain materials; and when it dwindles, there is either a lack of some materials, or the forces co-operate in a way different from that which produces growth. If a structure has varied, the implication is that the processes which built it up were made unlike the parallel processes in other cases, by the greater or less amount of some or more of the matters or actions concerned. Where there is unusual fertility, the play of vital activities is thereby shown to have deviated from the ordinary play of vital activities; and conversely if there is infertility."*

These statements respecting organic evolution can without any alteration be applied to the growth and decay of the social organism, the progress and the retrogression of civilization.

---
* "The Factors of Organic Evolution," *Nineteenth Century*, May, 1886, p. 749.

States, constituted of human individuals, must consequently represent the successive progress or retrogression of the human mind, and naturally keep pace, in their advance or stagnation in civilization, with the devolopment or deterioration of the moral principles of the mind. Every abnormal variation in the social condition of the state points to an unnatural state of society, and as the development of the state always takes place in conformity with the progress of the principles of the moral senses of the human minds constituting the state (comp. §42) it is evident that the fault lies in the fact that society is suffering under some abnormal causation, in disagreement with these moral principles, —through their decaying or having been outgrown by the material element of the festered state; which means that the moral elements must be restored to their natural equilibrium, or the whole constitutional system is endangered.

In the foregoing section the analogy between social organism and biological organism has been set forth; the natural consequence of this similarity of character is that the social organism must necessarily correspond with the nature and physiology of the individual beings, constituting the homogeneous particulars of the aggregate. Thus the physiology of the state is that of the man. It is analogous with the normally developed body and mind of its individual members.

§50. From these premises we can conceive the natural structure and organs, and the different faculties and functions of the body-politic called State, and we will find that the analogy of the physiology of the state with that of the human organism is as natural as it is logical.

Thus the state is an organized society, and, being a living phenomenon developed from human beings, it must naturally have a concrete body, that is, an independent individual existence, which, for its own preservation and growth, in conformity with the natural evolution process, has also the faculties corresponding with the physical and moral faculties of the physically and morally developed human beings of which it is a homogenous aggregate.

As such, the state must have a *head* and a *heart*, organs of Conscience and of Sympathy, which must work harmoniously together in order to preserve the constitution of the state in a normal, healthy condition, and to direct its *will*—the executive power of the State—in accordance with its Spirit of Law. The head is the sovereign and his government; while the assembly of representatives of the people constitute the heart, which, in harmonious relation with the head, keeps this latter in healthy control by the proper circulation of the *blood*—which is the public opinion of the people, forming the Spirit of Law of the State through the popular conscience (§33). Through this co-operation of the head and the heart of the state, the executive power of the government, *i.e.*, the will of the state—is directed in the path of justice and benevolence; which is the general welfare of *all*—the weak as well as the strong, the poor as well as the rich—for Justice, apart from the moderating influence of Benevolence, degenerates into despotism, and from despotism into tyranny, but Benevolence allows no rules to be imposed upon human beings except such as the frailest human power is able to bear without being crushed, or its development retarded. These are the natural premises of the law-giver of the state, *i.e.*, the process through which the subjective good, conceived by the moral senses conscience and sympathy, is brought into the objective form of practical social laws; in other words, the principle of legislation through mutual accord of Government and Representative Body.

When the head and the heart of the state are in normal activity, the constitution of the body—which is the mass of the people—is able to do its duty of feeding and strengthening the members which support the weight of the state and execute the decrees of its will. While national industry provides the means for physical strength, and public education supplies mental powers, morality and religion constitute the sinews and nerve of the state.

The body contains the material element, the national wealth, but the spinal cord, the centre and vigour of the whole living organism of the state, is the morality of the people, the national virtues, without which the whole structure must crumble into the formless materialistic chaos which constituted the state of human co-existence before the evolution of the Moral-Mental Organisms of men began to give form and harmony to Social Organisms.

§51. As the executive of the government represents the State under all circumstances, it has become customary to indicate the government by the term State. Hence the error of representing people and state as two distinct elements of a nation. But the expression "state" and "people" have one and the same meaning, for it is impossible to think of a state without the people constituting it, neither can an aggregate of human beings represent a nation or people without some form of organization in the nature of a State; *i.e.*, of a social organism which exists and acts as body-politic with rights and duties as the person of International Law. The State does not mean the Government in particular, but the Government and the People combined, as an individualized homogeneity with one head and one heart to direct and to control, to will and to execute its will.

The head of the state, as the centre of the government, represents the sovereign power of the whole state, internally as well as externally; externally as the organ of the State's individuality in its relations with other states; internally for the management of the state-affairs and the execution of the state-laws made with the co-operation of the people's representatives.

The representation of the people is not an opposing, but a regulating-controlling element. The functions of the assembly of the representatives of the people, with respect to the whole state or body-politic, is like those of the heart in the human body

—regulating and sustaining life through the whole organism. Morally as well as materially controlling and rectifying the activities of the State, the representative body is the practical expression of the Spirit of Law, and, as such, its agent in the law-forming process of legislation (§56).

From the conclusions arrived at in this and the foregoing sections, results the form of state-organism which may be called the *Natural-Constitutional* form. This is the normal form of government evolved in a society composed of civilized beings, *i.e.*, those endowed with normally developed moral senses. Emanating from the natural evolution process of the individual organism, and analogous with the human constitution, the natural-constitutional state's form is the standard form of the civilized state.

§52. In the foregoing sections (48—50) we have noted the natural analogy which exists between the social organism and the biological organism of man. It was then shown, while treating of the physiology of the State, that the normal development of society takes place in conformity with the development of the moral senses of the people composing it; this being the natural condition through which harmony is maintained between the different faculties of the State (§42). It was said then (§49) that if society suffers under some abnormal causation, in disagreement with the constituent principles of the moral senses—which condition readily manifests itself in the excrescenses of dissatisfaction—it means that one part of the system is decaying, or has been outgrown by the other, so that the harmony between the elements composing the natural structure of society is disturbed, *i.e.*, that the social organism is in an abnormal condition. In such case the harmony must be restored and the natural equilibrium of the structure maintained, in order to prevent the whole constitutional system becoming endangered. Thus we could fairly conclude that the physiological identity of the state with the human beings of which it is composed is manifest.

As a natural consequence of this identity of physiological

conditions between the social organism and the biological organism of man, results (as was shown in §50) the necessity of a relative identity in the corresponding faculties of the social organism with the organs of the human body. The undeniable natural analogy which thus exists between the organism of the state and the normally developed body and mind of the individuals constituting the homogeneous particulars of this aggregate of human beings, excludes the idea of anarchy, in any sense, as the normal result of the progress of societies composed of beings with normally developed moral senses.

Anarchy, in the sense of no-government, has no more reasonable meaning than the idea of a developed biological organism without the head. The more society develops itself towards the state of complete identification of altruism with egoism, as stated by Mr. Herbert Spencer, and noted above (§§32 and 40) the more government, in the sense of the concentrated consciousness of the social organism, becomes intensive, through the absorption of the individual particulars into the aggregate form, which can never exist as a body without a head. The theory of natural evolution is thus opposed to anarchy in all forms of social organism.

§53. The essential conditions of the natural constitutional state's form, as described above (§51), procure the necessary indications with regard to the requirements for the status of the head of the state, as well as the conditions attached to the quality or selection, the formation or election of the people's representatives and the principles of representation. History and the experience of thinking statesmen of all times, testify that the same danger which Government serves to avert from society, *viz.,* the danger of the stronger tyranizing over the weaker, and which makes government indispensable to preserve society, rises again in those who administer the government, in the tendency to abuse of their powers, when not checked by the control of the people; that also in this control is again perceivable the strong tendency of one party to overpower the other, which later danger can alone be brought to its minimum by a judicious system of representation. This is the natural consequence of the selfish propensities of human nature. Therefore absolute power, by right, is the attribute of no human being, for clear and right judgment and unbiased true sympathy constitute a state of perfection of the human mind as yet attained by none. But although perfection cannot be attained, it is the goal we all aim at, to the best of our ability and judgment.

Thus, actions for the practical and judicious conduct of human affairs are always guided by two different motives—1st, the desire to do what is conscientiously believed to be in conformity with the Moral Law, and 2nd, the selection of measures, with this aim in view, which are the most likely to succeed. The combination of these two motives is the aim of Government.

"Liberty," says an American statesman, "is little more than a name under all governments of the absolute form, including that of the numerical majority, and can have only a secure and durable existence under those of the concurrent or constitutional form. Having its origin in the same principle of our nature, *constitution* stands to *government* as *government* stands to *society*; and as the end for which society is ordained would be defeated without government, so that for which government is ordained would, in a great measure, be defeated without constitution. But they differ in this striking particular: there is no difficulty in forming government; it is not even a matter of choice whether there shall be one or not; like breathing, it is not permitted to depend on our volition; necessity forces it on all communities in some one form or another. Very different is the case as to constitution; instead of a matter of necessity, it is one of the most difficult tasks imposed on man to form a constitution worthy of the name."* The task is not alone difficult, but it may well-nigh be found impossible to trace, *à priori*, the conditions in

---

* CALHOUN: *Disquisition on Government*, p. 60, p. 8.

which people and government shall come to stand towards each other after the evolution process has gone on for some time.

Government and constitution alike are of natural growth; like the human mind from the evolution of which they originate, they are yet far from perfection, but their more or less successful harmonious working indicates the stage on the road to perfection which they have attained, and from this may be fairly traced the advance of a nation in civilization; for, without this harmonious working of a sound head and a fervent heart, there is no hope for progress, or improvement of the State.

§54. "If the human mind," says Prof. Bain, "grows dwarfish and enfeebled, it is ordinarily because it is left to deal with commonplace facts, and never summoned to the effort of taking the span and the altitude of broad and lofty disclosures. The understanding will gradually bring itself down to the dimensions of the matters with which alone it is familiarized, till having long been accustomed to contract its powers, it shall lose well-nigh the ability to expand. The laws of the body are those of the mind. Exercise and excitement strengthen and energize, indolence and habits of insensitiveness contract, debilitate and at length kill."*

A good Government is that whose first duty of internal policy consists in the care for the moral and intellectual development of the people : by opening, through suitable institutions, to all and every one, the opportunities for education and free individual development, in science, for the intellectual culture, and in philosophy, for the cultivation of well-directed thought and reflection, for the fostering and strengthening of the moral senses of the individuals composing the State—thus to awaken the moral conception of their real interest and duties in respect to themselves, their neighbours, and the laws of the State. The establishment of institutions to promote normal education and moral common-sense is the first duty of the civilized government (§33). The government which thinks to promote the well-being of the people by strong

---
* ALEX. BAIN: *The Emotions and the Will.*

state's discipline, usurps the power over human conscience, and estranges the minds of the people from individual self-respect and love of their country. Having no voice in the choice of their legislators and in the framing of the laws by which they are ruled, they are indifferent to the public welfare and are apt to look up to the government for all sorts of material support, instead of depending on their own exertions. Where there is no right, the sense of duty is very lax. Void of right, they are free from responsibility and are apt to discard all the moral obligations imposed on civilized members of a society. The Government having assumed the right to rule their private, as well as their public aspirations and destiny, it is natural that the people should give their government the blame of any increase in pauperism and crime.

If a short-sighted government can rule after its own pleasure, it cannot shape society to its own convenience. If the tendency to improvement gets awakened in minds of the people, society is always prepared to receive the beneficial changes which lie in the natural course and tendency of the human nature, by the ever-acting Moral Senses, without whose working on the minds of the people, progress would be retarded indefinitely. When the thinking minds are prepared, there will be the proper man forthcoming to throw the weight of their individual faculties into the scale, trembling between progress and retrogression, and if the governing class be even then neither able nor willing to prepare for the advent of the natural regeneration on the way to progress, the ever-growing current of civilization will swell to a power which will remove all obstructions (§39). The principles on which government is based belong to those primary and philosophical questions regarding the evolution of the social organism, the solution of which is the not-to-be evaded task of enlightened statesmanship; all sound politics form an integral part of this philosophy. The monarchical extravagance of Hobbes, and the strong individualistic prevalence of Herbert Spencer's theory, find their medium in the monarchical-constitutional government, as moderated and counterbalanced by the free development of the individual moral senses. Political discussions must have their value tested by the elementary social science, for our conscience is equally exacting in practice as in speculative thought, to arrive at truth with sincerity and earnestness. An apparently small incident of local interest in politics is an integral particle of the wider interest of mankind. Our knowledge of the state is not complete with practical experience only, but must be raised from the domain of experience to that of thought, to test experience by the doctrine of political rights and obligations. On the other hand, philosophical speculation is not merely an entertaining exercise for intellectual ingenuity, but provides for the basis of conduct and influences the details of action of the conscientious man. The meeting point of these mutually corroborating speculative and practical activities is where the impartial observer of facts and the honest searcher of theoretical truth are merged into the good citizen.

§55. As it is impossible for the mass of the people to assemble in one body, and for each individual member of the State to devote his active personal attention to the affairs of the State, in co-operation with the Government, as noted above, it becomes necessary to select a suitable number of individuals among the people to represent the whole nation.

These representatives of the people, when assembled in conformity with the constitution of the State (§§60 and 61), constitute what is termed the Legislative Body, which, in mutual understanding with the governmental element, has an active share in the affairs of the State.

We shall now proceed to treat, in this and the next sections, the fundamental requirements of this most essential organ—the assembly of the representatives of the people, called above the "heart" of the State (§50).

From the statements made in sections 50-54—we draw the **following principles, on which the representation of the people** must be based. Representatives must answer to this double qualification; viz., 1st, that they be the persons best fitted by moral character and intelligent culture, by knowledge and practical experience, to constitute a body able to co-operate with the Government in the framing of laws for the regulation of the affairs of State, *i.e.*, to form an active and efficient *element of government*. 2nd, that they be, at the same time, the most popular men, *i.e.*, possessing to the greatest extent the confidence of the people, in order that the assembly of the people's representatives may constitute, collectively, a body representing as nearly as possible *the true character and aspirations of the people.*

The method for the selecting and the election of the Representatives must lead to the comprehension of both these qualities combined in the Legislative Body, so that this element of Government be composed, as nearly as possible, of actual representatives of the different dispositions, opinions and interests of the people, by morally and intellectually developed individuals.

§56. As such, and as such alone, the representative body can be the exponent of *public opinion*, that is, of what the nation really thinks and desires—the real and serious demands of the popular will—in other words, the conclusion of the popular consciousness which constitutes what we termed above the Spirit of Law of the society composing the State (§33).

The government or the representative assembly which fails to discern this genuine Spirit of Law from the one-sided outcries of those bustling, loquacious and noisy party organs, so often mistaken for public opinion, are placed in a false position towards each other, fraught with the gravest dangers, as it makes harmony and co-operation between these two principal organs of the State impossible. The warning against the danger of this false position is the manifestation of an intelligent and influential public opinion *outside* the assembly of representatives and in direct contradiction to the opinion of the majority of this body. This indicates a defect in the mode of selecting the representatives and the formation of the representative body. To correct this abnormality, the assembly should be dissolved and reconstructed *de novo*, in the manner and form prescribed by the constitution, in order to secure for the Public National Conscience its natural right of legally expressing itself in the Legislative Assembly of the State.

§57. The foregoing sketch gives us an insight into the nature of the organism of the State, in its normal condition, when the different members and faculties are in harmonious working. This harmony is the condition of the State when advanced in civilization, and is what the State *ought* to be. But the egoism of despotic Goverments, on one side, and the not less selfish aspirations of revolutionary political parties on the other, are constantly disturbing this equilibrium of the State's organism. As soon as political actions come into life, they are found to oscillate between two extremes, viz., *despotism* and *anarchy*—the extreme of government authority and the extreme of individualism. From this condition two principal political parties emerge in the State, the one inclined to the side of absolute government, the other towards complete individual independency, representing the two main springs of State-policy, viz., the principle of *authority* and that of *liberty ;* each party asserting a truth but not the *whole truth*, for neither the one nor the other can have exclusive sway without the tendency of destroying the State. This shows the necessity of their counterbalancing each other; from which results—for the stability of the State—again the necessity that in the normal constitutional State, the actions of government and people be combined in the Legislative Body. When one organ absorbs more vital power than is consistent with the natural harmony in the distribution of function in the body, the other members must fall into decay, and the whole social constitution must consequently suffer from this abnormal condition. So in a State in which government and people have not the same main interest to support, each trying to overpower the other, the final result must be *despotism* or *anarchy*.

§58. Abnormal conditions exist in the internal policy of the State, when the harmonious co-operation of Government and Representative Body is not honestly adhered to by any one of the two parties in this, through nature's evolution, consolidated social pactum; for instance, when the absolute right of *veto* is refused to the chief of the Government while the assembly of representatives retain their full right of initiative and legislative power—or, on the other hand, when the right of initiative is refused to the representative body, which is then only called upon to sanction the bills proposed by the Government in disregard of the manifest aspirations of the people. In all such cases where the elements of the state do not co-operate, but each follows its own course, the tendency is the destruction of the natural constitutional character, which is the judicious equilibrium of the faculties of the State, as formed by the natural evolution process of the social organism (§49).

Through this judicious equilibrium of powers, the natural-constitutional Government finds strength to protect the *minority* in the State against the tyranny of the *majority*, without prejudice to the legal rights of the latter. This is arrived at by the *right of veto*.

The right of veto, in a general sense, as vested in the head of the State, is the corrective indispensable for the maintenance of the equilibrium of the natural-constitutional form of State. To exercise this right for the impartial benefit of all and every one in the State, it is an indispensable requisite that the Sovereign, as head of the State, be completely independent of all individual ties and party associations in the State, and to be such, he must not owe his high position to any individual or party influence, and must have antecedent individual existence outside the people of the State, of a source beyond all arbitrary human influence. Hence the head of the natural-constitutional State must be *a priori* designated by a condition unalterably fixed in Nature, which is the *birthright*. This brings us, inductively, to the conclusion that the naturally—through social evolution—developed State, with an organism composed of elements in equilibrium of power, must have the *Hereditary-Monarchical Constitutional* form of Government.

§59. A primarily independent Head is so natural and indispensable a guarantee for true liberty to all, in the unbiased maintenance of the equilibrium of faculties of the State in its natural constitutional form, that eminent republican writers, though far from inclining to the monarchical system, yet, when admitting the existence of a natural moral element in social evolution, are forced, by the logic of organization and the reason of the thing, to acknowledge the necessity of a general regulating and incontestably independent power as the Head of the State, to superintend and, when necessary, to rectify the equilibrium of functions in the organism of the State. The only point on which moderate republicans differ from our system is that they deny the necessity of the hereditary qualification, while we submit, that to be completely independent of all political parties, for the unquestionable benefit of all and every one, the Head of the Natural Constitutional State must owe his power of Regulator of the State to none but the unbiased and bribeless Law of Nature.

"J'aurait voulu maitre," says Rousseau, in his famous work: *Discours sur l'origine et les fondements d'égalité parmi les hommes,*—"dans un pays ou le souverain et le peuple ne pussent avoir qu'un seul et même interêt, afin que tous les mouvements de la machine ne tendissent jamais qu'au bonheur commun, ce qui ne pouvant se faire à moins que le peuple et le souverain ne soient une même personne ; il s'ensuit "—he takes care to add— " que j'aurais voulu naitre sous un gouvernement démocratique, sagement tempéré."

"*Sagement tempéré,*"—there is the rub! Rousseau does not venture to trust himself unconditionally to a democratic people who are their own sovereign and correcting regulator.

Democracy with a distinct legal individual Head, who has the power of regulation and moderation, is what Rousseau thinks to be the model Government. But is there any sounder bulwark of moral and material liberty than the Constitutional Monarchy with liberal or democratic institutions?

"De lui même," says this republican philosopher again, in his *Contrat Social,* "le peuple vent toujours le bien; mais de lui même li ne le voit pas tourjours. La volonté générale est tousjours droite, mais le jugement qui la guide n'est pas tourjours éclairé." The *volonté générale du peuple* is, single-handed, a well-meaning but a blind guide, and as such not to be trusted.

The mechanism of State must have its equilibrium restored by unbiased control, to secure impartiality in the execution of the popular will, to regulate the affairs of State with justice and benevolence; this consists in the execution of the will of the majority in justice to *all*, that is, with the least possible sacrifice to the minority in the State; in other words, the civilized State must have a guarantee against tyranny in every form, whether appearing in the absolute democratic majority of partyism or vested in the one-headed despot.

The Monarchical-Constitutional Government represents the natural equilibrium between material and moral powers in the State. It is the system born from the natural evolution of the human mind, leaving full scope to the moral development of the people, by keeping the individual mind free from the demoralizing influence of partisanship. While the despotic government tries to maintain its power by crushing out of the people's mind all interest in the progress of the State, the uncontrolled democracy tends to party tyranny. When going side by side with bribery and lawlessness, it crushes out the moral senses of the people, as there can be no respect for Conscience or Sympathy when partyism has its own, not being checked by a supreme power in the State which is perfectly free from all political party influences.

Thus the Monarchical-Constitutional Government is to be regarded as the only healthy normal medium between despotism and anarchy, the safe refuge to escape from the scourges of both.

The hereditary sovereign is the constitutional judge, with *à priori* well defined and regulated power to apply the right of *veto* on decisions of the majority, when measures decided upon by a relatively small *majority*, without being of great value to the State in general, may be, on the other hand, the cause of great affliction or injustice to the real interest of a large *minority* in the State. The State, as an organized association, has for primary object the physical, mental and moral well-being of the people, and is not merely an institution for the accommodation of a factitious majority who happened to be master of the polls for the time being. The end of the State, in the first instance, is to promote the happiness of *all*, if this be practicable, otherwise, the greatest happiness of the greatest number *(not that of the majority alone)*, and thus applying to *all* its Benevolence as well as Justice. The theory of Bentham, though proposed to deal with purely material interests, is yet true in the moral aspect of the well-organized State. In his work, *Constitutional Code*, he says: "The right and proper end of government in every political community is the greatest happiness of all the individuals of which it is composed, say, in other words, the greatest happiness of the greatest number."*

§60. The codification of the principles on which the form of the government of a State is based, is the fundamental Law, called *Constitution*. This contains the plan of the whole organism and the fundamental rules for the maintaining of the equilibrium of the elements of the State. The constitution, and other organic laws emanating from it—which latter could be called *Constitutional bye-laws*—are collectively comprehended under the denomination of the *Public* or *Political Law (Jus Publicum, Staatsrecht* of the State—see §61).

---

* BENTHAM: *Constitutional Code,* Book I., Introduction.

The Constitution of a State, however, is not a document of lawyer's conception, but, as noted above, State and Constitution are growing together. It is not the Constitution, as law, which produces the social organism. The spirit of Law (§33) of the society will mould the law to its own standard of civilization, progressing or retrograding in conformity with the popular consciousness. Not the people by the law, but the law by the people; *quid leges sine moribus?* (comp. §40).

The stability of the fundamental Law of a State is caused by the fact of its being gradually developed with the moral-mental organism of the people. In this natural development consists the moral relation between Government and People, and the guarantee for the equilibrium of powers in the State, so that in a State of normal development Government and People will advance together in civilization; while, the Government not checking civilization, the People will not become estranged from their rulers. In this harmonious development of both Government and People lies the strength of *self-government*.

Besides the definition of the territory of the State, the constitution contains, in the first place, stipulations with regard to the functions, power and prerogatives of the Head of the State, the mode of succession, and the members of the governmental organism. Further, the Constitution contains regulations with regard to the representation of the people as noted above (§54) and the basis of the Legislative Power of the State, in two branches, as described in the next section.

§61. The danger to which individual liberty is ever exposed, with regard to an autocratic head governing the State, does not the less exist with regard to the legislative body. The vesting of the power of legislation in the numerical majority of one single assembly of men, is equally despotic in principle, and a despotism which is the more hopeless as it comes from the elected of the people, having the countenance of a multitude, which, through party spirit, is too often only bent on what serves their own party-interest. The selection by popular suffrage of a number of individuals—be it few or many—assembled in a body, does not procure an adequate guarantee against mislegislation or oppression by the majority, unless this body be properly controlled by another independently-constituted body of representatives, equally emanating from the popular choice, but selected among those morally and materially independent citizens, who through their independent stand in society, are more apt to constitute a *controlling element* in the legislature of the State.

The lessons of experience having thus taught that *absolute legislative power* cannot be safely confided into the keeping of single authority, it was found necessary, with the intellectual and moral development of the people, to counteract this tendency to abuse, by dividing or distributing this power in more than one keeping.

This is arrived at through the instituting of *two* different assemblies of representatives, constituting two distinct legislative bodies, equally elected by the people, but with some different qualifications with regard to the status of the members, or by different systems of election, regulated in the Constitution. The Constitution also establishes and formulates, practically, the political relationship between these two branches of representation and the government of the State, their attributes as law-makers, collectively and separately, in the two essential requirements of the people's representation, noted before, viz., that of being genuine representatives of the people's interests, and at the same time that of constituting an efficient element of control in the legislation of the State (§54).

III. The Co-existence of Social Organisms.—External Social Life.—International Law.

§62. The internal policy of a State is closely connected with its external success as a Nation, and, as the basis of this policy is the entire range of its legislation, it is obvious that, in the present state of civilization and progress, the internal legislation of States exercises a growing influence on their mutual intercourse.

The duties of a civilized State are thus internal and external. In the first instance, those duties which constitute the *raison d'être* of a State and are essential to its existence, consist in the obligations which arise between the Government and the individual subjects or citizens *(Staatsangehörige)* in all matters pertaining to public order and to the moral and material progress of the nation. These are the internal activities of the State which may be varied or modified without contact with the internal or external attributes of any other State.

But, in the second instance, in order to be able to fulfil its internal duties undisturbed, and to its full extent, the State must enjoy the outward security and respect essential for the free exercise of its full faculties and all its attributes as a body-politic. This necessarily imposes on the individual State the duty of intercourse with other States in order to establish its rights, which, with regard to their external relations, are called *International Rights*.

These International Rights are enumerated as follows:—

1st. The right of existence; from which devolve the rights of self-preservation and of self-defence, with the accessory rights of redress, retortion, reprisal, seizure, interference, and that of making war and concluding peace.

2nd. The rights of sovereignty, independence, equality and respect.

3rd. The right of property.

4th. The right of legislation.

5th. The right of intercourse and international commerce.

6th. The right of legation, negotiation and treaty.

7th. The right of neutrality.

The principal features of these rights and their correlative obligations form the subject-matters of International Law.*

---

* See my *Manual of International Law*, etc., Edit. 1884, Vol. I., p. 79, *et seq.*

In the case of all well-organized civilized States, their mutual rights and corresponding obligations are, respectively, of the same nature. Owing to this similarity of attributes and interests, international rights and duties must devolve upon every State, as a natural obligation to respect the rights of every other State, and thus to maintain its own security for the proper fulfilment of its internal obligations.

A State which refuses all international intercourse, places itself outside the pale of the Law of Nations and has in consequence no guarantee for its safety.*

§63. From this it appears obvious that the interests and duties of States are indentical, and that the mutual interests of civilized States are so interwoven, that each, by the due performance of its own duty, promotes the welfare of all. Again, it is obvious that the substitution of might for right brings misery not only on the oppressed but also on the oppressor.

Plato observed that the just State differs in nothing from the just man, and Hugo Grotius maintained that ethical principles should underlie all transactions between nations as well as those between individuals.

In sections 36 and 37 we have given an account of the forming of the International Spirit of Law, and why International Law must be regarded as the manifestation of civilization. The rights and duties of Nation towards Nation—the basis of international intercourse—are gradually developed from the actions of the moral senses of the human mind, as described above (§§46 and 47).

When mankind began to form itself into societies, and when these different Societies, through having intercourse with each other, found it necessary, for mutual safety and for their own individual benefit, to abide by certain rules, tacitly or expressly

---

* Thus China and Japan, and recently Corea, after centuries of seclusion and exclusion of foreigners, entered into the family of Nations to secure their own interests.

admitted, the basis of these rules, which are wanted for material interest, found root in the human moral sense of Conscience which engenders *good faith* (§31).

In the same proportion as Nations advance in civilization, their rules of conduct towards each other are gradually brought into conformity with the principles of justice and morality, and find henceforth support not alone in material considerations and purely selfish motives of mutual preservation, but also in the awakened Human Conscience, which, when developed into National or Popular Conscience, tends more and more towards the practical observance of the dictates of the moral senses. This takes place not only in the case of States of equal strength and pretensions, but, indiscriminately, among all the members of the great commonwealth of Nations.

This constitutes what is termed *International Morality*, which is the principal agent in the forming of the International Spirit of Law (§36).

We find that civilized States, in their mutual intercourse, in times of peace as well as in times of war, invariably appeal to public opinion for the justification of their acts. This may be done sometimes in the manner in which Pilate appeased his conscience, but, however that may be, it is a plain acknowledgment that justice is expected to be observed in the intercourse of States, in the Society of Societies, as it is a constituent element of Society itself.

The civilized Nations of all ages recognized moral principles as binding upon themselves in their internal relations. There are historical facts which indicate that the observance of these principles, in external as well as internal relations (however imperfectly realized) were not unknown to Greece and Rome, the oldest of civilized Nations, on whose institutions modern European Laws are modelled. Cicero, in his great work on the commonwealth, maintains that God has given to all men conscience and intellect, and that, where these exist, a law exists of which all men are common subjects, and Plato repudiates the idea that any Society could flourish which did not respect the rights of other Societies.*

A State must be regarded with respect to its rights and duties, and to the consequences of its relations with other bodies-politic from two different points of view, viz., *de jure* and *de facto*. On the one hand, a State must be regarded as a moral person, as being an aggregate of self-conscious agents, if we are to comprehend the standard principles of its moral obligations. On the other hand, it is necessary, in order to avoid ambiguity in our conclusions, to bear in mind the difference which *de facto* exists in the nature of the respective rights and duties of the individual man in his social relation to his fellow creatures, and the societies of moral beings, called States, in their present mutual conditions; from which it results, that certain prerogatives and exceptional rights are attributed to States which could not be possessed by individuals.

Reason, therefore, which is the exponent of Conscience, through Common Sense, and as such a distinct source of International Law, guides the application of the dictates of the moral senses to the rights and duties of States, by following the International Spirit of Law † (§74).

§64. As we have seen in the preceding sections, the nature,

---

* PHILLIMORE: *Commentary on International Law*, Vol. I., Edit. 1879, Chap. iii, §§17-27. "The same rules of morality which hold together men and families, and form families into commonwealths, also link together these commonwealths, as members of the great Society of mankind. Commonwealths, as well as private men, are liable to injury and capable of benefit from each other; it is, therefore, their interest as well as their duty, to reverence, to practice and to enforce those rules of justice, which control and restrain injury, which regulate and augment benefit, which, even in their present imperfect observance, preserve civilized States in a tolerable condition of security from wrong, and which, if they could be generally obeyed, would establish and permanently maintain the well being of the universal commonwealths of the human race."—SIR JAS. MACKINTOSH: *Discourse on the Law of Nature and Nations*.

† PHILLIMORE: Vol. I., 1879, Preface, page 7., and Chap. iv., page 30, Vol. III., 1873, page 878. G. F. DE MARTENS: *Précis du Droit des Gens*, Edit. 1858, Note of Ch. Vergé, §4, page 41. KLUBER: *Droit des Gens Moderne de l' Europe*, Edit. Ott., 1861, §37, page 58. VATTEL Edit. Pradier Fodéré, 1863. Preface of Vattel, page 47, and Preliminary.

necessities and interest of States give rise to international concerns, which establish international claims or rights with their corresponding duties and obligations; hence comes International Law. There exists, however, in the great Society of States, no legislative power, and therefore no written code of International Law, but there exsist more or less generally acknowledged rules of reciprocity of conduct, in peace and war. Such rules have been sanctioned either by written agreements concluded between sovereign States, and called Treaties or Conventions, and forming the *Conventional Law*, which has direct binding force for the States under contract and serves as precedent in many cases, or they have been sanctioned by custom or usage of long standing among Nations, voluntarily admitted as the *Customary Law*. These two elements constitute what may be called the *Positive Law of Nations*. But as this Law, hedged in by the narrow limits of special and isolated conventions and tacitly admitted customs, could not supply all the wants of international intercourse, in the manifold conditions of peace and war, it is supplemented by a third element, which may be called the *Necessary Law of Nations*, and serves for all those cases for which no provision is made, either by treaty or custom. This third element, necessary to complete, through International Jurisprudence, the rules essential for the intercourse of civilized nations, necessary to cement the loose stones of the Positive Law of Nations, composed of customs and conventions and stray facts of historical precedents, into the solid international structure that constitutes the stronghold of social progress and civilization, is the *Law of Conscience*, which is the Law of *Justice* * (§31).

These three legal elements, viz., the Written Law, Customs, and Justice, form, in their combination, what is called INTERNATIONAL LAW *(jus inter gentes)*.

The introduction of the Law of Conscience, as an acknowl-

---

* VATTEL: *Droit des Gens*, Prelim. §§6-9. G. F. DE MARTENS: *Préces du Droit des Gens*, Edit. 1858, Note of Ch. Vergé, §4, p. 41.

edged element of International Law, is only practicable to the extent to which the fluctuating standard of international morality, as existing at a given time between nations, by virtue of the respective moral civilization of individual States, will admit of it. A State's capability of being subject to Law evidently depends upon the exercise of a sense of right and of a sense of the obligation to act in obedience to it, either on the part of the community at large or, at least, of the person or body of persons in whom the will governing the acts of the community resides (Hall, p. 13). International Law, being based on International Morality, depends upon the state of progress made in civilization. Hence arises the difficulty of giving an all-comprehending definition to International Law. What *ought* to be permanently understood among civilized nations as the main priciples and the basis of their mutual intercourse, we have noted already to be the condition of the moral senses which we called above the Moral Law of Nature (§32). But we have also seen that the Spirit of Law (§33) is the practical manifestation of this general Law of the human mind in the different stages of progress on the road to civilization. Investigating this spirit of Law, we find the definition of International Law to consist in *certain rules of conduct which Reason, prompted by Conscience, deduces as consonant with Justice, with such limitations and modifications as may be established by general consent to meet the exigencies of the present state of society as existing among nations, and which modern civilized States regard as binding them in their relations with one another, with a force comparable in nature and degree to that binding the conscientious person to obey the laws of his country.* All depends, thus, upon the capability of the "conscientious person," who represents here the International Popular Conscience, which is the International Spirit of Law.*

WHEATON: Edit. Dana, §14. W. E. HALL: *International Law*, Edit. 1880, pages 1 and 13.—"It is true, indeed, that a law controlling independent Sovereign States can only become such by their free consent; it must, as we

From this it appears obvious that, in the present state of international intercourse between states, no immutable system for a generally acknowledged Law of Nations has as yet been arrived at, although the principles of the Moral Law of Nature are individually upheld by all civilized states, by the impartial application of Justice to all included within the respective territories.

"Righteousness exalteth a Nation, while sin is a reproach to any People." This warning lesson of ancient wisdom, which holds good for the rational dealings of Nation with Nation through all generations, is fully acknowledged, but the influence which the Moral Law, the Law of Conscience, exercises on the actions of a Nation, is not regulated by its national moral standard only, but also by its relative freedom from powerful outward causes of pressure, which may sometimes be beyond the control of its most conscientious leaders. Thus it is that we sometimes see Nations act in contradiction to their popular Conscience, as exhibited by their popular organs, and this for want of a free will to follow the dictates of that conscience.

It is the aim of sound State-Policy, to keep clear of a position so degrading to the national character, by securing a free exercise of the National Conscience.†

It has been stated that there can be no law between Nations, as there is no palpable authority nor any acknowledged common superior, no international executive to enforce the precepts of in-

---

have seen, be voluntary. But this code of voluntary rules cannot, for that reason, be arbitrary, irrational, or inconsistent with Justice."—WOOLSEY: *International Law*, Edit. 1879, page 14.

† "The science which teaches the reciprocal duties of Sovereign States is not a vain and useless study. If it were so, the same thing might be affirmed of the science of private morality, the duties inculcated by which are frequently destitute of the sanction of positive law, and are enforced merely by conscience and social opinion. As the very existence of social intercourse in private life depends upon the observance of these duties, so the existence of that mutual intercourse among nations, which is so essential to their happiness and prosperity, depends upon the rules which have generally been adopted by the great Society of Nations to regulate that intercourse."— WHEATON: *Elements of International Law*, Ed. Dana, Preface, page 21.

ternational laws. No Nation will take up arms to punish another Nation which, whilst engaged in warfare, wilfully disregards the common law of Nations. And it is fortunate that such is the case; for it was the very attempt to set up such an authority of external nature over the affairs of Nations, which prevented so long the pure development which international morality might have enjoyed through the free progress of civilization. The inefficiency of such superior direction or international executive, which, in whatever shape it may clothe its authority, would never be free from the shortsightedness, egotism and partiality, which is the nature of all human institutions, is exhibited by history, in the struggle between Church and State for secular supremacy, in their claim to guide the destinies of the Nations of Europe, and in the feudal pretensions of the great Potentates of the East. What have they all led to but to a retardation of the free development of civilization. It is true, "*pour ce genre d'infractions, il n'y a pas de juge ici-bas*," * and it is natural that such is the case; for what human institution could sit in judgment over transgressions of this nature, over crimes committed by Nations. The Judge required is not personified on earth—no more than the Great Regulator of our moral obligations, who imparts to our minds, through the Soul, a ray of His Spirit for our guidance, so that, notwithstanding this absence of a visible judge, civilized humanity finds itself restrained by the irresistible power of the human conscience, which, in affairs of nations, has a sure agent in public opinion, the organ of the Popular Conscience, and whose reprehensions are not seldom the visible powerful factors of effectual retribution † (§37).

It is not the physical enforcement of a law which constitutes its legality. The principal condition for the existence and main-

---

* Letter of Count von Moltke to Professor Blemtschli, dated 11th December, 1880, *Revue de l'Institut de Droit Intern.*, Vol. XIII., 1881, page 80.

† HEFFTER: *Le Droit Intern. de l'Europe*, Trad., Bergson Ed., 1873, §2. page 3. HALLECK: *International Law*, Commentary by Sir Sherston Baker, Ed. 1878, Ch. ii., §§13–16.

tenance of all necessary laws is the moral sanction, for no power, be it ever so strong, can uphold an unjust law for any length of time. Justice is a Law of Nature and not the offspring of human power, for what becomes of the power which is not based on Justice? Let history speak and we shall find that where the two are combined, there it is that Justice above all is indispensable for the preservation of power. The pretension that might is right was regarded by Goethe as an infernal principle, when he put in the mouth of Mephistopheles the words "*hat man Gewalt, so hat man Recht.*" *

The broad basis on which the principles of International Law rest, makes it possible to comprehend all mankind in the sphere of this Law, as it is applicable not merely to the intercourse existing between Christian Nations, but also to the intercourse existing between these and non-Christian people, and to the intercourse existing between these latter, while it is also binding on all civilized Nations, as far as practicable, in their dealings with uncivilized Nations for purposes of mutual benefit. Equality of States, whether in civilization or in dependency, is not a necessary condition for the conception of legal relations existing between States on the basis of justice and benevolence, which form the Moral Law of Nature. †

Whenever Nations come in contact with each other, their mutual intercourse is subject to this Moral Law, as the law which is naturally binding before any regular compacts have evolved from such intercourse.

---

* *Le Droit règne à d'autres conditions que la Force; il suffit à celle-ci d'être toujours la force ou la paraitre; il faut qu'elle s'allie à l'ignorance. Le ressort de la terreur ce détent à la lumière, celui du droit s'y fortifie; la force se manifeste par la bonalité de ses attaques, le droit ne se revèle, ne se montre aux hommes que sous des formes intelligentes, ou il cesse d'être le droit; émané de l'intelligence, il ne peut s'adresser qu'à elle. C'est un élément qui recherche et poursuit à travers tout ce qui n'est que matériel, reservant accueil et sanction à tout ce qui a passé par l'ame et désavue à ce qui n'est pas marqué de ce scéau.*"—*Le Droit dans ses Maximes*, page 135. RITTIEZ: *Science des Droits*, etc., Ch. xv., §§4-7.

† H. I. H. The Duke of Leuchtenberg's letter to Prof. Martens, of St. Petersburg, of 19th February, 1881, with regard to the Laws of War (see *Revue de Droit International*, 1881, p. 307) proves practically that it is possible to respect these Laws under exceptionally trying circumstances.

Another essential consequence of the supreme government which this Law of the Moral Senses exercises as regards the affairs of Nations is this, that by applying or keeping in view the principles of conscience and sympathy combined, all differences which might arise between States, can on this basis be settled by arbitration, for when the absence of positive instruments and proofs might render the solution difficult or even impossible, there are the principles of Justice and Humanity in which all agree.

§65. As stated above (§§46 and 63) the basis of all intercourse, in the case of Nations as well as individuals, is *good faith*, *i.e.*, the respect which civilized men owe to the given word of promise. This principle is the first in the test of civilization, as the natural result of the moral development of the human mind described in §5. All agreements from which obligations result, must fulfil the following conditions, viz., 1st, that the contracting parties possess the moral and legal capacity to treat; 2nd, that the consent be freely and voluntarily given; 3rd, that the agreement be in harmony with the Moral Law of Nature, *i.e.*, in conformity with the Spirit of Law of the highest standard existing between the contracting parties; in other words, the agreement must be based on the standard of national morality and civilization of the party most advanced in morality and civilization, for those who have attained to the higher moral standard cannot, under any consideration, stoop to the lower one without polluting their conscience and retreating on the road to civilization. These principles determine the mutual duties of States.

With regard to the attitude which a civilized State ought to assume towards uncivilized Nations, and the mutual confidence which ought to exist between equally civilized States, in accordance with the Moral Law of humanity, we cannot give better evidence, in support of our exposition of the general principles given in the preceding chapters, than by quoting from the recent remarkable work of Prof. Lorimer, *The Institutes of the Law of Nations*, the following passages.

"The moment that the power to help a retrograde race forward towards the goal of human life consciously exists in a civilized Nation, that civilized nation is bound to exert its power; and in the exercise of its power, it is entitled to assume an attitude of guardianship, and to put wholly aside the proximate will of the retrograde race. Its own civilization having resulted from the exercise of a will which it regards as rational, real and ultimate, at least when contrasted with the irrational, phenomenal and proximate will of the inferior race, in vindicating its own proximate will, it is entitled to assume that it vindicates the ultimate will of the inferior race, the will, that is to say, at which the inferior race must arrive when it reaches the stage of civilization to which the higher race has attained. But the obligation and the right of a civilized Nation to interfere with a retrograde race, even where such interference might be for the benefit of the latter, is limited by the proviso that, in so doing, it does not so burden its own resources as to cause a greater loss of the means of progress to itself and others than it confers on the retrograde race."

"But," says Prof. Lorimer further, "time is an element in the action of civilizing influences, the importance of which is not always sufficiently kept in view. Neither warlike nor peaceful contact acts immediately, nay, the first generation subjected to the influences of either is frequently inferior to that which preceded it. The pagan temple is in ruins, and the Christian Church has not been built. The old rule of life has been abrogated, and no better rule has yet taken its place. In many cases it becomes a question of the utmost delicacy, whether appeals to the reason, conscience, and the self-interest, even of savages, through missionaries, traders and neighboring settlers, be not more potent than the closer contact and more direct guidance which results from political subjection, if unaccompanied by actual colonization. It is too true that colonization often acts as an improving influence only by improving those subjected to it off the face of the earth; but its action admits of being so regulated by the mother country as that it shall ultimately assign to her retrograde children the position for which they are suited by the characteristics of the race to which they belong, and the stage of progress which they have reached, or, in the case of old communities, at which they stand for the time being. The great difficulty always consists in understanding those whose circumstances differ from our own often more widely than their characters." *

With regard to the relations of mutual confidence which ought in general to subsist between civilized States, Professor Lorimer makes the following further remarks.

"The normal relations of States are relations neither of hostility nor indifference—as is alleged, not very justly, perhaps, to have been the ancient opinion—nor of mutual jealousy and distrust, which is still too much the modern opinion, but of amity and reciprocal confidence. This is the logical inference from the doctrines of Natural Law which we have elsewhere established. It is on this inference that all the doctrines of the Law of Nations rest, and its conquest, as a conscious starting point, is justly regarded as the greatest achievement of science in this department of inquiry. The much profaned principle of *fraternité*, when thus understood, brings the whole moral hemisphere within the range of scientific vision, and holds out to us a prospect of its practical exploration. Expanding from the person to the family, from the family to the State, and from the State to the community of States, the doctrine that "love, which worketh no ill to its neighbour," is "the fulfilling of the law," by bringing the law of Nations within the range of ethics, is preparing it gradually to assume the character of a positive jural system. But mutual good-will by no means implies mutual interference or even co-operation, in ordinary circumstances. On the contrary, the capacity for self-support and self-government being, as we

---

* Prof. JAMES LORIMER, LL.D.: *The Institutes of the Law of Nations*, Vol. I., p. 227.

have seen, conditions of recognition, non-interference may be enunciated as the primary duty which separate communities, simply as such, owe to each other. That, in the normal relations of jural entities, the negative takes precedence of the positive principle, is a maxim of universal application in jurisprudence, which follows as a corollary from the subjective origin which we have assigned both to rights and duties. As the first subjective right of every separate rational entity is the right to the unfettered exercise of the powers which God has conferred on him, and his first subjective duty is to exercise these powers in his own behalf, so, in like manner, the first objective right which this entity must acknowledge is the right of others to be relieved by his personal efforts of the burden of his support, and the first objective duty towards him is the duty of permitting him to energize for this purpose. Now separate States are such rational and responsible entities. It is on this ground, as we have seen, that their right to recognition rests—and in their case, consequently, just as in the case of individuals that are *sui juris*, the rule must be in favor of non-interference. As time rolls on, and the experience of ages accumulates, the importance of this rule, not only for the sake of those in behalf of whose liberties it is invoked, but of those on whose ambition, or philanthropy, or restlessness, its restrictions are imposed, comes to be more and more clearly admitted. The interest of each is felt to be the interest of all; and the interest of each, with few and often doubtful exceptions, will be better promoted by leaving him to follow the bent of his own genius than by any rules that we can impose upon him, or even by any aid that we can afford him." *

§66. With regard to States as well as with regard to individuals, every right implies a correlative duty. Accordingly

---

* Prof. LORIMER: *The Institutes of the Law of Nations*, Vol. I., p. 230, *et seq*. IDEM: *Institutes of Law*, p. 101, *et seq.*, 212 and 235.

all international rights are bound up with corresponding obligations. Hence proceeds the interdependence of States.*

From the point of view of humanity and civilization, the normal condition of Nations appears to be a relationship of mutual good will and peace. From the necessity and the desire to secure this natural relationship, devolve various measures, including even war, when the state of equilibrium is disturbed and all peaceable means are exhausted.

"The obligation of a State to render justice to all others," says Halleck, "is a *perfect* obligation, of strictly binding force, at all times and under all circumstances." No State can relieve itself from this obligation, under any pretext whatever. It is an obligation, according to Vattel, "more necessary still between Nations than between individuals; because injustice has more terrible consequences in the quarrels of these powerful bodies-politic and it is more difficult to obtain redress." The same rule applies to all the duties of a State which result from the *perfect* international rights of others, for whatever one Nation has a perfect right to demand of another, that is the other absolutely bound to surrender. The rule is absolute, and cannot be evaded by any technicality, sophistry, or under any other pretext. To refuse what is the absolute *duty* of a State to concede to another, under any pretext whatsoever, would be a violation of the positive rule and fundamental principle of international jurisprudence, and no civilized Nation can now be found to refuse to another an acknowledged and indisputable right. They may dispute the right itself, and deny its existence as a right, but there is none so low and debased in moral character as to deny the duty and obligation to respect what is a manifest and acknowledged international right of another. Moreover, this obligation of the State is equally binding upon all its rulers, officers, and

---

* Souveränität ist nicht absolute Unabhängigkeit, noch absolute Freiheit eines Staates, denn, die Staaten sind keine absolute Wesen, sondern rechtlich beschränkte Personen.—BLUNTSCHLI: *Völkerrecht*, §65.

citizens—in short upon each and every individual member that belongs to a State or body-politic.*

In the foregoing pages (§§62-66) are treated the data of civilization with regard to international intercourse between individual States; we shall now proceed, in the following sections, to examine the nature and requirements of the medium of this intercourse, and the means of its subsistence, viz., the Right of Negotiation and the International Treaties (§§67-69).

§67. Treaties and Conventions—forming, as stated on page 97, the *Conventional Law of Nations*—are the means through which international rights are created, modified or extended, by developing or regulating the natural moral obligations which exist between social organisms, as described above (§§62 and 63). Whilst moulding these natural moral obligations into practical rules, international agreements impose upon the respective parties, by mutual agreement, supplementary obligations to do or to omit to do, or to suffer third parties to do or omit to do, certain special acts by which parties calculate to arrive at a certain definite aim.

The constitution of every State determines the authority in which is vested the power to conclude treaties binding on the State as body-politic. As this power emanates from the Public Law of the State, international agreements are called public treaties or conventions *(pactum gentium publicum)*, in contradistinction from private contracts, which the Government of a State sometimes enters into with private individuals or corporations—whether native or foreign—with regard to loans or concessions of territories for agricultural, colonization, mining or any other industrial purposes. It is evident that only public treaties or conventions, as being agreements between States, belong to the domain of International Law.†

---

* HALLECK: *International Law*, Edit. Sir Sherston Baker, Vol. I., p. 392. VATTEL: *Droit des Gens*, Liv. II., Ch. v., §63.

† VATTEL: *Droit des Gens*, Liv. II., Chap. xii. MARTENS: *Précis des Droits des Gens Moderns*, §47. KLUBER: p. 141. ORTOLAN: *Dipl. de la Mer*, Vol. I., Chap. v.

§68. International treaties as well as international customs are the manifestations of the International Spirit of Law; in other words, they are the indications of the state of progress or of re-action in civilization, with this distinction, that the elasticity of custom renders it a far more sincere interpreter of this Spirit of Law than the formal treaty. Custom formed by moral obligations (§29) rarely mistakes actual circumstances, as is often the case with treaties, which are based on theories or presumed facts, or made to satisfy temporary exigencies. Custom, being unconsciously guided by the moral senses, causes men to follow the true direction without being able to explain to themselves the reason why they have chosen any particular course; while many treaties, which pretend to fix the goal beforehand, or to establish the right direction through premeditating conception of the material object to be attained, make men drift into the wrong way while they intended to go right.* Thus, treaties which serve to suit special interests are often serious impediments to progress. Finally, the existence of a custom is the unfailing evidence that its object was possible; while the real objects of many treaties are not always attainable.

A treaty ceases to be efficacious when the moral or material, the speculative or practical object of agreement on which its *raison d'être* was based, ceases to exist. The moral causes of the imperfect observance of international contracts must be looked for in the changes which take place in the standard of international morality, as treated above (§§62-65.)

§69. The practical causes of the imperfect observance of treaties must be looked for in their material and technical imperfections and defects. These causes are judiciously indicated, under four heads, by Professor Sheldon Amos, in his late work on the Science of Jurisprudence, as follows:—

"In the first place, treaties are often made to last for an indefinite length of time, during which the parties to them or-

---
* Prof. LORIMER: *The Institutes of the Law of Nations.*

dinarily undergo remarkable changes in their circumstances, both in relation to each other and to other States, to which there is no parallel presented in the circumstances of parties to a contract in National Law. In order to meet this difficulty, it has been suggested that either no treaty should be made for longer than a very limited period—say ten years—or that, if made for longer than that period, it should be known to be open to revision at the end of some such period. The objection to this recommendation is that some treaties must, from the nature of the case, be intended to endure for a far longer time than others, and that a prospect of a revision of them at a short distance of time would produce the very insecurity in the tenure of all rights under them which it is the main purpose of the treaty to prevent. In the treaties with Great Britain which followed the declaration of American Independence, and which had for one purpose, among others, a definite fixing of the relative claims of American and British citizens to fisheries along the coast of Canada and of the adjoining islands, any prospect of changes after the lapse of a definite period must have seriously qualified the nature of the rights themselves, and any prospect of a revision of the treaties at a fixed time must have not only had a like effect, but have operated very unfavorably in fostering a restless temper of political ambition. It should be admitted that just as a single State can acquire rights by prescription or by continued possession, or by the enduring consent of other States, so between two States certain treaties may be made which must be allowed and expected to operate as long as the two States exist. The responsibility incurred in making any such treaties, and the inexpediency of multiplying them, is sufficiently evident to all.

"Another cause which leads to the imperfect observance of treaties is the fact that the most important treaties, on the strict maintenance of which the peace and order of a complex society of States depend, are constantly made out at the conclusion of a war, in order to ascertain and fix the relations of the belligerent

States towards one another. A professedly moral engagement made under such circumstances can hardly fail to lack all the elements of choice and freedom which alone can create a personal sense or a general recognition of real responsibility. In all national systems of Law the presence of 'duress,' or *vis* and *metus*, are peremptorily held to invalidate the most formal and the most apparently voluntary transactions. When terms are imposed by a conqueror, with the terrible alternative to their adoption of a continuance of the war, and when, as it too frequently happens in times of war, opinions and feelings in the vanquished or worsted State are violently distracted, any engagement that can be made as to the future must always contain the suppressed clause that the treaty is only to operate so long as the weaker State is physically forced to tolerate its operation. The very consciousness of this latent infirmity, attaching to every treaty of peace, tends, of itself, to make the customary terms of such treaties harder than they might otherwise be. Thus violence begets distrust, and distrust increases the violence; from which terrible series of reactions springs the lamentable phenomenon that, while all the existing relations of the European States have been mainly determined by treaties of peace, following upon sanguinary wars, and depend, for their stability, upon the rigid observance of those treaties, nevertheless hardly a single State shrinks from breaking—or, at the least, from clamorously insisting upon a revision of—any one of those treaties, as soon as it seems conducive to its own interests to do so. A remedy for this cause of the prevailing infirmity attaching to treaties is to be found in multiplying treaties between States at peace with each other, and while each is enjoying a considerable measure of independence and dignity; such treaties would possess all the most hopeful elements of stability and cogency, and the States which were parties to them, instead of writhing under a hard and tyrannical chain—the memorials of past degradation—would cherish and honor them with a noble rivalry, as being at once memorials of a worthy ambition and continuing tests of the national honor.

"A third cause of the non-observance of treaties is undoubtedly to be found in the loose and inaccurate form in which they are frequently drawn up, in consequence of which there exists no universal canon of interpretation which is applicable to them. This fact is due partly to the political necessity of the case, and partly to the want of any common juridical language equally accepted by all the States of Europe. A treaty, when once finally agreed upon, is always the result of a series of compromises, especially when following upon a war. These compromises are the product of protracted negotiations, conducted by a body of men proverbially famous rather for deceiving one another in the politest language than for successfully communicating to one another the real meaning of their language and no more nor less. Those negotiations, again, are apt to be violently interfered with by all kinds of special influences and of indirect aims irrelevant to the main points at issue, which yet, however, in the general result, are not and cannot be ignored. Again, while there is an avoidance of purely colloquial language in framing a treaty, there is a current dislike to a purely legal style—founded no doubt on a reminiscence of the narrow system of interpretation, vulgarly, though not altogether unjustly, attributed to professional lawyers. It thus comes about that the style of a treaty runs a risk of having the special defects of a home-made will, and of containing just enough legal phraseology to generate disputes, and not enough to clear them up. It is scarcely necessary to say that the true remedy for this cause of the imperfect observance of treaties will be found in the general cultivation throughout Europe of the study of International Law. The age of secret diplomacy is passing away with that of autocratic rule. It is probable that the new era will be marked by a race of great and popular statesmen, carrying on the negotiations with foreign States, as far as may be, in the light of day and on principles which do not shun that light, and by a growing school of international lawyers who will assist to build up a truly humane code, expressed in precise language, to which the terms of every international document will bear explicit or implicit reference.

"The notice of the influence of popular movements in the present day suggests the last or fourth cause which need be noticed of the imperfect observance of treaties. It has always, of necessity, been a matter of the utmost solicitude to determine what amount of ratification, and by what persons, is necessary in order to impart to a treaty its binding force. Treaties are necessarily negotiated and executed by persons who reproduce, in International Law, the character of agents in National Law. As in the case of such agents, the special or general character of the representatives has to be taken into account in estimating the degree of their authority. In all States, ancient and modern, the capacity to make binding treaties with foreign powers has been held to rest exclusively in the Executive Authority of the State, though—as in the case of the share in such capacity possessed by the Senate in the United States—the Executive Authority has occasionally been, for this special purpose, modified in its constitution. This remarkable and enormous function of the Executive has maintained its ground, no doubt, in part from the traditional notions of the mutual dynastic relationships of the monarchical heads of different States, whereby all foreign transactions peculiarly adhered to the prerogative of the monarch, even where matters of internal government had gradually become encroached upon by the people; and partly to the possibility of sudden emergencies presenting themselves, needing instant settlement by conventions between States under circumstances in which the delay necessary for consulting a public assembly, or the publicity involved in consulting it, would seriously interfere with the accomplishment of the purpose in view. It is possible, however, that the capacity of making important treaties will, in all States, be more and more taken into its own hands by the supreme

Political Authority. It is much to be desired that this should be the case, not only to ensure more prudent and deliberate engagements being made, but in such a way to charge the whole Nation with the joint responsibility as to ensure their being kept."*

But whatever may be the inherent defects or imperfections of international contracts, their obligatory force rests on mutual good faith. All laws which have been formally enacted must be formally repealed, so treaties which have been formally negotiated must be formally renounced or revised, as they do not possess the elasticity and self-regulating characteristic of custom. As long as the material interests are in harmony with the moral reasons, the conscientious fulfilment of the mutual obligations, imposed by the compact, is as natural a task as it is an easy duty to accomplish. But, as we noted above, the progress of humanity, in conformity with its moral senses, is ever changing and moulding the International Spirit of Law, which manifests itself in the intercourse of Nations, and finds formulated utterances in different international transactions. As such, international treaties are the landmarks of the progress or the retrogression of Nations on the road to civilization, and when a treaty does not agree with the actuality of that state of mutual understanding between parties, which is created by and is existing through the International Spirit of Law, the treaty becomes naturally amendable. The natural defect of such a contract must lead sooner or later to its invalidity, and finally to a rupture of the inefficient contract, unless the treaty be in due time abrogated or altered. The aspects under which the successive degrees of inefficaciousness of a treaty, and its final peaceable amendment or abrogation present themselves, are conspicuous marks of the progress or retrogression of the International Spirit of Law.

Thus when we observe States entering into mutual obligations which afterwards become unduly onerous for one of the

---

* Prof. SHELDON AMOS: *A Systematic View of the Science of Jurisprudence*, Ed. 1872, p. 425, *et seq.*

parties, so that the contracted obligation "conflicts with the rights and welfare of its people" (Heffter); when we see a Nation having "inadvertently and gratuitously abandoned an essential natural right—such, for example, as part of its independence—holds treaties incompatible with its development to be null" (Bluntschli); or when we hear that "all treaties are to be looked upon as null which are opposed to the development of the free moral and material activity of a Nation, and that, by the light of this principle, such treaties must be held immoral, iniquitous and valueless" (Fiore)—then, in all these cases, the sole way by which it could be ascertained whether reasons given as above are vile excuses of unscrupulousness and ambition, emanating from a powerful party to impose on its weaker neighbours, or whether they are real principles, emanating from a progressing International Spirit of Law, is to put them to the test of unbiased righteousness, which underlies this Spirit of Law. This is done through the pratical solution of the question whether the contract under dispute is or is not compatible with the real welfare of the complaining party, as well as with the progress of civilization in general, and thus ought to be adhered to or modified for the benefit of all parties concerned. The solution of this question is the task of impartial arbitration, as will be described hereafter.

When justice and benevolence, which, combined, constitute righteousness, condemn an existing contract, the obligations emanating from such a pactum, though couched in the most solemn legal forms, are doubtless immoral, iniquitous and valueless, and when, under the disguise of justice or humanity, weapons of vile ambition are used, these are easily detected by unbiased common sense, for nothing is more inconsistent with our common sense than that Law, which is formed by our moral senses, should be intended to bring license and confusion, instead of restraint and order, into human dealings and transactions. But, as noted above, these dealings and transactions are products of the state of civilization of the respective parties to the transactions, and the changes which these transactions undergo keep pace with the moral progress or retrogression of Nations in their intercourse, in other words, with the International Spirit of Law.

§70. The accidental or momentary disturbances which are observed in the economical system of nature, both in the physical and in the moral organism, are phenomena caused by occasional perturbations in the regularity of occurences in nature, *i.e.*, in the Laws of Nature, moral as well as physical. These deviations are observable through all stages of creation, from inorganic matter up to biological and social organisms.

The variations in the dominion of the **Moral Law of Nature** —which, as described in the First Chapter, is the undisturbed evolution of the human mind towards the Good—are indicated by the phenomena which we call the Spirit of Law, described in §33. The causes of perturbations of physical laws, in other words, the origin of varieties in species, are often hidden to our senses; the inadequacy of our physical senses to perform proper observations among the milliards of active factors which cause the deviation of some particularly conspicuous physical law into the channel of another or several other laws combined, will remain a serious impediment to natural science, notwithstanding the most skillful contrivances made to bring to perfection the test of experiments. Under these circumstances our perception of physical causes must necessarily be deficient. This is, however, not the case, to the same extent, with regard to our consciousness of moral perturbations, provided we try to discover the causes of the variations of the Moral Law of Nature through our moral senses Conscience and Sympathy, which, when combined, represent in our mind this Law of Nature, and form our judgment, through genuine common sense, which is Reason and Feeling combined, as described above (§34).

The scientific moralist who accepts the moral-mental organism as part of the economical system of Nature, will not fail to obtain, through a well-developed common sense, a sufficiently clear conception of the National Spirit of Law and the International Spirit of Law; for, judging the history of mankind through genuine common sense (§34) he will easily comprehend the immediate factors which produced deteriorations from the Moral Law.*

We have noted before (§63) how civilized States, in their mutual intercourse in time of war as well as peace, invariably appeal to public opinion for the justification of their acts, and how it is proved by history that civilized nations of all ages have recognized the Moral Law to be binding upon them as the basis of mutual duties, however poorly the state of the Spirit of Law, which governed those mutual duties, might now appear to us by the light of a progressing civilization. This Spirit of Law, emanating from the moral senses, of which it is the manifestation in the practical life of nations as well as individuals, shows itself in different aspects (not unlike the normal varieties of species produced in the sphere of the physical laws), which are caused by manifold influences of social life at every stage on the road to civilization made by the subject whose immanent phenomenon it is. These are *normal variations* of the social organism, but differences, disputes and war between nations or states are *abnormal variations* of the Spirit of Law, caused by fundamental disturbance in the natural evolution process which governs social relations.

In international as well as in civil jurisprudence, a distinction must be made between the rights of parties and the legal means they employ to maintain and justify these rights and

---

* La perturbation accidentelle et momentanée de l'harmonie qui doit présider à tout système régulier, est un fait de l'ordre physique et de l'ordre moral. Ce fait s'observe dans la matière inerte et dans les corps organisés, chez les êtres animés dépourvus de raison, et chez l'homme, être essentiellement raisonable. Dans l'ordre physique, la découverte des lois qui président à cette perturbation est souvent un problème insoluble pour la raison de l'homme; les effets se perçoivent, tandis que les causes demeurent cachées. Dans les institutions humaines de l'ordre moral, l'interruption de l'harmonie prend sa source dans le conflits des intérêts individuels, dans l'antagonisme des droits de chacun et des obligations ou devoirs qui répondent à ces droits.—ORTOLAN: *Diplomatic de la Mer*, Edit. 1864, Vol. II., p. 2, Cause et objet de la guerre.

for the termination of the differences. Justice and Benevolence are ever influencing the human mind to bring the latter in harmony with the Moral Law of Nature. The standard by which the rights of parties must be regarded by an unbiased mind can therefore not be disputed; it is the means of adjudication which constitutes the difference between civil and international jurisprudence. Thus, differences or disputes between Nations or States, when not capable of being settled by amicable arrangement, compromise, arbitration or other normal measures of peace, are apt to throw society back into that state of semi-barbarism in which only brute force constitutes an acknowledged verdict, that is, into the state of war.*

In the first instance, the rules applied in order to arrive at a solution of the question in a peaceable way are called the *Laws of Peace*, while, in the other instance, when parties have drifted into a state of mutual violence, this state is yet subjected, as far as possible, to certain rules of restraint acknowledged by International Law, which are called *Laws of War* (*Jus belli*)—(§§72 and 73).

§71. There is, however, an intermediate condition between peace and war, a medium state, in which a crisis is formed by the alternative of adopting the one or the other course. In this state arbitrary acts are often committed, by one or both of the contending parties, in order to hasten the termination of the crisis. This brings parties into a condition of enmity, often accompanied by acts of violence, which fall short of actual war only by being more or less limited to a certain defined line of action or field of operation in conformity with the predominating social, political or moral conditions which the respective parties occupy in relation to each other. This intermediate condition between peace and war is called *retaliation* or *reprisal*.

The Laws of Peace give several remedies at hand to terminate

---

* G. F. DE MARTENS: *Precis de Droit des Gens*, Edit. Vergé, 1858, Vol. II., p. 19. KLUBER: Edit. Ott., 1861, p. 406.

differences among contending States. In the first place, the principles of the laws of peace require that the *facts* which have caused the difference or contest must be clearly established. In the means which parties employ to establish these facts lies not only the test of the sincerity of their appeal to the laws of peace, but these proceedings form a genuine standard by which one may judge their respective national morality.

When Great Britain, with the magnanimity really worthy of a great Nation, acknowledged the misconception of facts which had led to the Transvaal war, and ceased the bloody contest with those few brave sons of *het oude Vaderland*, which the colossus could have easily crushed but never made to yield, British statesmen never displayed a truer sense of the appreciation in which they hold inborn national-moral sense of justice and benevolence. Thus it was also in the case of the *Alabama* arbitration, when two great Nations avoided a bloody contest between kindred nationalities, by submitting to a sincere investigation of facts, and proved that, when the International Spirit of Law has attained to a high moral standard, bloody conflicts between States are almost sure to be prevented. Alas! that history could not have recorded the same of the latest differences between two of the most civilized Nations of the Earth, who, without any serious attempt at a peaceable solution, hurried two friendly neighbouring populations into a war which filled Europe with consternation and dread. But fortunately again, the chariot of the conqueror was checked by the genuine appreciation of justice and benevolence, worthy of the great Sovereign under whose sceptre a great people has succeeded to combine tribal nationality with political unity, and through the moderation of their great statesman who, while taking all responsibility on his great mind, yet never quailed in any difficulty, nor ever overstepped the limits of his great task to venture on feats of ambition, which would have thrust back the civilization of Europe for more than a century into a course of retrogression—leaving all the great and good minds, which have so zealously pleaded for the recognition of international morality, in profound despair of ever finding a clue to the problem of human destiny. And thus it was the ever self-rectifying power of the Moral Senses which, regaining its sway over the human mind, caused genuine common sense and moderation of leaders and people to prevail over the rapacious, selfish inclinations of the animal nature of man.

But, returning to our subject, it must be kept in mind that, although the ascertaining of the facts, which gave occasion to the difference, is logically the first stage of process in every attempt to discuss a matter of dispute between reasonable beings, yet, unfortunately, facts cannot always be proved to such an incontestable degree of certainty as to convince the party who is in the wrong, even presuming that he really and *bonâ fide* wishes to be convinced. And how seldom does this latter case happen; how often the so-called leading newspapers of the day stoop to become, maliciously, misleading chroniclers of history, refusing all rectification that could remove the national prejudices to which it is their interest to pander. Thus each party tries to establish such a statement of the facts complained of as would tell in its own favor, in which process almost invariably a one-sided subjective conception of the facts in dispute, or their effects, is, with all the characteristics of an *ex parte* statement, substituted for actual occurrences, which may in themselves have been very innocent acts, caused by *force majeure* or by some peculiar position of the parties. In this case an unprejudiced court alone can clearly establish the undeniable facts; this indispensable requisite is to be found in the system of arbitration, which is treated in sections 74 and 75.

With regard to the moral obligation resting on both parties, to ascertain the facts with moderation, Halleck says:—"The precepts of morality, as well as the principles of public law, by which human society is governed, render it obligatory upon a State, before resorting to arms, to try every pacific mode of settling its disputes with others, whether such disputes arise from rights denied or injuries received. This moderation is the more necessary as it not infrequently happens that what is at first looked upon as an injury or an insult, is found, upon a more deliberate examination, to be a mistake rather than an act of malice, or one designed to give offence. Moreover, the injury may result from the acts of inferior persons, which may not receive the approbation of their own Government. A little moderation and delay in such cases may bring to the offended party a just satisfaction; whereas rash and precipitate measures often lead to the shedding of much innocent blood. The moderation of the Government of the United States, in the case of the burning of the American steam-boat *Caroline* (1837), by a British officer, led to an amicable adjustment of the difficulties arising from a violation of neutral territory, and saved both countries from the disasters of a bloody war. The moderation of the British Admiral in the affair at St. Juan Island is deserving of the highest praise."*

When the facts which gave rise to the dispute are clearly established, it is the moral duty and thus the sound policy in the case of every State to try to settle differences in a peaceable manner before resorting to the decision of arms.

§72. War between civilized Nations is that abnormal social condition which is produced by the temporary degeneration of the International Conscience, which has then ceased to be susceptible of conceiving the practicability of any means for settling differences otherwise than by force (§70).

Degeneration or retrogression of the moral-mental organism of man is a condition he plainly feels to be contrary to his nature, and he strives hard, therefore, to raise himself above it into his normal state of existence, in harmony with the preponderance of his moral senses, which perpetually are urging the moral-mental organism to complete this harmony. Hence the strange phenomenon that, in the midst of the uncontrollable passions of their

---

* HALLECK: *International Law*, Ed. Sir Sherston Baker, Vol. I., p. 413.

brutish propensities, civilized human beings, *i.e.*, those which have reached the stage in creation called the moral-mental organism, are imbued with a longing, an innate desire to bridle these passions. This is the manifestation of the influence which the Moral Senses exercise on the moral-mental organism of man, and this influence is the origin of the usages which are called the *Laws of War*.

Thus war, though being a state of litigation between Nations, in which the force of arms must act as judge, and decide, is yet subject to rules which prevent it from degenerating into indiscriminate slaughter of human beings on either side, to end, as in the barbarian ages, with the extermination of one of the contending parties.

It is due to the influence of the Moral Senses on the human organism, which causes the development of civilization, that Justice and Benevolence, though far from being as yet predominant in the human mind, are becoming more and more conspicuous in the present stage of creation on earth (§5). Hence the possibility of laws between Nations, in warfare as well as in peaceable mutual intercourse.

Whilst in this condition of carrying on litigation by force of arms, the parties acquire, through the Law of War, certain accidental rights called *belligerent rights*, which impose also certain obligations on third parties, called *obligations of neutrality*. These obligations of neutrality are based on the principle of strict impartiality towards parties in litigation, and impose on neutrals the obligation—when called upon in certain doubtful cases to prove their impartiality—of granting belligerents, in special cases, the right of investigation and adjudication in matters which, in a normal state of affairs, would be entirely outside their jurisdiction. Among the rights granted to belligerents, is that to visit and search neutral vessels or conveyances, which are suspected to be in unfair relation with an enemy, provided these proceedings take place in conformity with the generally acknowledged rules, which we termed above the Laws of War.

§73. In section 70 we have noted the nature of the condition of war between civilized societies in its relation to the natural laws governing these societies, and in section 72 we have stated our views with regard to the origin of the restraint placed by civilization on the ravages of war, which constitute the **Law of War** (*Jus belli*). We must now proceed to note the status which is regarded as Law of War for the contending States, and for individuals as third parties.

War is a relation between States alone, and States being the only subjects of International Law, that Law takes cognizance of the individual solely through his State and as belonging to it, so that, except as a member of his State, the private individual has, in the eye of International Law, neither personal nor proprietary rights. From this principle—which is acknowledged by almost all writers on the Law of War—it naturally follows that where neither personal nor proprietary rights are acknowledged, there can neither exist any personal obligations nor any liability of property.

War affects, in a direct manner, States only, not individuals, for States are the sole international units. "The community and its members," says Mr. Hall, "except in their State form, being internationally unrecognized, any rights which belong to them must be clothed in the garb of State rights, before they can be put forward internationally." *

If this is the case with rights, it is a natural consequence that such must be also the case with obligations. As individual members of a State have no recognized international rights, the private individual cannot be involved in the international obligations of his State.

The state of war entails no *jus in personam* against every private individual in the State, for whose liabilities any human creature belonging to the Nation indiscriminately—widows and minors and their properties not excepted—may be sued *in solidum* and compelled *ad dandum aut faciendum*.

---

* W. E. HALL: *International Law*, Edit. 1880, p. 39.

The principle of the *jus in personam* is founded on the free-will of men, and results especially from the power which every individual has over his own acts, and nobody can ever possess such power over the acts of anybody else so as to bind the latter to any obligations without his free consent, for no one can acquire through another a *jus in personam* without distinct transfer. Thus the private individual can, *per se*, never be identified with the international acts for which his State as body politic, and its agents of all descriptions, are solely responsible, in conformity with the principle of International Law; consequently in war there exists a relation of a State to a State, and not of individuals *versus* individuals. The savage maxim that when war is declared between the two Nations, every individual member of the one is on the war-path against every person belonging to the other, is happily banished from the usages of warfare between civilized States, and what is still left of the individualism of those tribal wars of mutual massacre and plundering is gradually giving way before the progress of civilization.

The inevitable imperfection of our moral-mental organism entails the same condition of imperfection in social life, for States are collections of human beings and, as such, partake of their imperfections, but the National Spirit of Law, which is the outcome of the influence of the Moral Senses on the individual man, is distinct from the International Spirit of Law, which latter is the effect of Public Consciousness (§33) on aggregates of individuals in their combined condition called States or Bodies-Politic. It would be, therefore, contrary to Justice and Benevolence to refer actions and transactions of States, which are distinct unities, governed by the International Spirit of Law, to the responsibility of private individual members of these unities, which latter follow, in their mutual relations, the clearer and better defined rules of the National Spirit of Law. Their respective obligations can, therefore, not be identical. In the former condition the individual has no direct or active share as such, while in the latter he exercises a direct and active influence, being then in a position to obey the injunctions of his conscience and sympathy, through the direct individual control of these senses. It is, on the other hand, impossible for the private individual to exercise any control over the actions of a body in the management of which he has no share. Hence the distinction of the National Spirit of Law and the International Spirit of Law, as described in §§33 and 36, and the palpable injustice inflicted in making private individuals, who have no part whatever in the direction of the affairs of a State, and who do not possess any leading or executive functions, suffer for the result of actions beyond their control.

The hostile character of the public enemy (*hostis*), which is distinct from that of the private enemy (*inimicus*), results from political ties and not from personal feelings or personal wrongs. "Their status," says Halleck, with reference to public enemies, "is that of legal hostility and not of personal enmity. Private enemies have hatred and rancour in their hearts and seek to do each other personal injury. Not so with public enemies; they do not, as individuals, seek to do each other personal harm, and even where brought into actual conflict as armed belligerents, there is usually no personal enmity between the individuals of the contending forces. So far from this, when peace is declared, the military forces of the opposing belligerents are usually personal friends, and vie with each other in politeness and mutual kindness." *

The principles of the Law of War (*jus belli*), as described above, are established under the influence of the International Spirit of Law (§36) but the fortuitous *Usages of War (coutumes de la guerre, Kriegsgebraüche)* are not always in conformity with the principles of the Law of War, as laid down by human Conscience and Sympathy in their striving to bring the practices of actual warfare up to the acknowledged normal standard of civilization, *i.e.*, to bring about conformity with the existing International

---

* HALLECK: Vol. II., p. 52.

Spirit of Law. But there exists nevertheless a certain correspondence between these principles and the contingent usages or practices of war, which is sufficiently perceptible to serve as a guide that will enable us to find out what may or may not be deemed justifiable practices of war.

One of the most conspicuous deviations of the incidental usages of war from the principles of the Law of War is the peculiar custom, which yet exists, to seize and confiscate all private property of the enemy on the high seas—a custom which on land is called pillage, and as such banished from the practices of war among civilized nations.

This anomaly in the usages of war of a civilized generation is due to the tenacity with which some nations persist in adhering to the ancient practices sanctioned at one time by the barbaric propensities of former generations. This anomalous practice is the more surprising as it is maintained side by side with a military code characterized by the most conspicuous marks of an advanced civilization. The cause of this partial barbarism is to be looked for in certain influences predominating in State government, which are maintained by traditional national prejudices and fostered by narrow-minded selfishness; and this, notwithstanding all the most able and conscientious efforts made, from within and without, with a view to overcome these prejudices.*

---

* The writers of the last and present centuries, who have most effectually opposed the usage of capturing private property on the high sea, are the following:—MABLY: *Le Droit Public de l'Europe, fondé sur les traités*, Vol. II., p. 310. LINGUET: *Annales Politiques*, Anno 1779, Vol. V., p. 506. Prof. F. MARTENS: *De la propriété privée en temps de guerre*. Drs. AEGIDI and KLAUHOLD: *Frei Schiff unter Feindes Flagge*, 1867. ERCOLE VIDARI: *Del rispetto della proprieta privata fra gli Stati in Guerra*, Pavia, 1867. EUGÈNE CHAUCHY: *Du respect de la propriété privée dans les guerres maritimes*, Paris, 1866. BLUNTSCHLI: *Du droit du butin en général et spécialement du droit de prise maritime*, "Revue de Droit Intern." Vol. IX., 1877, p. 539, and Vol. X., 1878, p. 60. E. DE LAVELEYE: *Du respect de la propriété privée sur mer en temps de guerre*, "Revue de Droit Intern.," Vol. VII., 1875, p. 560. PIERANTONI: *Les prises maritimes d'après l'école et la législation Italienne;* "Revue de Droit International," Vol. VII., 1875, p. 618. FIORE: *Nouv. Droit Intern.*, Part II., Chapters vii. and viii. G. MASSÉ: *Le Droit commercial dans ses rapports avec le droit des gens*, Paris, 1874, Vol. II., Livre II. ERNEST NYS: *La Guerre Maritime. Etude de Droit International*, Brussels, 1881;—in chapter viii. of this valuable essay we find a very

All barbaric practices in war are the result of the mischievous assumption that war is a relation between individual members of the belligerent States, and not simply a relation between States only.

It is true that there are instances in which private citizens have taken an active share in a war waged between their respective Governments, and many may sacrifice their fortune on the altar of the common country and give freely their life-blood in its defence, thus contributing, at their own private risk, to the success of their country's cause; but can these single cases of heroism and devotion be used as arguments to upset all principles of Justice and Benevolence, or as motives to arrive at the conclusion that the war must be waged against every individual member of the enemy State? If this were so, there could be no legal reason against admitting the belligerent right to murder every single member of the enemy State, to plunder indiscriminately and to declare all that we can lay hand on, belonging to our enemy, to be legal prize, and this in order to reduce the whole enemy population, thus securing peace through the extermination, or at least utter prostration, of the enemy. A doctrine from which such conclusions could be derived is really intolerable. Its principal argument, that war will be the sooner terminated if the enemy is mercilessly attacked in his home industry, in his foreign trade and in every private interest of the individual members of the enemy, has no reasonable ground. All the wars which during this century have devastated Europe, serve more or less to prove that general hatred and animosity on the part of the mass of a people is invariably the natural result of hardship unjustly inflicted on the private individuals, and that a

---

clear and instructive review of the different efforts made during the last and the present centuries to establish the rules of maritime warfare, with regard to the private property of the individuals of an enemy State, in conformity with the usages of war as waged on land. "La contradiction est flageante," says the learned Judge of the Brussel Tribunal, "et il n'est pas besoin de démontrer que l'état actuel des chôses reclame impérieusement une réforme."—(*l. c.* p. 134.)

general desire to make peace is not brought about by cruel reprisals.* Truly, Goethe was inspired by his good genius when he conceived it as characteristic of Mephistopheles to rejoice in the doctrine that commerce was ever a fruitful source of war and piracy. When tempting Faust by exhibiting before him the glorious array of plunder which his piratical crafts had collected through war waged against peaceable commerce, Mephistopheles used, with a cleverness worthy of an evil spirit, the **ingenious** expedient of placing **the victim** on the same level of morality occupied by its spoilers. "*Krieg, Handel und Piraterie, dreieinig sind sie, nicht zu trennen,*" is the doctrine of a Mephistopheles. How often do we not find this Mephistopheles policy practiced, under different forms, when plunder of the defenceless **is** advocated.

But whence comes this desire, as unjustifiable as it is inefficient, to plunder peaceable commerce? For both parties are unavoidable sufferers in the long run, for there exists in reality **no such thing** as an exclusively enemy commerce amongst civilized nations.† **Are** the merchants of the belligerent State the most clamorous for war? Are they the instigators to upset the state of peace, which is the element of their existence? **No**, certainly not. With the exception of individual speculators fond of hazards, the body of the commercial population is naturally adverse to war. But the politicians, backed by those who prefer to fish in troubled water, the aggressive military party, and those who are fattened by the plunder of commerce, through privateering, prize-money or lawyer-fees,—they are the instigators of **war, for they** alone have nothing to lose but **all to** gain, whether **in glory or** in the shape of other more substantial acquisitions, **reaped by plunder,** through the prize court or from the public treasury.

---

* RAYNEVAL Liv. III., Chap. v., §1. PORTALIS, LE PERE: *Discours au conseil des prises du 14 flor. an. VIII.* MASSÉ: *Le Droit Comm.,* etc., Vol. I., p. 221. Lord PALMERSTON's speech at Liverpool on the 7th November, 1856.

† MASSÉ: I., p. 221.

Is it then to be wondered at, that at the present stage of development reached by the European International Spirit of Law, which has worked already such marked progress in the manner of waging war, that we still find the capturing of private property on the high seas an acknowledged usage of war? The cause of the persistency of this usage of war is to be looked for, not so much in the exigencies of war *(Kriegsraison)* as in the tenacity of national prejudice fostered by individual selfishness.

Dr. Woolsey says,—"There has long been a difference between the treatment of enemy property—including in this term the property of individual subjects of the hostile State,—on land and on the sea, or more generally between such as falls within the power of invading armies, and such on the sea and along the coast as falls within the power of armed vessels. The former is to a certain extent protected. The latter, owing to the jealous feelings of commercial rivalship, hardened into a system by Admiralty Courts, has been extensively regarded as lawful prey."*

Make commerce as free in times of war as is possibly consistent with the actual means of defence and with an effective carrying on of the war, abolish completely the ignominious systems of booty and prizes, as not worthy a place in the procedure of modern civilization, lop the excrescences of aggression from the noble stem of National Defence,—you will then have cut off the main stays of the instigators of war; and the object of war, which is peace, will be more speedily accomplished.

Attack the arch-instigators of war, and not the noble apostles of peace, who, as your own conscience ever tells you, are leaders on the right road to true civilization, such as the human Moral Senses indicate, though they be, perhaps, too far in advance of the present generation to serve as practical guides.

When narrow minded jealousy, aroused by the enemy's progress in commerce—which has been the only cause of so many maritime wars of the last century, and is not less threatening in

---

* WOOLSEY: Edit. 1879, p. 207.

our days—has no chance of enforcing its malevolence; when the **military** creed is purified from notions of aggression; when **prize-money** is no more to be easily pocketed as the reward for the hunting down of defenceless merchant vessels on the high seas, and lawyers desert the prize courts—you will be nearer to peace than ever Nations were in the golden age of plunder, general reprisals and privateers, enhanced by prize-court lustration.*

§74. When the facts are clearly established, it yet remains the moral duty as well as sound policy in the case of every State to try to settle differences in a peaceable manner before resorting to the decision of arms.

The means for peaceable **settlements** are:—1st, Amicable arrangement or compromise between the two interested parties, without the direct or open interference of any other Government. 2nd, Mediation or arbitration which takes place through the **good** offices of one or more friendly Powers, to which may be added Conferences or Congresses on general political questions.

The solution of international questions through amicable arrangement or compromise may in some cases be a mere palliative postponing open rupture and war, as the main question is then often **left** undecided, yet the peace is preserved, though it be only for the moment, and at all events it is a marked proof **of** the spirit of moderation and of good faith which prevails in **the** respective counsels **of** the parties interested.†

The difference between an amicable arrangement and **a** compromise consists **in** this, that the former indicates the settlement **of** the dispute by **a** mutual agreement to abandon the question, while a compromise implies an understanding arrived at, on **some definite** object of contention, by mutual concessions

---

* The **Usages** of War with regard to the seizure of the enemy's private property on **the** high seas **are** extensively treated in chapters xxxii. and xxxiii. of my *Manual of International Law*, Edit. 1884, Vol. II., pp. 308-387. From this "Manual" several passages, with regard to the principles of International Law, have **been** taken over in the present work.

† CALVO: *Le Droit Intern.*, Vol. I., Edition 1870, §661, p. **785**. HEFFTER: *Droit Intern.*, Trad. Bergson, §107.

in the same sense as in a case in civil law. Thus a compromise partakes also of the nature of an amicable arrangement, but an amicable arrangement is not necessarily a compromise. For the amicable arrangement of disputes between Nations, a settlement by negotiation or compromise is not always involved or necessary.

"Amicable arrangement or accommodation," says Halleck, "is where each party candidly examines the subject of dispute, with a sincere desire to preserve peace, by doing full justice to the other. In such cases, all doubtful points of etiquette will be yielded, and all uncertain and imaginary rights will be voluntarily renounced, in order to effect an amicable adjustment of differences. If no compromise of the right in dispute can be effected, the question will be avoided by the substitution of some other arrangement which may be mutually satisfactory. Such conduct is worthy of great and magnanimous Nations; weaker States seldom act with so much moderation. An example of amicable accommodation is found in the adjustment, by the treaty of Washington, in 1842, of the differences between the United States and Great Britain, with respect to the right claimed by the latter to visit the vessels of the former in search of slavers on the coast of Africa.

"Compromise is where the two parties, without attempting to decide upon the justice of their conflicting pretensions, agree to recede on both sides, and either to divide the thing in dispute, or to indemnify the claimant who surrenders his share to the other. For examples of compromise we may refer to the negotiations terminating in the treaty of 1842, by which the Maine boundary question was satisfactorily adjusted, and to the negotiations terminating in the treaty of 1846, by which the Oregon difficulty was formally disposed of. Accommodation is a peculiar kind of compromise, and has, therefore, been deemed by some to be improperly classed as a distinct measure." *

---

* U. S. Statutes at Large, Vol. VIII., p. 582, etc. HALLECK, Vol. I., p. 414.

§75. Judgment not being admissible when independent States are litigants, other modes of terminating disputes between Nations must be resorted to, whether by peaceable measures, taken *via amicabili*, or by forcible measures, *via factá*. To come to a solution of the question by the first mode of procedure, the disposition and full consent of both parties to a peaceable settlement are indispensable, while forcible measures to decide the contest *via factá* are invariably resorted to against the declared wish of both actors, at least such as can be drawn from diplomatic notes, manifests and proclamations, which are cast about at the approach of war like dry leaves before the storm wind. And yet with all this loudly proclaimed wish to maintain the blessing of peace, we have to witness throughout the history of civilization the strange fact that amicable arrangements of international disputes are but seldom preferred to war. (Comp. §63).

The main cause of such an abnormal state of the Spirit of Law is that the mutual consent to an arrangement, should it have any effect at all, must be sincere, and necessarily entails moral restraint and probably some material sacrifice. Besides, to rush into war with an equal antagonist is a sensation agreeable to inflated imagination when this fruitful source of evil is fostering the passionate brutish propensities of certain parties in the state, while, in the case of forcing a weaker State, against its interest, into war, it is found easier to keep timid Conscience aloof and to damp the weak voice of Sympathy, than to sacrifice some material interest on the altar of Justice and Benevolence (§20).

At the Congress of Paris, in 1856, the following recommendation was passed by the representatives of the Powers there treating for peace. "The plenipotentiaries do not hesitate to express, in the name of their Governments, the wish that States, between which a serious disagreement should arise, would, before appealing to arms, have recourse, as far as circumstances admit, to the good offices of friendly Powers." That this safe recommendation has not been followed during the differences which led to the recent wars in Europe might be explained by the foregoing observations.

The different modes of adjusting international disputes *viâ amicabili* have been variously enumerated by text writers on International Law. Besides the mutual arrangement between parties in direct dealing, as noted in the preceding section under the heads of amicable arrangement or accommodation, and negotiation or compromise, there are the various processes of mediation, arbitration and conferences, in which the good offices of third parties are invoked.

Mediation **may be** solicited or offered. When offered by a third party, it includes not seldom, in disguise, a threat of intervention, the intervenor offering his good services for the purposes of an accommodation **which** would suit his own individual interests.

When mediation is asked by parties, it takes the form of **arbitration**.

When real **and** impartial reconciliation is intended, the mediator submits his impartial propositions, calculated to enable the contending parties to arrive at an accommodation, which he simply offers, leaving the parties entirely free with regard to their acceptance or not.

"Le devoir du médiateur," says Vattel, "en interposant ses bons offices pour engager les parties à s'entendre, est de garder une exacte impartialité; il doit adoucir les reproches, calmer les ressentiments, rapprocher les ésprits. Son devoir est de favoriser le bon droit, de faire rendre à chacun ce qui lui appartient; mais il **ne doit** point insister scrupuleusement sur une justice rigoureuse. Il est conciliateur et non pas **juge**: sa vocation est de **procurer la paix**, et il doit porter celui qui a le droit de son côté à relâcher quelque chose, s'il est nécessaire, dans la vue d'un si grand bien." *

---

* VATTEL: *Le Droit des Gens*, Liv. II., Chapter xviii., §328.

Arbitration is the solemn settlement of a dispute, when **two States, by** common consent, refer the questions in dispute to the decision of a third party, on the condition that they will abide by **his** decision. Generally the scope and conditions of the reference are settled by special understanding. Mediation and arbitration are closely connected, but with this difference, that the former resembles more the above mentioned amicable **arrangement** between parties, **and the other** takes the form of compromise. **In** the case **of** mediation, parties retain their complete liberty **to** accept the proposed arrangement or not, while in **the case of** arbitration, parties having, beforehand, submitted themselves **to** the decision of the arbitrator, the award must be for them the **rule** of conduct,—barring, of course, judgments which are manifestly contrary to *equitable justice*, *i.e.*, Justice with Benevolence combined, and thus, *per se*, repudiated by common sense.

IV.—INTERNAL SOCIAL LIFE.—THE CO-EXISTENCE OF INDIVIDUALS.

§76. **The** agent of evolution in the **theory** of the struggle for existence and survival of the fittest is, in the animal world, physical **force prompted** by the instinct of material self-preservation, while the motor of evolution of the human mind, **and** through this **of** the social progress called civilization, consists in the strife of the **moral** senses with the lower selfish **nature** of animal propensities (§39).

With regard to the animal world, the process is thus described by Mr. Herbert Spencer. "Their carnivorous enemies not **only** remove from herbivorous herds individuals past their prime, **but** also weed out the sickly, the malformed, and the least fleet **and** powerful. By the aid of which purifying process, as well as **by the** fighting so universal in the pairing season, all vitiation of the race, **through** the multiplication of its inferior samples, is prevented, **and the** maintenance of a constitution completely adapted to surrounding conditions, and therefore most productive of happiness, is insured."

Such are the agents conducive to animal happiness, *i.e.*, the happiness of living creatures without moral senses and consciousness, and whose only end is the unconscious following of their selfish instinct. This is also the case with regard to men with whom the moral senses are yet dormant or temporarily overruled by animal appetites. These latter, though endowed with moral senses, yet often appeal to the animal rule of "*might is right*" in order to stifle their conscience and sympathy, for the better accommodation of their selfish animal propensities, which prompt them to shoulder aside a physically or intellectually weaker, though morally far superior, fellow-creature. Like the savage of Helvetius, thus they moralize to those on whom they prey. "Look up to the skies and you see the eagle swooping down on the dove; cast your eyes on the earth and you see the lion tearing to pieces the stag or the antelope; while in the depths of the ocean small fishes are destroyed by sharks. The old and weak lions or sharks are in their turn despoiled of food by their own stronger species and left to die, and their dead bodies are devoured by the weakest of living creatures, which are then the stronger in their turn. The whole of nature announces that the weak and the powerless must be the prey of the strong. Strength is a gift of the gods. Through it I become possessor of all it is in my power to capture!"

But can animal physical strength, deified by the materialistic dogma "might is right," be the natural agent through which our social condition of intellectual and moral as well as physical development must be maintained? If not, what have we then to do in sociology with the Darwinian law of "natural selection," or with Mr. Herbert Spencer's philosophy of the "survival of the fittest." And if so, what place is the moral element to take in the agency of evolution in these theories? It would certainly be doing great injustice to the philosophy of men like Prof. Darwin, Mr. Herbert Spencer, Haeckel, or any evolutionist philosopher of the present age, to imply that they simply ignore the

moral element in the human mind, or that they would seriously **propose** to explain the development of our present social order by **the** raw, primitive method of natural selection through survival of **the** fittest after material contest. This may stand good for the solution of the problem of perpetuating animal species, but has no real sense when applied to the evolution of the human mind. The fact is that as these theories deal only with **the material** instinct of man, they fall short of his moral nature. The **sharp** distinction **between the instinct of the** brute, in its struggle for existence, and the human mental organism, evolving into social organization, is manifested **even in the lowest human strata of** the wildest known savage tribes. With the **germ of social order,** though scarcely budding in the barren soil of a purely material yet *human* nature, there is, though dimly shining through the **mist** of animal propensities, yet perceptible the glimmering light **of a** higher mental organism with its dormant moral senses; to be **quickened** into life by the first intuition of the moral senses when **these are awakened** by suitable surroundings. Then, indeed, a struggle for existence sets in, but a struggle of widely different nature from that constituting the agency of evolution in the animal world—for it is a struggle of the animal propensities of man against the activity of his moral senses, which prompt to higher motives than that of material self-interest.

Mr. Herbert Spencer says that, in his view, "the struggle for existence as carried on in society, and the greater multiplication of those best fitted for the struggle, must be subject to rigorous limitations." * **But if** the law of natural selection through the survival of the fittest be really the law of nature, **according** to which the development of the human race in social order takes place, then there can be, scientifically, no restriction suggested **to modify its** operation, except through natural conditions forming **a new** law of nature. No artificial conditions can be framed under which—and *sine qua non*—the natural process

---

* "A Rejoinder to Mr. de Laveleye," *Contemporary Review*, 1885, p. 515.

of elimination of the unfit should be allowed to operate; no legislative power can be scientifically postulated to stem the current of natural events forming a law of nature. If the law is not wholly applicable in its principles, in all circumstances, its default, in any case where its wings are to be clipped and its forces limited to suit actually existing conditions, proves the inadequacy of the theory to serve as an explanation of the working of natural agents. It must, then, be rejected, or, if in reality limitations to such a law are apparent, then these limitations prove that there exists another counteracting natural force, whose effect is manifested by these limitations.

Now, that Societies, as aggregates of human beings, are conditioned by natural events is manifestly true, but by those events, principally, which constitute the law of the Moral-Mental Organism, where the moral element is primordial factor. But, as the human faculties are of two-fold conditions, viz., physical and moral, corresponding with the physical and moral senses, the conditions under which the social organism develops are likewise of two-fold nature, viz., the material conditions, causing the struggle for existence and survival of the materially fittest—which is the law of man's physico-mental organism, *i.e.*, of man as species, in the lowest human strata—and the moral conditions, which consist in proportion to the development of the moral senses. These moral conditions, caused by the moral Senses Conscience and Sympathy (§15)—called the law of man's Moral-Mental Organism or the Moral Law of Nature—form the limitations of the material law of natural selection in the social organism, by checking the animal propensities in the human nature (§5).

Here the *struggle for existence* is the strife between the animal passions, *i.e.*, the selfish inclinations of the material nature of man, and the higher moral element of his mind. Here natural selection does not exist in the "survival of the fittest," of those who possess the greatest physical strength or the mightiest material influence, but among those of the most morally as well as

most intellectually developed human beings who are as such, and as such only, the fittest for the requirements of civilized social life. **These** are not the industrially superior, who, through purely material propensities, favoured by suitable surroundings, *i.e.*, accumulated capital, protection, land properties, etc., get advantage over the weaker in physical energy, or the poorer in suitable surroundings, and settle by themselves the question of civilization—in the same way as the most ferocious animal species **would** undoubtedly get the upper hand and infest the world, were it not for the superior power of man, not superior, indeed, through greater physical strength and ferocity, but through the intellectual and moral faculties of his mind.

Thus, limitations are placed on material predominance by the *moral senses* of the normally developed human mind. Only by bringing into account this counteracting moral element of human nature, it is possible to apply the Spencerian or Darwinian theory of the survival of the fittest as the law of human society. Mr. Herbert Spencer could not have meant any other limitation, for the **natural** development of the moral-mental organism, with its moral senses, constitutes the only valid opposing force against the brutish propensities which cause the struggle for existence as taught by the "natural selection" theory. The bridle postulated **by Mr.** Herbert Spencer on the natural animal appetites, in the **process of** the struggle for existence, is the manifestation of a recognition of the Moral Element in Nature (§32) operating on the moral senses of the minds composing **the society**.

§77. In his rejoinder to Mr. de Laveleye, quoted before, **Mr. Herbert Spencer** says the following:

"**If there needs** proof that, in my view, the struggle for existence, **as carried on** in society, and the greater multiplication of those **best fitted for the** struggle, **must** be subject to rigorous limitations, I may **quote as** sufficient proof a passage from the *Data of Ethics*, premising that the word co-operation, used in it, must be understood in its widest sense, as comprehending all those combined activities by which citizens carry on social life."

This passage reads thus:

"The leading traits of a code under which complete living through voluntary co-operation (here antithetically opposed to compulsory co-operation, characterizing the militant type of society) is secured, may be simply stated.* The fundamental requirement is that the life-sustaining actions of each shall severally bring him the amounts and kinds of advantage naturally achieved by them; and this implies, firstly, that he shall suffer no direct aggressions on his person or property; and, secondly, that he shall suffer no indirect aggressions by breach of contract. Observance of these negative conditions to voluntary co-operation having facilitated life to the greatest extent by exchange of services under agreement, life is to be further facilitated by exchange of services beyond agreement; the highest life being reached only when, besides helping to complete one another's lives by special reciprocities of aid, men otherwise help to complete one another's lives."

"It will be observed," says Mr. Herbert Spencer further, "that in this passage are specified two sets of conditions, by conforming to which men living together may achieve the greatest happiness.†

---

* It must be remembered here that Mr. Herbert Spencer distinguishes two types of social elements, the "*militant*" type, which he characterizes as the *regime* of status, *i.e.*, *compulsory co-operation*, and the "*industrial*" type, characterized by the *regime* of contract, *i.e.*, the *voluntary co-operation*. The militant type, which was in ancient society the predominant social organization, is now, in the present state of civilization, represented only by the standing armies, in so far as these are composed of conscripts, in which each unit must fulfil compulsory duties under pain of death, and receives, in exchange for his services (materially viewed) stipulated wages, food and clothing; this is the regime of status or law. The industrial type is formed by the voluntary co-operation of workers, who agree freely to exchange specified services at a given price, and are at liberty to separate at will; this is the *regime* of free contract. Through progress of civilization and its reforms, based on Justice and Benevolence, the ancient "militant" state of society has gradually given way for the industrial *regime* of contract. —"*The State* versus *Man*."

† "A Rejoinder to Mr. de Laveleye," *Contemporary Review*, April, 1885, p. 515.

If we analyze the above quoted propositions, we find that of these two sets of conditions for the attainments of social life under voluntary co-operation, the first set requires that the life-sustaining actions of each individual shall be fully guaranteed to him, so that he shall suffer aggressions neither in person nor property, nor in his rights obtained by free contracts. **The** guarantee of the material existence of each is thus in human societies attained through Justice—expunging every tincture of the idea of "might is right." This is the work of the **moral** sense of Conscience, which—as the human mind is the agent of social evolution—replaces the brutish instinct of self-preservation through physical force. **But** the morally constituted human mind acts under the influence of Benevolence as well as of Justice, when protecting the weak against the aggression of the **stronger, so** that both the moral senses Conscience and Sympathy, equally **and** combined, form the agency of civilization, *i.e.*, to achieve the greatest happiness in social life.* This is proved by the second set of conditions of Mr. Spencer's above quoted rule of life, for here we find that, besides the guarantee of life, **property and** rights, these mere life-sustaining actions should be supplemented by mutual exchange of gratuitous services outside of agreement, which actions Mr. Herbert Spencer qualifies as "generosity," but which we call by the wider, comprehensive term *Benevolence*. But, says Mr. Herbert Spencer, the highest life is reached only "when, besides helping to complete one another's lives by specified reciprocity of aid (agreement), **men** otherwise help to complete one **another's** lives" (beyond agreement). Thus, while Benevolence, **of which** generosity is an effect, is exercised by the State in its attributes **of** distributing Justice—not merciless justice alone, but

---

* "The **root** of all the altruistic sentiments is sympathy; and sympathy could become dominant only when the mode of life, instead of being one that habitually inflicted direct pain, became one which conferred direct and indirect benefits; the pains inflicted being mainly incidental and indirect. Adam Smith *(Theory of Moral Sentiments)* made a large step toward this truth when he recognized sympathy as giving rise to these superior controlling emotions."—HERBERT SPENCER: *Morals and Moral Sentiments.* ("Essays Speculative and Practical," p. 32).

justice with reasonable mercy combined,—generosity, which is *charity*, remains the necessary requirement of social life among the private individuals composing the state. By this it is obvious that both sets of conditions, "by conforming to which men living together may achieve the greatest happiness," must be traced to the moral senses above named. This is the natural consequence of the human mind being the agent of the Moral Element in Nature as the motor of civilization (§39). Thus, whether the practice of benevolence in *all* its branches is or is not the necessary attribute of the State, it is a truth clearly felt by human consciousness, that the bringing into action of the moral sense of sympathy is, at all times, indispensable for the attainment of the highest life. And, if this be so, that benevolence is a necessary agent in the maintenance of our social order, then, where voluntary and unselfish mutual aid is lacking, the community, through its government, should undertake to administer Charity as well as Justice. Insuring to each citizen individual safety of person and property is *public justice*. Securing to each the acquirement of intellectual and moral training, and a fair chance in the struggle against unjust arrangements of existing and unchangeable social **conditions, is** *public benevolence*. The one is not less essential to the common safety and welfare of the community than the other. The one duty is not complete without the other.

The logic of the doctrinaires was sound as polished steel, but want of expansive capacity made their theory snap at the first pressure of the revolution. A reign of absolute justice, unqualified by benevolence, if possible to exist any length of time, would dry out the vital sap of society, while a **reign** of benevolence without **the** rectifying element of justice, would lead alike to dissolution. Justice is the framework of the State, Benevolence its generous expansiveness. The wholesome state is that in which justice and benevolence are combined in the actions of Government and Legislative Body, which, aware of the duties of their regulating as well as controlling, preventive as well as repressive, "positive-regulative" as well as "negative-regulative," functions, will fairly guide State's interference in the right channel, provided they can emancipate themselves from abstract theories, impracticable under existing social conditions, and follow unbiased and sincerely the dictates of conscience and sympathy, applied through common sense, which is the logic of reason and feeling combined (§34).

If the doctrine of the survival of the fittest be construed for social application as the survival of mere industrial superiority, it must mean the struggle between capitalists and laborers, as well as between empty-handed laborers mutually; for the struggle for existence as carried on in society is open to *all*, without distinction between physical and financial strengths; and as no limitation whatever can be allowed on this score by Mr. Herbert Spencer's system of "negatively-regulative" state-action, it is obvious that citizens who have like claims to carry on their activity, but are totally deprived of the financial strength, find no protection whatever in this negative kind of state-action, which is positive state-inaction, and may, from their stand-point, as well be called state-injustice.

Unfortunately, social chances are not the same for *all*, even when equally morally and intellectually developed. As long as this is not the case, and this inequality of chances is due to unjust social arrangements, brought to light by a progressing civilization, it is simply justice to diminish the suffering of those unfortunate and inferior citizens who are neither idle nor vicious, and owe their misery to the abnormal arrangements of society. Where such unjust social conditions cannot be radically rectified, there state-action *must* help to produce organized arrangements which can tend to mitigate the mischiefs caused by the chronic abnormal form of society, developed from former unnatural "militant" **types.** This is State-Benevolence, the indispensable requirement of social life in its corporate capacity, which gives vitalizing, expansive power to the iron *doctrinaire* cuirass of the negatively regulating State-Justice. Indispensable, indeed, especially in our present social conditions, in order to regain, as near as possible, by counterbalancing chronic injustice, the normal equilibrium, and thus avoiding the threatening catastrophe of a social revolution, which will then in reality establish "new injustices for the purpose of mitigating mischiefs produced by old injustices."

This is the state-benevolence, **the** state-interference, which is styled *State* or *Scientific Socialism*, an unwelcome sound to the doctrinaire ear, **but** surely the only corrective to recover the equilibrium in disturbed social conditions. Positive State-action, when based on genuine Benevolence with Justice combined, is the natural counteraction to those destructive agents of society called *Communism* and *Anarchism*, and other theories of social dissolution. These, fostered by the coercive logic of State-inaction, the negatively acting doctrine of State-justice **without sympathy**, are destructive indeed, as they work from within, threatening to burst through those iron-manacled boundaries, void of generous expansiveness, which are the desperate imitations of the dethroned "militant" type of ancient society, tending toward barbarism, **after having drowned** the last vestige of civilization in the flood of social dissolution.

Justice alone is not sufficient to secure happiness, as true happiness is understood and felt by every moral **being, whose** moral senses shape his motive of action (§17); **it** is justice and benevolence combined which constitute **virtue, and** virtue is the basis of civilization. The end of social life is individual happiness, combined with the greatest happiness of the greatest number. This end is the guiding star of State-action (§52).

§78. *Socialism* versus *Communism.*—Civilization is young in comparison **with** the vast career the human race has before it. Sociology has yet grave problems to solve before the natural evolution process of the moral senses has completed the development of the human mind.

Sociological theories for social reform are manifold, but **one** and all, when they find their source in the science of political **economy,** are based only on the material element of civilization.

After the peaceful theories which found their experiments and failures in the well-known socialistic schemes of the Owenites, the Simonians, Fourierists, Icarians and other one-sided artificial forms of philanthropic communism, followed the *Socialism* of the present transitional period of society, in a completer aspect and with defined programme. Socialism distinctly differs from that economico-revolutionary movement, with widespread and vigorous propaganda, called *Communism,* whose tendency is to effect a social regeneration without keeping account with the complexity of the social organism, as developed from the human organism. Communism is division of wealth with or without division of work; "to take from the worthy the things they have laboured for, in order to give the unworthy the things they have not earned." Its doctrine tends to the absolute reconstruction of society, on the principle of division of wealth; to be achieved either by mastering the Government or by anarchy and terrorism. **This serious occurrence in the social evolution** process **is brought** forward by the **process** of civilization, **of** which it **is a** preternatural product. **Like all** abnormal protuberances and excrescences, it saps the **main stem of** the social organism, which it reduces to a morbid condition.

The term Socialism is as ambiguous **a word as ever used in** economical, mental or moral philosophy; **for every altruistic system** may be called socialistic, and all **religious and social** movements, intended to benefit **humanity** in general. The labours **of** all great minded philanthropic philosophers—from Plato to Herbert Spencer—as well as any act of government or legislature, carried out with a view to the controlling of social abnormalities, by suppressing crimes and modifying anti-social egoistic **actions,** together with the maintaining of the altruistic course of society by **the** founding of benevolent institutions and public education, in **fact,** all measures, moral as well as material, which confer general benefit on all members of the society in an equitable manner, *i.e.*, with justice and benevolence combined, are objects of State or Scientific Socialism (§77).

By this it is obvious, that State or Scientific Socialism does **not** mean State-patronage, to be administered at the expense of the State, or by the plunder of capitalists, which is the communistic principle,—but simply means the regulating, on scientific bases, of sociological questions, by legislation, through **the** natural **organs of** the State. Socialism is distinct from communism, as it causes no disturbance in society, for it touches no man's fortune; it seeks no plunder of the rich to foster poverty, by unproductive, ill-gotten help; it enters into no secret associations which endanger the State's organism, but openly advocates legal State-actions, organized on sociological bases, in harmony with all the functions of the State's government. Its promoters and leaders **are no** demagogues who, from factious motives, seek to stir up and influence the people against their natural rulers; neither is socialism an indolence-creating, materialistic self-insurance association, as it breaks no faith with the industrious, the intellectual or the **moral** elements of society. It does not affect the functions of a **special** providence for the working man, for it is simply a rational speculation on the physical, mental and moral capacities of man, aiming not only at the material but equally at the intellectual and moral development of society.

Political Liberty.—We have noted above (§57) how, through selfish political aspirations, despotic governments, on one side, and revolutionary political parties, on the other hand, are constantly disturbing the equilibrium which the natural social evolution process is ever inclined to establish. The moral nature of the representative form of government ever manifests itself in its influence on the development of the popular conscience. When **the** representation of the people is judiciously constructed,—as demonstrated in §§54 and 55,—it represents the popular conscience, and thus indicates the means for the re-establishment of the disturbed equilibrium between the different social classes and political parties of the State. But the popular conscience depends on the individual minds of which it is constituted; individual culture, intellectual and moral, having direct effect on social conditions, are moulding the State, and, reciprocally, the policy of the Government of the State reacts on the development of the people in general, *i.e.*, on the forming of the popular conscience, which, when moving the representative or legislative body, is called the Spirit of Law (§33).

For this reciprocity of influence, which is necessary for the normal growth of the social organism, *freedom of action* is indispensable, that is, exemption from all restraint which might emanate from any arbitrary agency, strange to the internal process of social development.

These are the principles of social political liberty, but political liberty,—like the free-will of the human mind,—may produce many social evils, and when not under control and checked by the moral senses, it fosters abnormal social conditions which, as stated above, create communism, anarchism and other theories, which, deviating from the natural end of society, tend to social decomposition. Thus liberty is not absolute but conditional, as it is a destructive as well as constructive agency of the Natural-Constitutional State's organism, for although political liberty be indispensable for the normal development of society, it may, at any time, through retrogression of the moral element, become the germ of dissolution to any society in which the equilibrium of the elements of the State is not properly maintained, and thus not in a healthy condition, suitable for expansion, in conformity with the growth of public opinion. In such a State, liberty is the source of revolution, engendered through the distrust which exists between the wealthy and the labouring classes of the society; as the latter, despairing of remedial measures, seeks to overthrow private property in the exaggeration of their griefs. Thus the natural development of society is often retarded, and the most solid-looking social system, the work of ages, threatened with dissolution—on one side through the despotism of the government, and, on the other, by the abuse of political liberty. To control this danger a regulative power is necessary, and this is the expansive power of society, called State-Socialism which we have endeavoured to place in its proper light (§77).

Equality.—The social organism of the natural-constitutional form of government, with its system of free emulation and competition open to the moral and intellectual powers of all and every individual member of the community,—of labour as well as capital,—is the result of a natural evolution process, carried on through ages.

If the communistic "equality" were to be realized, emulation, *i.e.*, free competition, must necessarily be suppressed. But emulation, that manly strife to equal or excel the examples of others, by *fair means, i.e.*, in conformity with conscience and sympathy, is the natural agency of civilization; its developing influence is marked by the slow but surely constructive power of the social-evolution process. When upsetting this, anarchy sets in, which will bar all further progress or amelioration, by degenerating the elements of civilization. The natural result would be the thrusting back of society to the lowest social stage, bordering on the primitive savage condition of life.

Those who fancy their political party to be able to reconstruct society by sudden changes, to fit a model of their own imagination, attack Nature's work, to place on the ruins of society their artificial construction, which, having not the vital power of an organism grown from natural evolution, is easily swept away by the destructive waves of human passions. All sudden social revolutions can be traced in history by the bloody track of social retrogression.

The Co-ordination of Labour and Capital.—At this juncture we arrive at the contemplation of the labour problem, *i.e.*, the relation between labour and capital, the great social question of the present generation and for many yet to come.

The normal relation between Labour and Capital is that of joint enterprise on equitable conditions, the first condition being the securing of the rights of each by eradicating the wrongs of both, and, consequently, the fixing on a system of enterprise through which, without infringing on right of property, labour will receive its due reward.

Many systems have been proposed but failed to satisfy the equitable mind, as being one-sided and entangling the problem, by treating questions only indirectly related to labour and capital; they inclined either to the communistic view, *i.e.*, to question "why few are in opulence and many are poor,"—or, on the other hand, losing sight of the personality of the labourer, they treat human activity, *i.e.*, his physical energy, as an article subjected to the trade law of demand and supply.

As to the communistic view of the labour question,—which, in fact has more to do about how to pull down capital than how to elevate labour,—we have already disposed of by the above proposed definition and qualification of communism itself (page 143). With regard to the opposite view,—the sale and purchase of human labour, which is the theory of orthodox Political Economy, —we must say a few words here.

That this theory of classifying human labour is inconsistent with the nature of the social organism, as an aggregate of moral beings, is obvious, for labour, physical as well as intellectual, is a living element of this organism, and one of the active agencies of its natural evolution process. It is a cause, not an effect; a producer, not a product. As such it stands outside the sphere of market quotations, for labour,—the physical and intellectual energies of man,—cannot be separated from the individual;

and the individual, being the producer, cannot at the same time be the product; hence the absurdity of classifying human activities, under the name of labour, with commodities which can be used or let alone at convenience, and the necessary failure of all systems based on this assumption.

This is abundantly proved by **practical experience**. In a contract of sale, **parties are not further** implicated than the material value of the commodities, bartered for, **actually amounts** to; the result being simply a more or less pecuniary gain or loss. Not so in the **case of a labour contract**; the personality of the labourer **is here the principal** object; the price of his labour is for the loan **of his physical** strength and intellectual skill, which **compose his** only capital, from the interest of which he must live and support and educate his family at the standard of a civilized society, just as the capitalist must live on the interest of his money. For production, capital and labour must co-operate, but with this **marked** inequality of power, that the money-capital requires no outlay to exist, no life-expense, while the labour-capital, which consists of the qualities of the human body, must be fed and clothed;—of the first the interest is pure gain, while the other is subject to an unavoidable and persistent reduction of the interest, for life-sustaining expenses, before there can be any question of gain. For this reason the interest of the labourer's capital cannot be regulated by the market-value of production, but is dependent on the standard of living, in conformity with the actual conditions of civilization. The labourer's wage must keep equal pace with the state of the social civilization under which he lives; hence the resentment of the labouring class of a civilized community, at the introduction, for competition in their community, of labourers of a lower standard of civilization and, consequently, **lower** standard of living, which make the competition unfair, as the physical and moral wants of these latter are so much less than those of the civilized labourers. The abolition of slavery—the greatest socialistic measure of our age—and the subsequent working of estates on an improved basis, have proved the difference between civilized and uncivilized labour.

The Income Tax.—Legal Interest.—" If any would not work, neither shall he eat" is the dictum of Christianity and of science equally, *i.e.*, for those who can but *will not* work. The correlative to this law should be the rule that there shall be work for those who can and *will* work. As to those who *cannot* work, by any means, these are dealt with under the head of charity; but those who can and will work have the right to claim something more than mere charity in a civilized community. Capital can sometimes exist and make gain without the help of labour, by investing in government loans, where a small but sure interest is secured without any exertion, while the labourer is left to starve. In this case, government is procuring work for capital to the detriment of labour; for this reason it is just that capital which is not employed for industrial purposes, should be charged with an income tax. On the same ground a legal interest—a *maximum rent*—for capital not used to promote social industry, should be fixed by legislation, to prevent such capital being used in usury, to the detriment of industry.

Labour, intellect, and capital, form, as the producing elements of the state, the factors of the material progress of civilization. Capital which does not serve as a producing factor should be made otherwise useful to the state through revenue taxation.

Labour Legislation.—We have seen that manual labour is comprehended as a living element in the social organism which, with the other producing elements of society, viz., intellect and capital, is an indispensable factor of civilization. The people who, in the struggle for existence, apply the most efficient labour, *i.e.*, labour on intellectual method, is the most progressive in national welfare. If this be true, it follows that the fostering of the physical and intellectual power of labour is a state's duty.

Political economists, often men who have grown opulent, treat the subject of labour from a standpoint of guess rather than experience, and, more familiar with opulence, the production of wealth is to them of supreme importance. How or why such wealth, in the hands of few, might remain useless to society, from a sociological point of view, is with their system not a matter of consideration. But the knowledge of the manner how to get rich does not teach the causes which keep the masses poor; and not to study the agencies by which the distribution of wealth is to be effected,—or may be impeded,— among the labouring class, is criminal neglect on the part of those who influence society. On the shoulders of the labouring class falls the heaviest burden of depression in trade, and, consequently, restricted industrial enterprises. When capital is safely kept out of the storm, in government bonds and other securities, the labourer keenly feels the brunt of want of credit and *malaise* in trade.

He who must work with his physical power that he may eat, has no other property than his bodily strength; this is his only possession, and he has a claim on society for the protection of this, which is his capital, against possible extortion on the part of the other element of production, in order to spare him, unnecessary wear and tear, and to economise his physical and moral powers for the benefit of society itself. If he is to waste his strength under unusually unfavourable circumstances, for wages which are inadequate to support himself and family; if the necessary relaxations of body and mind are denied him, through an unjust regulation of work-time; if he is to work uninterrupted from twelve to fourteen hours, in places where fresh air and daylight are excluded, or in places where no precautions against dangerous accidents are taken; if his children also must be put to work at an age when culture of mind and body cannot be neglected without the risk of ruin to the individual health and morals,—and this from sheer necessity,

in consequence of the shortness of the parent's wages,—then
surely, under such damaging influences, the result shall not fail
to show itself in the physical, mental and moral degradation of
the working class, **to** the detriment of the whole society, for
without a healthy and contented labouring class, there is no
chance for a **wealthy** middle class, and no security for the **cap**-
italist. But **is there** no remedy for these social maladies? The
remedy is State-action, **as stated** before (p. 141), *i.e.*, **measures**
of State-legislation, based **on** the principle of state or **scientific**
socialism. These may **be classed** as follows:

I. *Moral Measures.*—These **are:** (1) Prohibition and
actual suppression of prostitution. (2) Laws for the prohibition of the sale of intoxicating **liquors, opium,** and all
descriptions of drugs which can be **used to** produce inebriat-
ing excitement, when **not** prescribed for medical purposes.
These measures have never been disputed as being the most
efficient steps to the moral and material improvement of the
people at large, and especially for the working **class,** which
is helplessly exposed to so many temptations. And **yet,** what
has been **done on** these scores by the so-called guardians of
the people, the representative legislators? **As** long as society
is not delivered **from** the curse of licensed debauchery,
as long as these **hot-beds** of immorality and poverty are not
cleared away, schools **for the** intellectual training of the young,
and religious and charitable institutions for old and young, are
working against tide. Religion and Education alike are permanently set at defiance by chartered licentiousness.

II. Under *Material* and *Economical Measures* can be
classed: (1) The legalizing and regulating of the "Trades'
Unions," **in the form** of *Chambers of Manual Industry,* (on the
footing **of the present** Chambers of Commerce)—as legal advising
bodies **to the Government** in matters regarding labour. (2) The
appointment of stipendiary *Labour-Inspectors, i.e.,* government
officials for the **controlling of** the faithful maintenance and

compliance with the legal regulations regarding labour, for the technical inspection of factories, workshops and other working places, and for the enforcement of measures of safety in behalf of the workers employed therein. (3) The fixing of a *normal work-day*, that is, the maximum of hours during which a labourer is allowed to work, within the twenty-four hours, for a day's wage; this to be regulated with due regard to the nature of the work, the normal work-day being reduced for the manufacturing of articles in the composition of which any health-injurious compounds are used, and also for exceptionally fatiguing or dangerous labour. (4) The establishment of *Labourers' Pension-Funds*, by compulsory contributions of labourers, to be placed under the control of the **Chambers of Manual Industry;** the statutes and bye-laws of these funds to be sanctioned by the Government, on the footing of life-rent insurance companies and chartered institutions. (5) Regulations with regard to the *labour of women and children.* These regulations should contain indications of the kinds of work which alone are allowed for boys, under sixteen years of age, and women to perform—other factory-work being beyond their physical strength and constitution—and also the prohibition to let children, boys under eighteen years of age, and women of any age, work during the night and on Sundays. A fixed rest-time of at least *two hours* should be allowed to divide the day's labour-task. Further, exemption from labour-tasks for women before and, at least, four weeks after child-bed. (6) These protecting rules should be coupled with *compulsory education*, in public government schools,—for boys until their fourteenth and girls until their twelfth year of age,—and, after that, *technical education* in public trades' schools. (7) The fixing of a legal rate of interest, as maximum interest for the loan of capital for all purposes of labour, industry or commerce. (8) The *regulation of wages* for manual labour, through the Chambers of Industry, which are to replace the Trades' Unions.

Economists, contending that a minimum of wages, for different manual labour, could not be regulated by legislation, have built this their doctrine on the false premises that labour is subject to the law of demand and supply, like any marketable commodity, and statesmen, following in their wake, refused to legislate for the maintenance of the equilibrium between the three elements of the material welfare of society, viz., intellect, capital and labour. Schools are established at great expense to the state, for the fostering of intellect; public works are erected by the state, at far more cost yet than public education, to facilitate the increase of capital; but what is being done, by state-action, to protect and strengthen the most essential of these elements of production—Physical Labour? This living agent of social progress,—the wear and tear of the units of society,—which cannot be neglected physically without injury to the moral element of the social organism, is simply left to be regulated by the mercantile law of demand and supply, or by the law which communism tries to impose on society. Side by side with measures for the improvement of the moral and intellectual man, physical labour must have equitable protection. If to maintain efficient healthy labour is necessary for society, then society must take logical measures to secure this end. Usury is bridled by a legal rate of interest, so also ought the living of the labourer to be secured by a legal minimum standard of wages. If the necessary complexity of the subject might make legislation on wages less practicable, then the minimum rate of wages can conveniently be periodically fixed by the legally instituted Chambers of Manual Industry, above mentioned.

Poverty versus *Political Economy*.—The science of Political Economy, as said before, does not deal with social questions except to speculate on the rules by which the few might get rich. The great problem of the causes which make the many remain poor, however instrumental they may be in the process by which the few get rich, is not within its scope. Mr. Henry George, in his work, "Progress and Poverty," makes an inquiry into the causes of industrial depression and of the increase of want with the increase of wealth. "I propose," says he, "to seek the law which associates poverty with progress and increases want with advancing wealth." We acknowledge that especially in great industrial centres, where Mr. George got his experience, progress of the few leaves often the rest in poverty, and that, side by side with accumulating wealth, often the greatest want, moral as well as material, is observed. But this condition is far from being the social law; it is the violation of the natural law of social development, the violation of justice and benevolence, which causes this abnormal condition in society, by disturbing the natural equilibrium of equitable co-operation between the three elements of material progress, Labour, Intellect and Capital. The main cause of demoralization and poverty is the want of labour-protection by state-action; no opportunism, but state-action based on scientific socialism, the state-interference described in the foregoing section (§77).

The end of political economy is the scope of wealth,—*i.e.*, the possession of utilities for material pleasures of all kinds, as long as they can be estimated at market value. Consequently, it does not cover those super-economical political duties of the state, called state-socialism, which find effect in practical sanitary regulations, the restricting of prostitution, gambling-dens, sale of spirits, and other licensed temptations to anti-economical dissipations, tending to the ruin, in the first place, of the labouring class in great manufacturing centres. These dissipations are fostered by wealth and the *laisser faire* of the doctrinaire political economy. Thus the absence of state-socialism, with its measures based on justice and benevolence combined, is the cause why "poverty is associated with progress," and "want increases with advancing wealth," and why the poverty and want are the labourer's, while the progress and wealth are the capitalist's.

While Political Economy has left all these vital questions of the intellectual and moral aspects of society unsolved, sociology, the science of the natural evolution of the state's organism, has taken them up and inscribed them in her rules under the head of state or scientific socialism.

Co-operation.—State or scientific socialism is thus the term for the sociological aspect of Political Economy, where attention is given to the development of society through the moral senses of the human mind, conscience and sympathy, as the combined regulators of equitable wealth. It is a higher stage in the development of science, keeping pace with the evolution process caused by the struggle between the moral senses of the human mind and man's selfish animal nature (§76). It substitutes the former Law of Wages, by the Law of Co-operation, under which is comprehended all concert acts for organised self-help by honest labour and honest trade, whether by work of hand or by work of brain, profits and losses being *equitably* divided among those who create them, in conformity with the pre-established rules of the contract of co-operation.

Co-operation does not mean equality of individual social conditions, but *equity*—which is justice and benevolence combined—in all its operations. As such, *honesty* is the basis of co-operation in the civilized society,—for, if the concert-acting is a thief-association, to cheat or rob the public, or a "ring" to plunder the public treasury by undue state patronage, it is, like all other organised frauds and crimes, punishable by criminal law, and thus outside the social law of co-operation.

Free-trade versus *Protection*. We have seen above that, without state-action and legislation, it is impossible to arrive at some amelioration of the condition of physical labour, in the present state of civilized societies. But, at the same time, it is obvious that, by mere enactment of laws, the labour-problem is not finally solved, however much would be done toward this end if a normal work-day were established together with the regulation of the labour-tasks for women and children. Only when,—labour being legally protected, as above proposed,—workmen and their families find sympathy with capitalists, while workmen cease to look upon capitalists as their natural enemies, but rather stick to them as their inevitable co-partners in the national industry, and when, through the suppression of the fatal enticement of public houses of intemperance and debauchery, the workman becomes able to elevate himself, morally as well as materially,—the national industry will develop into a normal condition, and society be in a fair way to civilization.

But here we see a lion in the path,—the spectre of international competition, claiming the cheapest national labour, is barring our way towards an improved condition through labour-legislation. Thus we are checked in this working out of national progress, by the threat of foreign competition, and compelled to serve *protectionism*,—that usurer under the disguise of a helping friend to all unsound state-finances, who pretends to be able to perfectionate home-industry by excluding all competition from abroad. But analyze the question, and you will find that this fear of *international competition* simply means the alternative of working our labourers to imbecility or into revolution, or, to compensate capital, by heavy import duties on foreign manufactures, for the losses sustained by the aforementioned amelioration of the labourer's condition. Here Capital-Protectionism and National Labour-Protectionism are brought face to face, and the alternative cannot be doubtful.

But also where no State-action has ever been attempted for the amelioration of the labourer's condition, and depression of prices is put forward as the cause of low wages, there the cry is, nevertheless, Protectionism to revive national industry—that is, to get better prices for the products. Thus protectionism anyhow, whether as compensation for capital,—in consequence of labour-legislation,—or as hope for better wages for the labourer, through better prices for products. Of these two motives we choose the first; if there must be protectionism in industry, by all means let it then be in consequence of state-measures taken for the amelioration of the condition of the workman; in other words, first labour-protectionism and then, if need be, import duties for the compensation of capital,—but let us never be fooled by the argument of the protectionist *quand-même*, that any branch of industry can ever be fostered by shutting out the *free-trade* competition. The so-called "fair-trade" protectionism is a sham, and not even a good sham, for everybody knows that governments mean by import duties simply fiscal measures, either out of necessity, to get money anyhow,—even by drafting on the energy of the national industry,—or simply to please capitalists, by making their competition with labour more easy. If "fair-trade," through import-duties, makes the price of the produce to be protected higher for the national consumer, it is to be qualified *unfair*; as its burden falls then on the shoulders of those who can hardly afford to pay the higher price for the better foreign article, and these are the labourers themselves, whose industry is so-called to be protected. This is another sham. But people will buy the foreign goods anyhow, if they are better than the home-made ware, and, if not, well then, their inferior quality bars competition, even without any import-duty,—so that, after all, protectionism through import-duty does not protect the national industry, comprehending both labourers and productions; and this is the greatest sham, for protectionism has proved to be no protection, and the so-called **fair-trade to be an** injustice.

Heavy import-duties seem to be relished, as a relief to his envy, by the artisan out of work, when, full of spite and despair, he sees the arrival, from foreign manufactories, of wares he himself could have produced, and be kept from starvation. But must the cause of his distress be looked for in free trade? Does protectionism help *him?* **In** spite of him and heavy duties, foreign manufactures will continue to flood the market, if their better quality is worth the price. This is proved by the increasing revenue of the import-duties in countries where protectionism is maintained, with or without the cry of "fair-trade." And does the outbeaten workman who clamors for heavy import-duties as a protection for his trade, know the answer to this simple question:—On whose shoulders falls the heaviest burden of those extra taxations, and for whose benefit is the sacrifice made?

Thus the lion in the path proves, on closer inspection, to be but a stone lion, a representation of the inert obstructiveness of protectionism, which, instead of being in reality a living, active power of defence and protection, is simply an object of obstruction in the path of progress and civilization. But, fortunately, this obstructive stone lion is, at the same time, a warning-post of partisan selfishness, where this crosses the high way of the State's justice and benevolence, which is the course of State's common sense. As common sense, aiming at *healthy* national self-preservation, rejects fallacious "protectionism,"—which, while filling the public treasury with money extorted from our own consumers, injures the mass by fostering the material interest of the few,—so does Scientific Socialism object to the protection of capital by import-duties, without protecting labour also by State-action.

State's common sense can agree with a *direct* protection—*i.e.*, by subsidy from the public treasury—of some particular national enterprise, where national industry or trade is gathering the necessary strength to enter the arena of free competition with those of other nationalities. Although such State-action might lead to abuses, when prompted by more benevolence than justice, it has, at all events, the merit of being an open act, free from sophistical complications, and, as such, a measure fit for fair, straightforward and comprehensible argumentation; but the jugglery of protectionism, under the allurements of "fair-trade," is an abnormal measure which can only be defended by pure opportunism, and, unfortunately, a fatal opportunism, which singularly fails to find a practical remedy for the social evils of depressed industry. It is the opportunism of uncivilized societies, where human labour must be protected by the prohibition of machinery, and where public roads are kept in such state, that no other means of communication are possible than the *porte-faix* and the wheelbarrow.

Protectionism, in fact, is either an indication of retrogression in civilization, or a work of bad statesmanship, when not merely an opportunistic measure of convenience to improve the distressed condition of the State's finances. In this latter instance it proves that the national legislature is dominated by parties imbued with narrow-minded national jealousy, or with a selfish, sneaking policy, which lacks the moral courage to enforce measures of *direct taxation*, on the logical and equitable basis of the income tax, and to leave international trade free for the necessary scope of a healthy development of the national industry.

Laws.—We have seen in Chapter II., containing the Institutes of Law, the origin of law explained to be National Customs, growing from the National Spirit of Law (§33)—*i.e.*, from the habits of thinking of the gradually developing individual minds composing the society,—and which have thus become established as the objective expressions or manifestations of subjective conception of Justice and Benevolence. These customs, when consolidated through progress of civilization, into the ethico-legal obligations which form the rules of conduct for the individual co-existence in society, are called *Laws* (§40). When laws emanate from the government or legislature of the State, they are State-actions, and having for origin the conception of Justice and Benevolence, they are, evidently, based on the principle of State or Scientific Socialism, as described above.

Laws being state-actions, based on State or Scientific Socialism, it follows that they are, as indicators of the Spirit of

Law, the test by which civilization can be gauged in the normal condition of Society (see §41).

As noted before (§62), the exclusive right of legislation and jurisdiction in all matters within the State's territories,—and with regard to its subjects or citizens, with certain modifications, also outside its territory,—is an essential sovereignty duty of the State, as the internal legislation of states exercises an important influence on their mutual intercourse, and thus on the growth of universal civilization. All individuals within the territories of a civilized State, aliens as well as its own subjects or citizens, whether domiciled or temporarily residing,—save some special exceptions established by treaty, or through the usages of international comity, and the rules of private international law,—all are subject to the legislation, jurisdiction and control of the State's laws. They have, consequently, equal right to protection and equal claim to legal and practical security of person and property, and in the transaction of their lawful business; wherefore the tribunals of a civilized State ought to be open to foreigners in the same manner and to the same extent as they are open to its own subjects, to have justice administered to them in conformity with laws and usages.*

The laws of a civilized State can be classified under the following heads, viz., Public Law (*jus publicum*), the Law of Persons (*jus personarum*), and Private Law (*jus privatum*).

Public Law has reference to the constitution and sovereign government, the state-policy, finance, general management of the State's internal and external affairs, and the care of the moral and material welfare of its subjects or citizens (*staats-angehörigen*). Under Public Law are comprehended the subjects treated above, in sections 52–61, under the head of Social Organism.

Public Law is composed of *Political Law*, *Penal* or *Criminal Law* (which contains also Police Regulations), *Commercial Law*,

---

* HUGO GROTIUS; *Dutch Jurisprudence*, Ch. xiii. Sec. iii.

and *Maritime Law*.* To the system of Public Law belong also, in Civil and Criminal Legislation, the rules for the examination, instruction, proceedings and judgments of judicial questions in Courts of Justice (*ordinatoriæ litis*). Under the general head of Public Law is also classed *International Law*, which comprehends the data of civilization described in sections 63–75, as the co-existence of Social Organisms or external Social Life.

Political Law embraces those legislative acts by which are established fundamental rules with regard to the criteria of what constitutes the political nationality *(jus civitatis)* of the State, and the conditions for the naturalization of aliens; comprehending also the regulations with regard to emigration, domiciliation in foreign countries, and expatriation of subjects or citizens (§44); together with the right of *asylum* and *domiciliation* of foreigners, *i.e.*, the principles on which foreigners are admitted to unmolested passage and peaceable residence in the State, and the cases in which their prohibition, extradition or expulsion is allowed. To the domain of political law belongs also the regulation of questions of exterritoriality, *i.e.*, all special exemptions and privileges enjoyed by foreigners and their corporations within the jurisdiction of the State. These and other matters regarding foreign intercourse find, however, more suitable places in International Law.†

The *Law of Persons* establishes the legal status of the individual, with regard to his personal conditions, his age, profession, parentage, affinity, and right of succession, including the rules for the registration of births, marriages and divorces, and deaths, and the formalities appertaining thereto; for the affirmation of the relative legal consequences, rights and obligations entailed by the respective personal status. The Law of Persons

---
* With regard to Maritime and Commercial International Law, I venture to refer the reader to my *Manual of International Law*, Edit. 1884, Vol. I., p. 395, *et seq.*

† For all further elucidation with regard to Determination of Nationality, *Droit d'Asile* and Extradition, Domiciliation, Naturalization of Aliens, Emigration and Expatriation of subjects or citizens, and Exterritoriality, I must refer to my aforementioned "Manual of International Law," Vol. I., p. 117, *et seq.*

establishes further the principles with regard to the individual capacity to possess and to acquire rights and things, movable and immovable,—which are termed *personal* and *real property*. The law of persons includes, finally, the individual capacity to make wills and bequests, and the relation in which the individual stands with regard to private law,—*i.e.*, his capability of performing legal acts and transactions, with the obligations which correspond to things and to rights.

While political law regulates the relation in which the individual stands with regard to the State, the law of persons governs his natural status and the mutual relations of individuals, in co-existence in and outside family life.

Private Law is the term by which are comprehended the principles on which the private interests of individuals are regulated with relation to things and to rights, and the obligations which correspond therewith *(res, jura, obligationes)* embracing the *Law of Contracts, i.e.*, the rights and liabilities *ex-contractu* and the legislation which regulates rights and claims to things movable and immovable; the transactions originating therefrom and the means whereby rights in general may be judicially vindicated and executed or realized.

The law of persons and the private law constitute together what is termed *Civil Law (jus civile)* with the legislation, jurisprudence and judicature appertaining thereto. This includes *Private International Law (jus gentium privatum), i.e.*, that part of the general international law which regulates, not the mutual relations of States, but the private relations which occasionally occur between individual members of one State and the laws of another state.*

Political Rights *(jus civitatis)* is the constitutional capacity acquired by Political Nationality (§44), and, in some instances, also by Domiciliation, to take part in the government and the

---

* Private International Law is treated in my Manual aforementioned, Vol. I., p. 142, *et seq.*

legislature of the state; from these rights aliens are thus excluded, but with regard to Civil Right *(jus civile)*, there is rarely any distinction made between aliens and subjects or citizens.

The Criminal Law of a State is co-existent with its National jurisdiction, as mentioned above (p. 160). The legislative and juridical powers of a State cover offences committed by any individual within its territories, whether native or alien, with the exceptions which, in particular cases, may exist by the rules of International Law, or by virtue of International Treaty, as in the conditions called Exterritoriality and Concurrent Jurisdiction.*

In some particular instances, these powers extend also beyond the territories of the State, viz., (1) In the case of offences, as specified and prohibited, under penalty by law, committed against the integrity, internal or external safety of the State, its public institutions of commercial, domestic and foreign credit, and its financial establishments, when guaranteed by legislation,—wheresoever and by whomsoever such offences be committed,—when the offender is found within the jurisdiction of the State, or his extradition is obtained. (2) In the case of all offences against the Laws of Trade and Navigation of a State, committed anywhere by its own subjects or citizens. (3) In the case of all offences, committed anywhere, by a subject against a fellow-citizen, when both—having their domicile within the native State—are temporarily abroad. (4) In cases —independent of the question of domicile—when murder or other grave offences and serious crimes have been committed, anywhere, by a subject against fellow-citizens or foreigners, or by an alien against subjects, whenever the culprit is found within the territory of the State, or his extradition is obtained; provided judgment has not already been passed and sentence delivered in the case by the competent law-court of the foreign State within whose territory the offence in question has been

---

* L. C., Vol. I., p. 137, *et]seq.*

committed. By a general rule, the offences for which subjects are punishable in their native State, although the offences were committed on foreign territory, are of the same class for which *extradition* is asked and granted between States, by virtue of extradition treaties; thus, a State rendering this class of offences—committed by its subjects abroad—punishable by its own laws, can always fairly refuse, on this principle, any demand for the extradition of its own subjects. (5) In the case of offences committed on board of a vessel of the State, in any part of the world, on the high seas as well as within the territory of other States, and without regard to the person by whom such offences be committed. (6) In the case of offences committed on board of private vessels (merchant ships) of a State, when the vessel is on the high seas; and, in foreign territorial waters, also for all acts regarding the internal ship's discipline, and, when stipulated by treaty, also for some other offences among the members of the respective crews. (7) Cases of piracy and those acts which are declared to be piracy by the Laws of the State. Piracy under the Law of Nations *(jure gentium)* includes acts over which every State has equal right of jurisdiction—to try and to punish, without regard to the question of nationality or the place where the acts of piracy have been committed; this class of offenders against the Law of Nature and Nations, being out-laws, have no legal claim on any Political Nationality. On the same principle, every civilized State is entitled to take action for the suppression of the Slave-trade, all over the world.

In the Civil and Criminal Codes, as well as in the Laws of Procedure and Rules of Court, regulating the modes of instituting and settling of judicial questions *(ordinatoriæ litis)*, of civilized States, there are also found certain provisions establishing the principles on which the law-courts of the State shall treat questions regarding *conflicts of law*, occasionally arising between the laws which govern transactions in foreign countries and those of the State, treating on the same matter or affair. The International usages regarding conflicts of laws constitute what is called Private International Law, as stated above (p. 162).

The Right of Legislation and Jurisdiction, possessed by a Sovereign State, extends over all persons within its territory, with the exception, however, of those cases in which the claim of jurisdiction on the part of some other State operates within its territory, reciprocally, to the same amount as its own jurisdiction extends into the foreign territory. These are cases of exception on the general rule of national jurisdiction, regulated by special international treaty,—establishing the conditions of *exterritoriality* and *concurrent jurisdiction*, above mentioned (p. 163)—or generally adopted through common usage of International Law, viz:—(1) With regard to the reigning Sovereign or First State-Magistrate of another state and their immediate followers, whilst temporarily residing within the territory, on an amicable visit. (2) The representatives of foreign States and the members of their legations. (3) Vessels of war of friendly powers entering the territorial waters. (4) Armed forces of a friendly power passing through the territory of a State, with the expressed or implied consent of the latter. (5) Foreign merchant vessels and their crews, in the cases expressly stipulated by treaty, or by *comity*, in conformity with International Usages.

The Theory of Criminal Law.—The important branch of jurisprudence, known as Penal or Criminal Law, constitutes, when in conformity with the National Spirit of Law,—*i.e.*, with the outcome of the development of the moral senses of the human minds forming the society,—essential data of civilization. These we are now going to consider.

All acts which are wrong, ethically considered, are likewise wrong within the meaning of the Penal Code of a civilized community, and are punishable by the Criminal Legislation of the State, whenever the result of such conduct or acts happens to be a violation of the altruistic principles of individual co-existence,—*i.e.*, injurious to any individual member of the society, in his public rights, or to society itself, as a social or political organism. This is the general definition of *Crime*, as the outcome of conduct based on motives of cupidity, avarice, ambition, revenge and other egoistic passions. Crime is thus the temporary suppression of the moral senses by the selfish propensities of the animal nature of man. The end of human punishment is the forcible repression of these passions in the criminal, without crushing out the individual moral senses. This end must not only be kept in view in the dealing out of punishment, but also in the process of accusation and the trial of the accused, as we shall see later, when treating of the Code of Procedure,—*i.e.*, of the method of proceeding in criminal cases.

Capital Punishment.—It has been stated above (§18), on the theory of the *free will* and the *motives of action*, that man's moral-mental organism, when in a normal state, could never be completely destitute of moral senses, so that, man in a normal mental condition, living in a civilized society, is ever accountable for his moral actions, and that, on the same ground, the regeneration of a criminal is never to be despaired of. The first named characteristic of man makes him subject to justice, while the other claims mercy. The accountability of man's free will and his recoverability from fall, through the regenerating influence of his moral senses, constitute, combined, the basis of Criminal Law, which involve sympathy as well as conscience. These principles form the *Theory of the Penal Code and Procedure* of a civilized society,—*i.e.*, the scientific basis for the definition of offences and the admeasurement of correlative penalties, and for the *ordinatoriæ litis* of Criminal Jurisprudence. From these premises follows the *principium juris*, that the administration of justice, in the prosecution and punishment of crimes, is not only aimed at the suppression of *evil*, but also at the promotion of *good* in society. On this basis only it is possible for Criminal Jurisprudence to keep pace with the development of society, and no nation can claim any reasonable degree of moral civilization whose Penal Laws have no other end than that of retaliating revenge.* The *lex talionis* of the barbaric periods of the history of mankind is greatly disproportionate to the end of justice, and discordant with civilization, as this is now moulded by the developing moral senses of the human mind. The end of punishment, in conformity with the human moral senses,—*i.e.*, "conformable to the dictates of truth and justice, the feeling of humanity and the indelible rights of mankind,"—for all offences committed against the constituent principles of society and its members, collectively or individually, is *retribution*, through penitentiary repression, as atonement for the crime. In this aspect, it is *repressive* as well as *reintegrative*, but, at the same time, it is *preventive*, as being essentially *cautionary*. These characteristics give the law an earnestness and truth, without needing the unnatural help of capital punishment. The theory of inspiring fear, with the aim of deterring others by the dread of capital punishment, has not the effect intended. When execution in public had been found to brutalize the people more than to caution against committing crime, and civilization was becoming loath of this barbarity, the aversion of the popular conscience and sympathy was met half-way, by the killing of the culprit in seclusion. But this compromise between civilization and barbarism cannot satisfy the moral senses of society. The plea of "depriving the party injuring of the power to do future mischief, by put-

---

* "In proportion to the importance of the Criminal Law ought also to be the care and attention of the legislature in properly forming and enforcing it. It should be founded on principles that are permanent, uniform, and universal; and always conformable to the dictates of truth and justice, the feelings of humanity, and the indelible rights of mankind."—HENRY JOHN STEPHEN, Serjeant at Law, *New Commentary on the Laws of England*, Edit. 1863, Vol. IV. p. 87.

ting him to death," is as irrational an argument as whipping at the post and execution in public have proved to be inefficient measures of dread for deterring future crimes,—for, if we have to weed out evil-doers from society, by the simple process of extirpation, where shall the executioner draw the line? As capital punishment has proved to be no measure of dread for deterring others, it continues now simply as a measure of human punishment on the principle of the *lex talionis*; of which a great English jurist* has observed, "That, as the difference of persons, place, time, provocation or other circumstances, may enhance or mitigate the offences, retaliation can never be a proper measure of justice; that the quantity of punishment can never be absolutely determined by any invariable rule, and that it must be left to the arbitration of the legislature to inflict such penalties as are warranted by the laws of nature and society, and such as appear best calculated to answer the end of precaution against future offences." Thus, the origin, quality and degree of punishment must be traced to the "Laws of Nature and Society," and from these laws it is proved that the only real precaution against social offences is the moral development of the human mind. But morality cannot be preached from the gallows, and dread of capital punishment has universally failed to restrain the ungovernable human passions. When the mind is not, at the same time, brought under the influence of the moral senses, no human punishment can be of any benefit to society. Putting to death is not even punishment; it is expiation, but without the moral fruit of atonement. The ghastly files of victims for the block, daily led to the places of public execution in the Asiatic states, are awful evidences that capital punishment, like all revengeful retaliation, instead of producing dread, only hardens popular feeling. Instead of repressing crime, it retards civilization;

---

* HENRY JOHN STEPHEN, Serjeant at Law, *New Commentaries on the Laws of England*, Edit. 1863, Vol. IV., p. 100.

for civilization is not fostered by the executioner, but by the human moral senses. Conscience and sympathy alike are revolted by this dreadful retaliation; for when the innocent is executed, and thus no chance is left for redress or rehabilitation, at whose door must the guilt of blood lie?—at the door of the judge and the erring procedure, or at that of the legislature which misinterpreted the extent of its warrant?

Codification.—The necessity which is gradually felt by all nations, with the growth of civilization, to insure to all dwellers within their jurisdiction, equally strict, cheap and expeditious justice, is the manifestation of the spirit of Law, which is formulating itself in conformity with the development of the popular conscience (§33). The principal requirement to arrive at this end is the Codification of the Laws of the State,—*i.e.*, the systematical arrangement of the laws and usages emanating from the development of society.* As each of the branches of Law,—enumerated above (p. 160)—has its own system, moulded by civilization and the natural condition of the people, each forms a separate Code of Law, representing as many data of civilization; but none so characteristically represents the outcome of the moral senses of the people as the Code of Criminal Law, which, of all the branches of Law *(jus)*, being the best indicator of the Spirit of Law of the society, is treated here in particular.

Codes of Criminal Law.—In conformity with the aforementioned principles, by the light of which the nature of crimes and punishments must be considered, criminal jurisprudence consists of two main branches,—viz., (I.) the *Penal Code*, containing the definition of crimes and the penalty for each special offence, and (II.) the *Code of Procedure in Criminal Cases*, which consists of the modes of proceedings by which crimes are detected and proved and the offender is brought to justice,—in other words, the formulation of the mode in which criminal justice is administered.

---

* What can be done in this way, in behalf of civilization, is proved by the codification of the British-Indian Laws into Western shape, completed in 1872.

I.—The *Penal Code*. Of all subjects of legislation, the codification of the criminal laws is the most necessary in a civilized society. The Penal Code, which is the definition of crimes and the specification and admeasurement of the correlative punishment, must embrace the whole subject of which it professes to treat; not being merely a digest of existing usages and laws, it must repeal, and remould into forms, evolved from the science of Jurisprudence, which is the outcome of the Spirit of Law, the whole of the Common Law, *i.e.*, the traditions of law, handed down from former conditions of society, and reduced into writings, and the "Statute Law," which consists of different desultory Acts of Legislature. But especially should the so-called "*Case or Judge-made laws*" be consolidated into systematic rules; these are the "*precedents,*" *i.e.*, the decisions given in similar or nearly similar cases, but pronounced by different judges, in different states of mind and degrees of intellectual culture, at different places and at former periods of social development—in other words, at less advanced stages of civilization of the society. Where no codification of the Criminal Law has yet been accomplished by legislature, there the uncertain state of Jurisprudence causes a wholly unmerited scientific predominance to be attached to the "precedents;" which is the more unwarranted, as these judge-made fragments of "laws" are often scattered in large numbers of volumes of case-reports, without any attempt at arrangement or system of legislation.

If completeness of the Penal Code is indispensable for the popular knowledge, then more especially ought this to be observed with regard to the definition of crimes; which, in order to reach popular understanding, should be put in simple and plain language, free from unnecessary technicalities. When laws are formed on the mental common sense, *i.e.*, on reason and feeling combined, with the *good* of society in view,—that is, the good, as defined by benevolence as well as justice,—then and only then, it can, in justice, be ordained, that no rational member of the ociety should be excused,—in no instance, not even in the case of the most uncultured subject,—on the ground of ignorance as to what the laws condemn as *evil*. A law which has for its immutable maxim: "*Ignorantia juris, quod quisque tenetur scire, neminem excusat*," must, in truth, be based on the human inherent consciousness of good and evil, impressed on the mind through our moral senses of conscience and sympathy, which also govern our common-sense (§34). This is the natural test of all theories of Criminal Jurisprudence, for it is the origin of Law itself. On this basis of common-sense, only, it is possible to formulate all laws in plainly and tersely expressed terms, with the use of plain, clear and concise grammatically acknowledged language, and which, from the determined wish to be understood by *all*, guards the law-texts from being swamped by multifariousness and prolixity of words,—the tedious verbosity of the so-called lawyer's technicalities.

Thus, a regenerated Penal Code, in conformity with the actual Spirit of Law of the society, forming a complete system of clearly defined "Statute Law," will keep pace with the progress of civilization. The data of such a Code consist in the following: 1—The distinction of public wrongs from individual wrongs, *i.e.*, of *crimes* from *private injuries*. A wrong done to an individual member of the society, in his *personal* rights, when the offence is not, at the same time, a violation of the *public* rights of individual co-existence, or of the altruistic principle of society (which is, as stated above (p. 165), the definition of crime), is a *private injury*, while the act, from an ethical point of view, is condemned as *sin*, if it does emanate from any egoistic or vindictive motive (§28). The social or public aspect of the wrong claims the human punishment, by the laws of the society, while the private injury is to be redressed by restoring the violated right, whether *in natura*, or through an equivalent. The *public* scope of a wrong brings it under Criminal Jurisprudence,—our present subject,—while its *private* aspect belongs to the domain of Civil Law *(jus civile)*, with its special jurisprudence, and which, as noted above (p. 162), is composed of the Law of Persons *(jus personarum)*, and Private Law *(jus privatum)*. 2.—The accountability with regard to crimes. It has already been noted that man's moral-mental organism, when in a normal state, could never be completely destitute of moral senses, so that every person in a civilized society, who is in a rational mental condition, must be held accountable for his actions. Thus, accountability for crime does not exist in individuals of whom the moral senses are not in a normal condition of development—*i.e.*, in the state of the mind as described above in §12, p. 16. When the mind is morally or physically unfit for moral or rational conception, the *ego* is dislocated, and, the will not being under control of reason, the individual is not accountable for his deeds; to this category belong infancy, idiocy and insanity, *i.e.*, children under the age of seven years, and persons who, by reason of undeveloped or defective mental powers, are incapable of knowing the criminal character or quality of the act committed by them. 3.—Accidental impunity. Besides moral and physical unaccountability, there are incidental causes which make offences, to a certain degree, excusable from criminality; these are ignorance, mistake, compulsion, necessity and other chance conditions, to be proved by established facts. 4.—The accountable offenders are distinguished into *principal criminals*, *i.e.*, the *absolute perpetrator* of the crime, and he who is an actor in the facilitating, aiding or abetting of the crime—and *without whose help the act could not have been done*—and the *accessory*, who is not an actor in the offence, but, in some way or other, connected with it, either before or after the committal of the crime, but *whose help was not strictly necessary for the perpetration of the act*, and which could have taken place even without the instigation, encouragement or help of the accessory. 5.—The classification of crimes into:—offence against the person, against property, against the government and public administration, against the administration of justice, the public peace, the public

health and the police; against public trade and economy; against public morality and religion, and against the Law of Nations. 6.—The rules of prescription of crimes.

II.—The second branch of Criminal Jurisprudence—*i.e.*, the *Code of Procedure*—the administration of Criminal Law, contains the modes of proceedings by which crimes are detected, and the rules by which the offence is proved and the offender brought to judgment. The data of this Code are the following. 1.—The means of preventing the perpetration of crimes. The object of Criminal Jurisprudence is to deter from crime, not to entrap into crime and then punish, for to tempt its commission is encouraging and abetting crime. This principle of Criminal Procedure must ever be kept in view by the detective or prosecuting agents of the law, if they aim at the moral end of society. 2.—The modes of detecting and prosecuting crimes; officers for the detection and for the prosecution (the *fiscal*); preliminary examination of the accused and witnesses. 3.—The Court of Criminal Judicature, consisting of an aggregate or judicial body of three or more judges, and the Court's Recorder or Registrar *(griffier)*, represents the *Righteousness* of the State, *i.e.*, of the Benevolence as well as the Justice of the social organism called State (§48), while the State's Attorney or Public Prosecutor represents the *Legislation* of the State, and claims the infliction of the legal penalties for the violation of its laws,—thus constituting the accusing party *versus* the accused offender as defendant; this latter, in order to have a fair chance, is assisted by a legal adviser of his own choice, or is, otherwise, supplied with one by the Court. Between the two thus contending parties, the Righteousness of the State decides. 4.—The arraignment of the accused, to answer, *personally*, on the plainly stated, comprehensible and definite *Act of Accusation* of the Public Prosecutor; the examination of the accused and of the witnesses, on both sides, to be done by the presiding judge, before the full Court, the Recorder taking notes of every question and answer. Cross-examination is allowed to parties, reciprocally, but only with regard to facts connected with the case; each of the two parties—the accused or defendant, as well as the Public Prosecutor—has the right to repudiate any witness as "*to credit,*" on the terms and for reasons as determined by law; the objections of parties with regard to the credibility of witnesses, can be overruled by the Court. The witnesses shall be examined upon their oath, but the accused shall not be allowed to give oath, for when being cross-examined by the prosecution, or confronted with the witnesses of either side, he shall have the right to add any explanation or addition he may desire. The moral senses of the accused shall be roused; therefore the Court, as representing the Righteousness of the State, shall address to the accused such words of exhortation and caution as may be suitable to the occasion, in order to revive in his mind the consciousness of his moral obligation to tell the truth and the whole truth, without in the least—through threat, or any pain-inflicting or fear-inspiring means—influencing his *free will* of confession. A mere confession of guilt does not form a complete proof for the condemning of an accused; besides his confession, there must be some direct or circumstantial evidence of the truth of his self-accusing statements, for, to administrate justice with righteousness, the facts must be clearly proved before the law can be judiciously applied to the case. 5.—The Court, constituted of an aggregate of judges, gives judgment by majority of votes after direct investigation, pronouncing:—firstly, as to the guilt or innocence of the accused as proved by the *facts*,—which must be carefully described,—established through the evidence, in accordance with common-sense; secondly, the definition of the offence of which the accused has been found guilty, and thirdly, the *application of the law*, in conformity with the merit of the case. The Judgment is thus the conclusion arrived at as to the point of the Positive Law bearing on the case, legitimately arising from well-ascertained facts and well tested reasoning; it is to be read at the public session of the full Court, in presence of the parties,—*i.e.*, of the accused and the Public Prosecutor. 6.—*Appeal* or *Revision* of the Judgment. 7.—Commutation, Remission, and Pardon. 8.—The execution of the Sentence.

These are the principal data, derived from common-sense,—as this is formed by the moral senses of the human mind, when in condition of civilization,—for the construction of a Code of Criminal Procedure, which, next to the Penal Code, is the most essential part of the Public Law of a civilized state. Here the National Spirit of Law finds its most notable expression; here, on the threshold of the temple of Justice, it abjures vindictive punishment,* and pledges itself to combine humanity with justice, —barring, at the outset, all attempt at the arbitrary invading of popular rights or individual liberty; acting with common sense it guarantees simplicity of form and language, in the framing out of the Act of Accusation and all legal instruments, so that these may be intelligible to all ordinary understanding. Its Law of Evidence is based on straightforward direct investigation of *facts*, in the face of the accused. As such, the direct examination of the accused is a point of righteousness, coming from the moral obligation of the Judge to give an offender the chance to relieve the burden of his conscience, by making full confession of his crime, and atone for it through the well-deserved punishment. By this provision the end of Criminal Jurisprudence is attained, and human punishment is sanctioned by the moral senses. But the system of conviction, by the so-called *jury trial*, is immoral, for there the accused is practically forbidden to plead for his own innocence, or to comply with the dictates of his conscience by confessing his guilt.†

Such an arraignment of Justice, where the mouth of an accused is closed, where he is neither competent nor compellable

---

* "Vengeance is mine; I will repay, saith the Lord" (Romans xii. 19).

† With regard to the question "*Ought the accused person to be examined?*" we can refer to the ample arguments put forward for the affirmative by Mr. EDWARD DILLON LEWIS, in his "Draft Code of Criminal Law and Procedure," Edit. 1879, Pref. p. xliii. *et seq.*

to give evidence in his own case,—a trial for crime, during which the offender remains in a hardened malignant condition of mind, or simply like a party interested in a betting between two skillful peformers at a game,—is immoral, as well impolitic, in Criminal Procedure; for the moral end of punishment is defeated, while the political view, viz., the precaution against future offences, is lost, through the baneful hardening of the offender's mind, in the suppressing of the free action of his moral senses.

The Trial by Jury is a precious relic of the past. It was one of the first essentials to success in the struggle for political and individual liberty between the "commoner" and his feudal lord. The commoner's right "to be tried by his *peers*," was conceded as a compensation for political and social inequality. In the face of the distrust which was fostered between different classes of the same society by the regime of autocratic governments and despotic nobilities, the trial by jury was surely a most valuable guarantee to the less favoured class of society, to secure them from being arbitrarily deprived of their liberty by the governing class; it was a sort of permanent *political "certiorari"* or "*habeas corpus cum causa*," obtained by the people against the judges, which belonged to the upper class or to an opposing political party. But now, after centuries of immense strides of social development and the growth of the Natural Constitutional Government, the judges,—at present appointed for life, with salaries and emoluments granted by legislation and unchangeable by government,—are completely independent from class influence and from the government, which is controlled by the representatives of the people. Thus the progress of civilization, having produced socially and intellectually independent judges, properly educated in the science of law, which they have made their profession for life, the trial by jury has no more *raison d'être*, and could safely be abolished. In the system of judicature with the *single judge*, where the verdict, as to the evidence of facts, emanates from a single mind, the jury-verdict is surely a safe shelter for the judge's conscience, and here lies the mischief, for the jury is neither responsible for its verdict nor bound by the law of evidence, and besides, the verdict of the jury, in criminal cases, is absolutely final, without appeal.* But where the court consists of an *aggregate* of trustworthy, able and independent *judges*, there the appreciation of facts, to prove the guilt or innocence of the accused, must naturally be left to the full court to decide, in conformity with the law of evidence; in order to bring the whole administration of justice,—viz., the finding as to the facts, as well as the application of the law,—to the competency of the Court of Justice, with the end of securing to *all*, without distinction of rank or social standing, equally strict, cheap, and expeditious justice, in conformity with the demands of a morally progressing civilization.

The so-called "*habeas corpus ad subjiciendum*," in English jurisprudence, is a remedy to obtain relief from illegal confinement, through a *writ* issued, in certain cases—on special demand, in behalf of the arrested person—from a superior to an inferior judge, commanding the appearance of the prisoner before the superior court, *ad faciendum, subjiciendum et recipiendum*—to do, submit to, and receive—whatsoever the judge or court awarding such writ, shall consider in that behalf. But a completer guarantee against illegal detention or imprisonment exists in states where the Criminal Code clearly defines the times, the causes and the extent,—when, wherefore and to what degree the imprisonment

---

* "In every civil cause, however small the interests involved, the litigants have the absolute indefeasible right of applying for a new trial. It is difficult, then, to understand upon what true principles it should be a portion of the law of England that, under no circumstances whatever, can a new trial be had in a criminal case, and that if a jury pronounce a verdict dictated by passion or prejudice, ignorance or mistake, or, upon the face of it, senseless and unjust, the person against whom it is pronounced is without appeal or redress; his life declared forfeited, perhaps; his liberty restrained; his honour blighted; his prosperity and prospects ruined; nothing left but an appeal to the clemency of the Crown—a clemency which, even if it be extended, comes in the form, not of rehabilitation to an injured and innocent man, but as an act of grace; in the most illogical form of a free *pardon:* pardon for an offence which has never been in fact committed."— EDWARD DILLON LEWIS: *A Draft Code of Criminal Law and Procedure.* Preface, p. 30.

of any individual, within the jurisdiction of the state, is lawful.
Where no arrest can be made, other than on an *a priori* writ of
the competent Court of Justice, save *in flagrante dilecto*, and,
even then, immediately to be followed by judicial examination;
where no imprisonment for debt exists; where no arrest of person
or property, nor any restraint on personal liberty whatsoever, can
be ordered or ruled, by any Governmental, Administrative or
Executive authority—however exalted his rank or position
may be—without having been previously sanctioned by legislative
act, or through a legal warrant from the competent judge;
there, surely, the constitutional rights of personal liberty of no
individual in the state, can ever be violated without immediate
and severe repression. And this is not the effect of an occasional *writ of habeas corpus*, but this condition is the natural
sequence of the permanent security which an effectual self-work-
ing judicial system, as based on the natural-constitutional
state-form (§51), affords to individual liberty. When appeal
is allowed in criminal as well as civil cases, toward a Supreme
Court, from which is emanating a permanent supervision over all
the Courts of Justice and all the Public Judicial Officers of the
State—without any exception whatever—by means of the ever-
watchful officers representing the Laws of the State, viz., the
State's Attorneys and Attorneys-General, who are constantly
present at all sessions of the courts, conducting the prosecution
for crimes of all degrees, and watching *all* law-cases, in civil as
well as criminal proceedings, in behalf of the integrity of the
State's Laws,—then it is obvious, that the *jury* can be
dispensed with; that the examination of the accused and the
witnesses can safely be left to the court of judges,—when the
loathsome treacherous *cross-examination to credit* shall cease
to profane the dignity of justice,—and that no writ of *habeas
corpus* shall be found necessary here. However valuable political
institutions might have been, in former ages of less development
in judicial education, and less trustworthiness of magistrates and

officers, they must give way before measures grown up on a firmer moral basis of the social organism, or they will encumber this natural growth, with its promising fruits of justice and benevolence, and thus retard civilization.

V.—The Intellectual and Moral Activities of Individual Co-existence.

§79.—Civilization is a fact, and not merely a speculation on certain relative conditions. This fact is the total outcome of the individual co-existence, forming the social organism called State. To arrive at the knowledge of the condition of a nation's civilization, it is thus necessary, first to consider the social organism or state as a whole, in its integral condition in relation to other States, *i.e.*, the State as a unit of the society of States, in the co-existence of social organisms, and then to proceed with the examination of the social organism in the modes of its integration, through the co-existence of the individual units composing the society. This method was observed above, in the delineation of the sociological status with regard to external social life,—the co-existence of social organisms,—as this appears in the contemplation of International Law (§§62-75), which was followed by the closer investigation of the internal social life,—the co-existence of individuals,—as exhibited in the Legislation and Jurisprudence of the State, especially in the Code of Penal Law and Procedure (§§76-78). We shall now continue and conclude this summary enucleation of the data of civilization, contained in normal human societies, by following up the social phenomena to their physiological source, viz., the intellectual and moral activities of the human mind;—thus recurring to the main propositions set forth in the first and second chapters of this essay.

Science, Industry and *Trade* emanate from the intellectual activities of the mind, but, as data of civilization, they merge into moral ends. The moral feature of manual industry, before the era of machinery, was the fostering of industrious habits in family life; this the gregarious character of the factory system,—when left to the inevitable consequences of human rapacity, unchecked by the moral senses,—is tending to destroy, to the detriment of civilization. When productive industry underwent the stimuli which science brought on through machinery,—beginning in the eighteenth century with the improvements for spinning, and steadily increasing in inventions for all branches of industry,— the effect upon manual labour was the absorbing of separate domestic industry by the collective labour in large establishments. The new devices for spinning with machinery, followed by machinery-weaving, brought the whole of the textile fabrication —which was, as old as history, a household industry—from the country fireside to the great centres of manufacturing towns. WORDSWORTH's ideal of modest contentment—in the picture of his beautiful sonnet—

> "Maids at the wheel, the weaver at his loom,
> Sit blithe and happy"—

was lost; for it could ill fit the "mill," where the power-loom is worked by steam, and the spinning machinery is watched by overworked, ill-fed and ill-housed "hands." And this is the case also with other branches of former domestic labour. The private industry of little shops, which might be started with such amount of capital as a thrifty artisan could save out of his wages, is incompetent against the competition of the factories. The shoemaker's shop, the shop of the blacksmith, the wheelwright, the carpenter, the cabinet-maker—one may still see them, in their modest exhibition of products, but the sphere of these household industries becomes more and more limited. The greater proportion of boots and shoes, and products of all other manual industry, are turned out by the large establishments, working by the aid of machinery, and constantly augmenting.

With the reign of machinery began the labour question, which culminated in hatred and strikes and communistic propaganda; the effect of which, through the tardy comprehension of the principles of State-socialism (§77), has not yet been counterbalanced and neutralized by the remedies of trades' unions and co-operation. But the cause of the evil which degenerated the social condition, when these great changes in the industrial organization of society occurred, must not be looked for in the vast increase of man's productive power,—for this is the material basis of civilization, and, in itself, a blessing to society, as it is the outcome of the natural development of human intelligence, and the consequence of scientific culture and free trade;—it is to be found in the disproportionate increase of the *material*, in overwhelming superiority to the *moral* element of civilization. The introduction of machinery had entirely changed the condition under which manual labour was procured; the monopoly of work was henceforth the capitalist's, as the enormous outlay of funds needed for the establishment of factories, necessitated the accumulation of capital, vastly in excess of the average possessions of the individual. When industry was carried on in private establishments, any intelligent and industrious workman might strive to accumulate, besides the means for sustaining life, enough to lay by, with the reasonable prospect of setting up a business of his own. Habits of thrift, which kept debauchery aloof, brought on a moral boon, even when the material ends aimed at were not always attained. Here human labour was free, and competition a healthy emulation between socially free powers, with no need of other capital or resources than intelligence, combined with a frugal, industrious life of self-improvement. Here the moral element could control the baneful tendency of purely material progress; but now, as the war of competition between the great factories is going on, national and international, and raging fiercer and fiercer, there are heart-burnings on the part of the producing labourers, and growing animosity between the elements of civilization!

And yet, the inequality of social conditions, which is the natural stimulus of civilization (p. 146), is not the cause of the antagonism of the working man towards the capitalist,—not even the social abnormality of a few very rich employers and the multitude of extremely poor labourers,—for all this could be mitigated if emulation had a fair chance; antagonism originates with the despondent views of the industrious, intelligent workman, that his social condition of hand-to-mouth existence is *despairingly permanent*. The position in which intelligent labour, combined with moral conduct, stands at present in society, is not alone that of an unprotected social condition, but it is also manacled by the political theory of *laisser faire;* the doctrine of "negative state-action," whose teaching is, that to leave a life competition "free" between two vastly unequally equipped forces of the State,—for the fostering of communistic hatred, to be followed by the forcible suppression by arms,—is the height of Political Wisdom.

The fault does not lie with the genius of human intellect, which is teaching, more and more, how to use the treasures of Nature's forces in behalf of mankind,—for it causes and perpetuates the natural development of the material element of civilization,—but with the social disease, which is now seriously threatening civilization, the fatal preponderance of the rapacity of the selfish animal nature of man, which, stimulated by the fierce war of material competition, will soon be developed beyond the usual strength of the moral senses, if not met by efficient measures, through the judicious combination of justice and benevolence in the leading minds of society. Instead of rational, practical treatment of the evils of society, statesmen and philosophers and leading economists have none but their quack medicine for all social maladies—the incantation of their magic formula: "*laisser faire, laisser aller!*" The moral element is left unsupported, but free scope to the animal nature is the result of the *negative state-policy*.

Yet, notwithstanding the obstruction caused by this *laisser faire* indifference, earnest efforts are being made, with more or less success, in Europe and America, by the leaders of moral civilization, in respondence to their moral senses, to counteract the baneful influences of gregarious labour in factories, through regulations based on justice and benevolence, by which the material conditions are adjusted to moral ends.*

The rational activities of the social co-existence of individuals take different forms of mental products, which constitute the material basis of civilization, and are distinguished by the general appellations *Science*, *Industry* and *Trade*, in conformity with the prominence of mental culture or physical activity, or both. These are the *intellectual* activities, which spring from the development of Physical Truth in the mind (§30), forming thus the physical or material element of social life, and which, when stimulated by the moral senses, co-operates with the *moral element* of society in the development of civilization. The *material* element is the consciousness of the mind, based on the recognition of the relations between *pleasures* and *pains*, and resulting in the intelligent adaptation of means to ends, on that basis, while consciousness of the good, through the impulses of the moral senses, conscience and sympathy—*i.e.*, the moral sentiency of man—form what we call the *moral* element of civilization (§§39–41).

Æsthetics.—The Arts.—Between the two above-delineated conditions of social activities, resulting from the physical and moral nature of man,—viz., the culture of mere intellect, through

---

* In England, where the abnormalities of this material social development were strongest felt, the passage of Lord Ashley's bill through the British Parliament, in 1833, established the first system of Government inspection of factory-labour.

With regard to the effect produced on the working population and general morality by gregarious labour in factories, and the consequent necessity of positive State-action, we must refer here to the struggle for labour-legislation in Great Britain, from the efforts of Robert Owen and Sir Robert Peel and his son, down to the "Factory-Acts Extension Act of 1867." The mischief to which the materialistic theory of *laisser faire*—which does not take into account the moral result of special social conditions—could lead, is effectually illustrated in the Autobiography of R. D. Owen, *Threading My Way*, and in Messrs. J. M. Ludlow and Lloyd Jones' joint essay on the Progress of the Working Class. To this may be added the Report of Mr. Robert Baker, one of the Inspectors of Factories, 1864, and—last not least—chapter vii. of the Duke of Argyll's *Reign of Law*.

empirical science, and the purely moral development of the mind, through the moral senses,—lies the medium condition of moral-intellectual development, called the *æsthetic* quality of the mind. This is the mental faculty to conceive the *good* and the *beautiful* combined, and to reproduce the subjective conception thereof into objective products of the *Arts*,—in plaster or paint, in poetry or music. Nature is immersed in beauty, but our taste and appreciation remain dormant, our æsthetical vision remains dim and unintelligent, if the mind cannot perceive with moral feeling. Like reason, to become *common-sense*, so taste, to be *æsthetic*, must be inspired by the moral senses. Then only the office of the Fine Arts becomes the education of the people. Like the great thinkers who inspire, through their philosophy, the popular writers, and through these, the multitude, who, though scarcely knowing their names, yet form thoughts and customs after the impulses emanating from the great master-minds, so shall the culture of the beautiful, ennobled by the good, through the combination of intellect and feeling, mould the popular taste for the development and progress of industry in all its branches.

The power which the fine arts, poetry and music exhibit, in the impulses given to the development of intellect and taste, is due to the culture of the moral senses, for when the mind is morally developed, intellect and judgment are ennobled, habits and taste are refined; all being moulded after the inspiration of the good. When intellectual culture has formed the tone of the mind for the systematical combination of proportions, which constitutes the *beautiful*, the moral senses seal the verdict that only what is *good* can be *true* and *grand*. Then the moral and intellectual powers of the mind are united, the æsthetic element forming the link between physical truth and moral truth,—between the material and moral element of civilization,—and the effect, in the civilized society, is conspicuous in the combination of material means with moral ends; which is the manifestation that the Moral Law of Nature is the motor of Civilization (§§39-41).

§80.—The vastness of the field to explore, under this section of the *Intellectual and Moral activities of Individual Co-existence*, makes it necessary to mark out our course with discrimination and clearness. We have therefore divided the subject-matter into sub-sections, under the following heads, viz:—

GOD.
CHRIST.
The DIVINE SPIRIT in the Universe, the *Moral Element in Nature*, the basis of
ETHICS. Absolute Ethics and Relative Ethics. The *Moral Senses*.
RELIGION.
The CHRISTIAN FAITH.
MAN'S PLACE IN NATURE; the Christian Duties of Society form the *Test of Civilisation*.

GOD.

The Spirit of Creation. Scientific manifestations of the Creator's work.—It is to matter and force, empirical science insists, that all phenomena must be traced. The Cosmic Philosopher, with his speculations on the nebula systems, must, if he wishes or not, go to the physicist to corroborate his "mechanical theory" of the universe, and it really looks as if the laboratory has to say the last word. But yet, chemistry with artificial evolution forced on it, fails to support the "mechanical theory" *versus* Life. The laboratorium can produce a complicated molecule, by employing some twenty distinct chemical and physical processes, under a temperature where life is an impossibility, but this product is not even "dead white of egg," much less living protoplasm or moneron,—the simplest living cell.

Not Häckel's calling the moneron but "primeval slime" and "individual lumps of albumen," nor Mr. Herbert Spencer's proposition that the lowest living things are not, properly speaking, organisms at all, for they have no distinctions of parts, no traces of organisation,[*]—can give any relief to the disappointment

---
[*] *Principles of Biology.* Vol. I., p. 482.

caused by the credulous assumptions of those who believe in *"artificial evolution."* The microscopical lens, of which the power is immensely increased by latest contrivances, shows too plainly complexity and structure in both the animal and vegetable cells, to admit of any link of artificial production between *matter living* and *matter not-living*. Giving names to its ultimate cells is not explaining the mystery of Life nor the working of the Motor of Evolution. The physical and biological truths, revealed by modern improvements of the microscope, bring to light the utter incompatibility of Häckel's definition of the animal ovum as "a little lump of albumen, in which another albuminous body is enclosed,"—the "nucleus." Truly, of this savant can fairly be said what Darwin said of Mr. Mivart:—"I conclude, with sorrow, that, though he means to be honourable, he is so bigoted (with 'Darwinism') that he cannot act fairly." * But the light thrown by the lens is impartial; the minute nucleus,—the "little lump of albumen" of the minutest organisms,—often not more than one tenth part of the infinitesimal body itself,—is now proved to undergo profound structural changes which precede all the great cyclic changes of the organism as a whole. The nucleus is the centre, in fact, of all the higher activities of the least and lowest infusoria; and is the centre of most delicate but clearly demonstrable structural changes. †

Nature does not admit the small to be insignificant nor the great to be marvellous. Her unit is the constituent of the atom.

The elements that make up the living structure of organisms are the most common substances in nature; carbon, hydrogen, oxygen, nitrogen are well known in all their qualities; the question is only *how* the elements that make up protoplasm can be so combined as, by their combination, to acquire the properties of that which lives,—and so we are not the less puzzled with regard to the mystery of life. Life in its structures and qualities is so

---

* "Life and Letters of Ch. Darwin." Vol. III., p. 145.
† Journal Roy. Micro. Soc. Presid Address, 1886.

utterly unlike, and sharply marked off, from what is not-living, that, at the present stage of human knowledge, biology gives no clue as to the origin of life without the postulate of a creative power. Can the not-living, without the intervention of living things, by any process of science, be changed into that which lives? Science answers: "life originates in life only." "The properties of living matter, says Professor Huxley, distinguish it absolutely from all other kinds of things, and the present state of our knowledge furnishes us with no link between the living and the not-living."* Sir Henry Roscoe, President of the British Association, an acknowledged authority on the subject of chemistry, in his recent address, says:—"But now the question may well be put. Is any limit set to this synthetic power of the chemist? Although the danger of dogmatizing as to the progress of science has already been shown in many instances, yet one cannot help feeling that the barrier which exists between the organized and the unorganized worlds is one which the chemist sees no chance of breaking down. It is true that there are those who profess to foresee that the day will arrive when the chemist, by a succession of constructive efforts may pass beyond albumen and gather the elements of lifeless matter into living structure; but whatever may be said regarding this, from other standpoints, the chemist can only say that, at present, no such problems lies within his province. Protoplasm, with which the simplest manifestations of life are associated, is not a compound but a structure built up of compounds. The chemist may successfully synthesize any of its component molecules, but he has no more reason to look forward to the synthetic production of the structure than to imagine that the synthesis of gallic acid leads to the artificial production of gall-nuts."†

The persistent motive power, called the Spirit of Creation, which, "in the beginning," gave the first impulse to the

---
* Ency. Brit. Art. Biology. Vol. III., p. 679.
† Sir H. E. Roscoe. Address before the British Association at Manchester. August, 1887.

homogeneous cosmic nebula (pregnant with all the germs of universal development) is manifested here as the motor in the evolution of the inorganic and not-living into living matter, by the operation of the same persistent creative power which acted at the outset, carrying on, without discontinuance, the evolution process, by natural laws primordially inaugurated. Thus the primordial germ of life on Earth originated, by the ever working Spirit of Creation, at a time when, in the scale of evolution, the highest point of development of the inorganic, the not-living, was reached and the stage of organic nature was to set in. This is the first *break* in the chain of natural evolution development, bridged over by the conspicuous manifestation of the Spirit of Creation.

How this was brought about and how evolution got over its dead-points is not demonstrated by empirical science. The link between the inorganic and the organic is not yet explained, not more than the question with regard to *matter* and *force* and the problem of *mind*.

Three mysteries elude and, so long as the human intellect remains in its present state of development,—will constantly elude the grasp of physical science:—they are, the mystery of life, as noted afore, the mystery of matter and force, and the mystery of the human mind. They all belong to the one great mystery of Creation.

Matter and Force have been partially explained as bases of phenomena, through their effect on our physical senses, by which certain physical laws have been defined and comprehended by human intelligence. It is from this partial experience that physical science insists that to matter and force all phenomena must be traced (p. 3). They constitute the primary manifestation of Creation, but we are not therefore to infer that matter and force are the only realities in the universe. Professor Stokes says:—Admitting to the full as highly probable, though not completely demonstrated, the applicability to living beings of the laws which have been ascertained with reference to dead matter, I feel constrained, at the same time, to admit the existence of a mysterious *something* lying beyond; a something *sui generis*, which I regard, not as balancing and suspending the ordinary physical laws, but as working with them and through them to the attainment of a designed end. What this something, which we call *life*, may be, is a profound mystery. . . . When from the phenomena of life we pass to those of *mind*, we enter a region still more profoundly mysterious. We can readily imagine that we may here be dealing with phenomena altogether transcending those of mere life, in some such way as those of life transcend, as I have endeavoured to infer, those of chemistry and molecular attractions; or, as the laws of chemical affinity, in their turn, transcend those of mere mechanics. Science can be expected to do but little to aid us here, since the instrument of research is itself the object of investigation. It can but enlighten us as to the depths of our ignorance and lead us to look to higher aid for that which most nearly concerns our well-being."*

Matter did not exist, in the homogeneous primordial cosmic cloud, in the nature in which it now presents itself to our physical senses as the structural essential of phenomena. The present groundwork of Creation on Earth is the result of Evolution, worked out by Force, from which originates Motion. Force appears as matter affected by Motion, i.e., as *Modes of Motion*. This Motion is brought into action by a Creative Power, which determined the external motion, by modes of motion transcending the human power of conception (§32). We are thus conscious of the Creator through the Forces in the universe, not by comprehending the creative actions and the Motor of Evolution, but by the effects of the creative power, perceivable in Nature through our physical senses, working out

* Presidential Address to the British Association at Exeter.

the conviction on our Moral Senses; which conviction, thus consolidated, constitutes *Faith* (§26, p. 33).

"Any finite mass of diffused matter, even though vast enough to form our whole sidereal system, if it were of absolute sphericity, absolute uniformity of composition and absolute symmetry of relation to all forces external to it," would be homogeneous and eternally incapable of change.* The primordial nebula or cosmic cloud, being denuded of energy and motion, was consequently simply dimension in existence, infinitely powerless and inert, without any other qualities or phenomena. When what is now called matter became a compound of this primordial nebula, through the introduction of energy—by the Motion caused by the external Power, as above said,—it also became divisible into molecules and substance. These are the chemical "elements," known to empirical science, and their introduction in the universe is what we postulated above as the First Stage in Creation (p. 7).

"We must not refrain, says Mr. Herbert Spencer, from dealing with matter as made up of extended and resistant atoms." † But "if you ask the naturalist, says Prof. Tyndall, whence is this matter. . . . . who and what divided it into molecules? . . . he has no answer." ‡ The answer might be given, as appropriately as empirical science is able. Mr. Crookes' splendid analysis gives a clue as to how the cosmic nebula was evolved into matter. He observed that matter (the "elements" of chemistry) was built up from a primitive element which he calls *protyle* or "first stuff," out of which the chemical elements were evolved. From the presence of this protyle it is conclusive that the chemical elements, as we know them, are not simple and primordial; that they have not arisen by chance or been created in a desultory and mechanical manner, but have been evolved from simpler matter, or,

---
* HERBERT SPENCER. "First Principles," p. 407.
† "First Principles," p. 176.
‡ "Fragments of Science," Vol. II., p. 396.

perhaps indeed from one sole kind of matter." * This protyle or first principle of matter, is more complex than the atoms of the "etherical" or homogeneous nebula, the cosmic cloud, the infinite primal nebula, from which (in conformity with the "cosmic nebula-theory" of Kant and Laplace) the worlds are evolved. Consequently *protyle* is also a product of evolution through force.

Forces are Modes of Motion, originated from the original impulse of the primordial Cosmic Motor, and, having served to evolve Matter, are consequently primogenial to Matter and elemental to it,—so that Matter could be called consolidated Force (p. 7).

On this proposition the hypothesis could be formed, that, as matter has been evolved through motion caused by force, and thus enclosing force as potential energy, *Gravitation,*— which is the ever constant affection of matter in motion,—is the result of that primordial potential energy being transformed into Motion. It is manifest that our idea of matter is built out of our experience of force.† To demonstrate matter, science is compelled to do it in the terms of force or motion, and the presence of *natural* or *phenomenal force* can only be manifested through evolution, i.e., through motion in matter, which we call development.

Thus development is Motion, and Motion originated from the Primordial Cosmic Power we called Spirit of Creation. If thus professor Tyndall asks:—Whence this matter?—the question is supplemented by asking: Whence that Motion? What is this matter which imprisons Force? Whence that Power from which Force originated to evolve Matter? To answer these questions the human mind should be able to cover a range that far transcends all sequences of physical phenomena, and enter into the domain of the unseen universe;

---

* " *The Genesis of Elements.*" Lecture at the Royal Institution (Reprint. p. 2.)
† HERBERT SPENCER. "First Principles," §167.

whence the Supreme Creative Power,—outside and far beyond all that we can contemplate through our physical senses,—is manifested by the visible universe.

All physical phenomena are different groupings of matter through force, under different appearances,—or like the phenomena of light, heat and electricity, the results of *modes of motion*; but motion can begin in force only. The modes of motion that produce the varied phenomena are balanced by a general dynamic law, called the *conservation of energy* or *persistency of force*. This means, that different forces or modes of motion are interchangeable,—viz: light may go over into heat, heat may become electricity,—without there being any loss of energy, which can neither be diminished nor increased in the present system of Creation,—so far, at least, as science has been able to conclude. The vast amount of energy which, under the form of light or heat, radiates from the suns into the endless space is not lost but remains potential in the ether, and is returned by friction to the revolving bodies in their career through the etherial medium.

This transformability of forces shows their common origin from *one* potential Energy, the primordial power of the Spirit of Creation. This persistent or indestructable Energy is the unity of all the activities of the visible and the unseen universe. The existence of this Power is conspicuous in the *breaks* in the chain of the natural evolution-process which science is unable to bridge over. As stated before, we find that the researches of science, in subtile and minute deductions, have proved that the so-called chemical elements are composed or evolved from the more primitive elements, "protyle" or "first stuff." The evolution-process thus begins with the development of the primordial protyle out of the homogeneous cosmic nebula into the seventy different chemical elements; carrying Nature, through all the stages of creation, to the Moral-Mental Organism of Man (§§3–6). All is clear to the *evolution*—and *mechanical theory*, but the links between these stages are yet wanting to bridge over the breaks in the process of creation on Earth.

To complete now this system of *mechanical evolution*, Cosmic Philosophy is bound to acknowledge, as necessary postulate, an original motive power, working from outside the inert nebula cloud, to set it in motion and keep the machine going. It is evident that the most perfect mechanical contrivance thinkable, based on the completest dynamical principles, is dependent for action on the conservation of the primitive impulsive force; to get through the dead-points, caused by the gravitation of atoms, the impulsive propelling energy must be continuous, in order to counteract the persistent tendency of gravitation to stability and inertia.

We have thus seen the physical necessity of this Primordial Power or Motor, for the originating of motion, i. e. to set the cosmic evolution process agoing; but, not less impressively, the study of natural science teaches the necessity of the continuous persistency of this Power in Nature as the Motor of Evolution, conspicuous in the bridging over of the breaks in the evolution career of Nature. Nay, more,—if the theory of evolution, as taught by Herbert Spencer and Charles Darwin, be true, this theory is the living testimony that the creative Power of God was not alone necessary "in the beginning" but is yet ever continuous and irrefragably constant in the universe. In every vibration of atoms, in every phenomenon,—from the first grouping of protyle into atoms of matter and the quickening of vital energy, through all the stages of creation on Earth, to the loftiest thoughts of the moral-intellectual mind,—the Motor of Evolution is necessarily acting in direct relation to this Primordial Power, that gave the first impulse to creation.

Through the persistency of the energy of this Power,— from which arrived the first impulse "in the beginning,"— thrilled the stupendous incoherent mass of the homogeneus cosmic nebula, from its inert equilibrium stability into heterogeneous atoms of matter. Then began development through Motion; the same Energy, carrying on the evolution-process over the vast structural difference of the *first break* in Nature, between the not-living and the living, throbs forward into the developing struggle of organic life; this struggle to be transferred from the vegetable into the animal life over the *second break*. Further and further on it works over the *third break*,—*i.e.*—the moral-mental dissimilarity between man and the lower animals,—which consists, *physically*, in the difference of the concomittants of thought in the brains of man and those of the lower animals, and *morally*, in the deep chasm which exists between the selfish instinct of the *dumb* animal and the moral-mental organism, with its moral senses, conscience and sympathy, of the self-conscious *speaking* man.

For all these riddles with regard to the breaks, where science cannot find the links in the evolution-process, there is only one solution, viz: the persistent energy of the Motor of Evolution. In this persistency of energy, through all stages of evolution, consists the congruousness of the cosmos, and therein is the manifestation of the intelligent cause—the primordial cosmic force—to be found.

We have now considered, scientifically, the continuity of the natural evolution-process on Earth, from the first impulse of that inscrutable Power, we call Spirit of Creation, on the production of the visible universe to the production of life, the consequent production of animals and man, and, finally, of the moral-mental organism on Earth. We have thus contemplated Nature's miracles, as the most clear indications of the Creator's work. The breaks, occasioned by the missing links,—which less conscientious scientists than Wallace, Darwin and Huxley pass over with obvious *sans-gênes*,—are recognised by these foremost advocates of the evolution theory, as unaccounted for through their theory of evolution, as explained by Darwin and his followers. They have simply confirmed the breaks and allow them to remain unaccounted for. But these breaks, we may safely admit, are so many occurrences in Nature where the Creator is made manifest to humanity.

Thus, by diligently investigating Nature's work by the light of physical science, we find the avenues leading to God.

Motor of Evolution. With life, the basis of organism, the development of the living organism sets in, through the Motor of Evolution, acting on the coincidence of atoms and molecules, when these are in the precise position for combination and general development. It is not only impossible for empirical science to disprove the existence of the Motor of Evolution, but it is also bound to admit that the coincidences which produce the conditions adapted to "natural selection" plainly indicate a power,—" a something *sui generis,* lying beyond,"—which could not be better defined than by the term Motor of Evolution.

This is the same energy which originated the modes of motion, "in the beginning;" which caused the collision of molecules in the most favourable conditions, adapted to form isomeric molecule compounds from the nebula atoms, and assisted in the formation of chemical compounds;—so that, when the first and germinal molecule was formed, this had at once the property of assisting the further formation of its like,—nobody knows why. This is the mystery which is called the "evolution of non-organic matter,"—the "affinities" which form the elements into the beautiful and wonderful crystalline forms; the "motions in matter" by which the elements manifest that there is a living power, working among their atoms, which links the evolution of matter from non-life into life,—nobody knows how.

This permanent Energy, called Motor of Evolution, which appears now passive, now active,—potential or kinetic,—does every thing in the universe, organic and non-organic. Gravity is the result of its originating action on the Cosmic Nebula, creating the Mechanical Force. Chemical Forces, the qualities of atoms, are its work, by evolving the "protyle" into "elements"—binding together particles of atoms into cohesion, or resisting their attraction, through contracting and identifying molecules,—atoms undergoing changes in their relations, through combination with other atoms. Producing now action, now reaction, by binding forces in atoms or releasing them into motion through "transformation of energy,"—the Motor of Evolution fabricates all forces, called mechanical, chemical, or otherwise, and manifests *design* in the evolution-process, by employing all these forces for the formation of Species, by evolving Variations in the conditions of organisms.

All changes in evolution are due to motion, but to an intelligent motion, going over an ever improving scale of species; so that,—as one species is transformed into another species of a higher grade in the scale of development,—a species which has once served as a step to development, passes from the Earth, never to occur again. And though abnormal conditions may sometimes retard the development, in special cases,—causing the appearance of a retrogressive evolution,—the tendency of the Motor of Evolution is ever pointing towards perfection.

Science versus Theism. The materialistic cosmic-philosopher does not start with the real beginnings of the cosmos, but takes up a process already initiated, by means about which he entertains no opinion; and yet, he cannot possibly do without causes and beginnings, and, while he ignores an intelligent Ultimate Cause, he forgets that this unknown "cause" is already admitted in his philosophy as a reality, as an activity and really originating power; which he would simply call the "Creator," if he could only shake off the prejudices of materialistic dogmatism.

We have seen that Science is the supporter of an intelligent Motor in the Universe,—of an intelligent Motor of Evolution;—by what right now does Atheism assume the name of Science? Science does not breed atheism; from what we have seen empirically demonstrated, we must conclude that,—viewed in its proper light, free from materialistic superstition,—Science will be found to point to the Creator, and to Christ as the result of Creation on Earth.

By the fundamental law of dynamics, it is asserted that the conservation of Energies in Nature is the outcome of their mutual influence in transformability. This mutual influence, as known by Newton's Law of Motions,—viz: that Action and Reaction are equal and opposite,—is necessary for the conservation of the equilibrium of the physical universe and points to an Ultimate Power, outside the direct reciprocal actions and reactions, productive both of potential and kinetic energy, of active and reactive motion. Like the touch of the loadstone, causing the two opposite poles of the magnetic staff to come into action, or, like friction producing the two kinds of opposite electricity, it originates transformations of energy into the "apparently constructing and destructing," composing and decomposing Forces of Nature, which are necessary for the maintenance of the equilibrium of the system of creation as a whole.

The same primordial Power, which caused, by integration of the diffused masses of cosmic nebula, this primordial gaseous existence to be evolved into planets and satellites,—is ever working, as Motor of Evolution, over millions of millions of miles, outside the pale of our universe, with the same forces and energies as in our own body and mind;—yes, still going on working, with the same master-fact, that called the first atom into motion, and whirled out worlds in Creation.

"Natural selection" and "survival of the fittest," "inheritance of functionally produced modifications," "successive changes of conditions through multiplication of effects," etc.—or whatever name might be given to the factors of organic evolution,—are all indications of the ultimate operative agent, called Motor of Evolution. The suborganic instinct of plants and animals, for the adaptation to surrounding conditions, manifests the existence of this creative power, which pushes on the evolutionary process, causing the variations and adaptations which science can assert.

Häckel, in his theory of *abiogenesis*, pretends that the organic comes out of the inorganic, as its adequate cause, by a process similar to that whereby the molecules of dead crystalline bodies assume regular form. With this physical explanation of life, Häckel acknowledges no other activity in organic evolution than the chemical and the mechanical. "The cell, he wrote to the German Association in 1877,—consists of matter, called protoplasm, composed chiefly of carbon, with an admixture of hydrogen, nitrogen and sulphur. These component parts, properly united, produce the soul and body of the animated world, and, suitably nursed, become man." With this single argument the mystery of the universe is explained, the Deity annulled and a new era of infinite knowledge ushered in. Not to speak of the crystalline-theory;—for we all know what has become of it,—one cannot help observing, how easily some great ideographical scientists can manage to step over the most serious physical problems. Some big terms, representing notions without facts, like: "persistency of matter and energy," "correlation of forces," dissipation of forces, etc. sufficiently explain all Nature. But such arguments as Häckel's are simply ideas,—not even logical ideas,—and, by no means, scientific,—much less could this protoplastic ideography be the ultimate conclusion of science. But the idea of ascribing to science the aspiration of Atheism is conspicuously unscientific, for how could science prove that there is no God,—as long as science completely ignores what matter is and whence motion comes. All what the genius of the school of Häckel could teach us, is that there are experimental matter and energy in the universe, and that, combined, they produce peculiar structures. That is all;—nothing more than the child knows of the structure of his father's watch, when he can peep inside, and sees that "the wheels go round."

With the same scientific claims,—and not a whit less,—as the scientific atheist insists on the discarding from the visible universe of all but what he can empirically test through his physical senses,—his antipode, the scientific spiritist, is filling up the universe with a teeming host of spiritual agents,—and overdoes the work at the same rate as his materialistic antagonist. Both fall short from grasping the truth; for this common reason, that both follow a wrong track:—the one by depending solely on his intellect, the other by following the creation of his imagination;—while both lack the Moral Senses, the sole guidance to truth.

Dr. Thomas Young shows us the invalidity of the basis of scientific conclusions, on merely materialistic views of experimental matter. In his lectures on Natural Philosophy, he has the following passage:—"Besides this porosity, there is still room for the supposition, that even the ultimate particles of matter may be permeable to the causes of attractions of various kinds, especially if those causes are immaterial; nor is there anything in the unprejudiced study of physical philosophy that can induce us to doubt the existence of immaterial substances; on the contrary, we see analogies that lead us almost directly to such an opinion. The electrical fluid is supposed to be essentially different from common matter; the general medium of light and heat, according to some, or the principle of caloric, according to others, is equally distinct from it. We see forms of matter, differing in subtility and mobility under the names of solids, liquids and gases; above these are the semi-material existences, which produce the phenomena of electricity and magnetism, and either caloric or a universal ether. Higher still perhaps, are the causes of gravitation, and the immediate agents in attractions of all kinds, which exhibit some phenomena apparently still more remote from all that is compatible with material bodies. And of these different orders of beings, the more refined and immaterial appear to pervade freely the grosser. It seems therefore natural to believe that the analogy may be continued still further until it rises into existences absolutely immaterial and spiritual. We know not but that thousands of spiritual worlds may exist unseen for ever by human eyes; nor have we any reason to suppose that even the presence of matter in a given spot necessarily excludes these existences from it. Those who maintain that nature always teems with life, wherever living beings can be placed, may therefore speculate with freedom on the possibility of independent worlds; some existing in different parts of space, others pervading each other, unseen and unknown, in the same space, and others again to which space may not be a necessary mode of existence."

In contemplating the exposition of Nature's progression from the formless moulded into form, from the inorganic to the organic, from blind forces to instinct, from animal instinct into the self-consciousness of rational intellect, and, finally, into the morally as well as intellectually developed human mind,—we must necessarily admit a Motor of Evolution, as an independent intelligent power, which causes this development of matter and energy, through all stages, into the evolved moral-mental organism of man;—forecasting, through this progressive evolution, that perfect altruistic moral-mental development of the perfect human being, which is the utmost consequence of evolution, as represented by Christ when on Earth (§26). Thus science destroys Atheism, in the theory of natural evolution,— as this scientifically intelligible theory is naturally correlative to the existence of an intelligent Ultimate Cause.

Design. Physics is essentially the science of the physical senses. The chemist, from his standpoint, is bound to ignore what he does not find in his crucibles and retorts, when analysing the elements in their forms and combinations;—and yet, the stupendous discoveries achieved by physical science in our ago are so many revelations of the Creator's design in Nature and form the most reliable forecastings of the future of man, for by disclosing his origin they foretell his destiny.

Cosmogony, geology, palaeontology, physiology, and, above all, the evolution theory,—when disclosing the wonderful combinations of matter and energy,—reveal the physical necessity of development; this is the natural law of necessity, from which follows the motive power of the world's mechanism and the production of phenomena. This primordial necessity, causing the process of continuous development of all and everything in the universe, is the natural agent of the original design in Creation.

Astronomy, more than any other science, has rendered us capable of conceiving the design, expressed in the law of gravitation, which causes the majestic harmony of the cosmos. The astronomer, when he sweeps the heavens with his telescope, *must* come to the conclusion that reason demands a reasonable purpose for the universe. As Mr. Herbert Spencer once said: "We are ever in the presence of an Infinite and Eternal Energy, from which all things proceed." * For *chance* there is no place in Nature; here all and everything proceeds from *necessity*, and where is necessity there must be *design*, *i.e.*, a determined end to meet the necessity. This, both physical science and logic teach us. Chance can never be congruous with necessity, for necessity implies a definite want, while chance has no definite cause or definite end,—for if chance had an end it would not be chance but a necessity required by the end. If necessity exists in Nature, it is not chance that will meet it, but some, also by Nature, prearranged, *i.e.*, *preordained*,—contrivance, in conformity with the law of necessity; otherwise what would become of the so-called "mechanical" order of the universe. A mechanical system could not exist without purpose; chance would be its destruction; it must work by a certain necessary law, or not work at all.

* Nineteenth Century. 1884.

Nothing thus gives better testimony of the existence of an intelligent and provident design than a thoroughly mechanical system. The mechanical system of the universe, as insisted upon by modern science, is a mechanism of vast intelligent design,—postulated above as Motor of Evolution,—with a purpose we cannot comprehend. Gigantic mechanical contrivances, continually but slowly and steadily moving, not alone in its infinitely detailed branches, but also slowly but steadily changing its basis. The system of the universe is gradually changing, and with it naturally the species of organic life. Not hazard or chance, but the necessary sequences of changing external conditions,—caused by the motive power of evolution,—produce the regular correlative to form the characteristics appertaining to types of species.

Could now "natural selection" be mere chance, while these external conditions are naturally and regularly originated through the cosmic evolution process? These are necessities which exclude chance as indeterminate variability.

To matter and energy we can reduce all phenomena, but behind these our intellect is, as yet, blind; for here our physical senses are of no avail. And when the highest point of inorganic, the not-living, was reached in the process of evolution on our globe, and a new power was to become active,—*i.e.*, the dead matter to be quickened and life imprisoned in its shrouds to be set free, to act as the powerful factor of organic evolution,— what great cause brought this on? Following up the plainly written history of creation, *i.e.*, the growing process of Nature, we come again and again to this question, for, again and again we come to sharp breaks in the continuity of this chain of evolution, for the solution of which we have no faculties at the present stage of human mental development. As stated before, we miss, in this concatenation of events, the links between the non-living and the living, the inorganic and the organic, the vegetable life and the animal life, the animal instinct of the dumb brute and the intelligent consciousness of the human being, endowed with speech and moral senses, which gradually carried him, from the primitive state of the brutish materialistic-egoistic mental condition of the savage existence, to the developed moral-mental organism crowned with the Christian Faith.

Whence this motive power, working wonders **upon** wonders in the continuity of the chain of events on our globe ? **Can science give the solution ? Yes, says the** Atheist, "It is all mechanical force, following the **necessity of law!**" We are apt **to smile con**temptuously **at the conceit of the** half-civilized heathen, who fancies he knows all about an engine, coming straightway from the workshop of civilized intellect, with all its subtle and highly elaborate workmanship, in which the smallest details or atoms of power are balanced by the laws of mechanism; his conceit jumps at conclusions, with simply a superficial conception of the principal **pieces,** through which the effects of the working are conspicuous, **but to his** limited comprehension nothing is known of the principles **of the** laws which underlie this rhythmical working. Such is the attitude **of** the Atheist with regard to the great mechanism of Nature's evolution process. Like the conceited half-civilized child **of Nature, he** thinks **he** understands all creation, and sets forth to dogmatise from a few apparently mechanical effects, conceived through **his** short-sighted physical sense;—and **yet, he** claims science as his revelation!

The potentiality **and congruity** of the universe, through all its duration, were laid up for development "in the beginning," **by the** predetermined creative action of **impulse, and** from "the beginning" up to this day,—judged by **the inference drawn** from scientific experience,—the persistent energy of this Power is ever constant **in** its mission of development;—often incomprehensible **to science,** in its present stage of progress,—but **also** often pouring forth its light on our path, and making clear **our course in the** grand career of the human race on earth.

The **germ cast at that awful** "beginning" **by the** Creator into the boundless space, has proved capable of development. In the natural process which science calls "evolution," every stage succeeds to maturity at its congenial time, through the primordial persistency of the Creative Power,—the Spirit of Creation,—infinite and "extending through all extent, as the fountain of all beings." This is the Motor of Evolution. Every contrivance of Nature, ever investigated as natural phenomenon, proves this assertion, and, at all the "stages of creation," when a new "factor of evolution" is evidently indispensible to explain the link between a lower and a higher stage of development, the modes of Nature's motions are not comprehensible to the human intellect, without the admittance, in the logical course of reasoning, of the active agency of this inscrutable Energy as Motor of the process of Evolution on our Globe.

"Belief, says Professor Huxley, in the scientific sense of the word, is a serious matter and needs strong foundations. To say, therefore, in the admitted absence of evidence, that I have my belief as to the mode in which existing forms of life have originated, would be using words in a wrong sense. But expectation is permissible, where belief is not; and if it were given me to look beyond the abyss of geologically recorded time to the still more remote period, when the earth was passing through physical and chemical conditions, which it can no more see than a man can recall his infancy, I should expect to be a witness of the evolution of living protoplasm from not-living matter."*

Professor Huxley's opinion, as expressed in this "expectation," with regard to the genesis of life, amounts to the proposition:—that it is—at the present stage of the cosmic evolution-process—as much possible for chemists to create life from not-living matter, as it could have been possible for any rational being to stand, as a living spectator, at the stage of the pre-geological era, watching how the process was going on of evolving living protoplasm from not-living matter, while

---
* "Critiques and Addresses," p. 239.

the primordial germ, from which his own brains were to be developed, was in process of construction.

Thus, with suitable design, different **agencies have been at work** at different eras of creation, in **the world's** history, **and through forces** not now in **operation within the present range of** our experience. Not alone **the organic structure of life, but** metals, and **some material compounds, of which the** composing elements **are known, elude, at present, all attempts at chemical** synthesis; **the time and congeniality** of the agencies **which** brought **about their development or** construction **have passed away, and as these agencies were neither mechanical nor chemical, they cannot be put in action by man.**

From the foregoing it is obvious **that, besides the** dynamic and chemical relations of **matter, that is,** besides the affection of atomic matter with any **amount of** mechanical motion,— **there exists** an all-pervading energy **behind** this mechanical **action of** the world's evolution; while it is clear that the **so-called** material philosophy, with its mechanical system of **creation, is** incomplete, and thus, **by itself alone,** insufficient **to explain the cosmic** evolution process.

Such incompleteness is observable in Mr. Herbert Spencer's definition **of evolution.** "Evolution, says he, **is an** integration of **matter and** concommitant dissipation **of motion,** during which **the matter passes from an** indefinite incoherent homogeneity to a definite coherent heterogeneity and **during** which the retained motion undergoes a **parallel transformation."***

It is obvious that all **this is merely the** effect of the evolution process; how the motion originated **is left not** alone **unexplained but** also unobserved; **the same with regard to the power that** determined motion, primarily, to change the homogeneous **mass** into hetergeneous matter, which, without this power,— **the originator of** primordial motion,—**would have remained eternally in equilibrium, incapable of change. And** the same

---

* **First** Principles, p. 396.

omission of cause occurs again with regard to Mind and Matter. "Nothing," says Mr. Herbert Spencer, "can be within the whole realm of thought severed by a wider interval than consciousness and thought on the one hand and matter on the other."* This entire and unqualified difference between mind and matter does not allow of mind being evolved from matter in the process of evolution, without the help of an outside power,—a postulate, which is able to constitute the *self-consciousness*, which,—instead of being evolved from motion on matter,—can create motion, through a *Free Will*, which *knows* that it exists. This power, as we have seen before, is the originative power of creation,—the origin of the first cause of evolution,—and is manifested by *mind* and *self-consciousness* and *free will*, which are the highest manifestations of the Creator on Earth.

To human common sense any belief or expectation, whatever, is superstition, when the conception is not based on natural phenomena; no power is in existence which has not its manifestation in Nature. On these premises our Faith is based.

From manifestations in Nature we know *design*, which is the appropriate action of the forces of Nature, but, like these forces, as yet a mystery to Science. We are conscious of design under two aspects, viz: as the objective design of the Motor of Evolution, (the primordial motion described on page 195, et seq.), which underlies the physical factors of organic evolution,—and as the subjective design of individual organisms, conspicuous in the inclinations and "habits" of plants, the instincts of animals and moral will of man; these are so many manifestations of the *modus operandi* of the Motor of Evolution, in the individual adaptation or modification of structures in species. (See Introd., page XVIII).

Design in Nature is thus manifested by the power of adaptation, conspicuous in all organisms, even in plants,—as we see in the vine,—and developing from instinct in animals to the Free

---

* Principles of Psychology, Vol. II., p. 484.

Will of man. Here design in Nature exhibits more conspicuously its moral end, for the free will in man is intuitively guided by the Moral Senses, Conscience and Sympathy.

One of the principal factors of evolution is "adaptation," *i.e.*, organisms adapting themselves to environments and circumstances, by force of necessity. "Necessity is the mother of invention" is an old truism, but invention is *design*, sprung from the *will* to suit the necessity, and moulded into adaptation to the environment. This Nature teaches us, by her process of evolution. It was a necessity for the blind creature of lower organism, when groping in the dark for its food, to have an organ of sight, and when it arrived at a certain stage of development, the eye was evolved from a primordial nerve, and made to suit itself to light. Here necessity brought out design. But, whence this design; is it that of the poor developing creature, or was it the power of development, laid up potentially in the primordial germ of its organism, which cast forward the suitable variation? It is evidently not the creature who creates its eye, but the evolution of the germ, laid primordially in the organism, which answers to the necessities of life in the designed form. Thus, the eye being designed to suit the necessities of light, is formed through the agency of light, but it is obvious that this agency alone could not produce the effect, if the structure were not previously designed in the germ of the organism.

Design in creation is manifested by adaptations and the regularity of events that we call "laws of nature," but principally by those continuous forecastings of development, which are known as *variations*, forming new bases for new species.

But design in Nature must not be looked for alone in the species, but precedently in the general congruity of the universe, which observation learns is steadily progressing. The Creator discloses his plans to human intellect in matter and force,—at least in the effects of what we call by these names,—but, behind matter and force, we cannot fail to be conscious of a purpose and a will and a method, while our intellect may, as yet, not be able to grasp the end of all these wonderfully working contrivances and adjustments, composing the method of creation which is called Evolution.

The Ultimate Cause. The Personal God. The perpetual craving of our reason to get at the knowledge of the primal and real cause of things is the idea of the *unity of science*. If science is continually exhibiting and proving the interdependence of phenomena, it must consistently arrive at a primal and real cause of things or, at least, be forced to acknowledge a necessary postulate as such, and while grouping facts into generalizations, it cannot fail to acknowledge the links between interdependent phenomena, which as series of design, mark the classification of things. This tendency of reason to presuppose a final cause corroborates the innate faith in a Creator,—the craving of the Soul, which finds its analogy and support in the generalizing tendency of science. The belief in God is no more a delusion than the belief in the Unity of Science.

It is preëminently unscientific to imagine that variations are fortuitous. This wrong notion results from an inadequate conception of the Universal Energy which pervades and guides the structures of atoms in the universal evolution of matter, through its various transformations;—the universal energy as postulated above under the name of Spirit of Creation. Variations are not caused by environments; these only mould adaptations. When the blind polype felt the necessity to look about for its food instead of being solely dependent on its olfactory organs for its support,—it is evident that the latent germ of the organ of sight in the system of the species is the cause of this craving for sight, which finds outlet in a new variation of species.

The Design which can be traced through the whole universe is intelligence and foresight. It is manifested throughout organic creation by what is called *inclination* in plants, *instinct* in animals and *moral will* in man. In plants and animals it has to act only on the necessity of its environment, but, in the case of man, it has to struggle also with impediments of higher pressure and of various kinds, which surround the moral being. We trace design in the plant, which suits its roots and branches to its surroundings:—in the vine, which—swinging its shoots in the air, as feelers in search of proper support, deliberately avoiding some dead hollow posts in which hidden insects lurk for its life-sap—clasps its tendrils in lusty winding spirals round healthy branches, for sound support in its struggle for existence. But it is in the animal instinct that the manifestation of this universal life-energy becomes a struggle for existence in its roughest material form, for the evolution of the species into the higher order of creation.

By way of conclusion to what has been said in this sub-section, we now come to the question: What gave primal origin to and governs the universe and all *developing phenomena*,—culminating in the human moral-mental organism,—Chance or Design?

Darwin writes to Asa Gray: "If I saw an angel come down to teach us good, and I was convinced, from others seeing him, that I was not mad, I should believe in design."* But why should he *then* believe,—the scientific man? The testimony of a so-called supernatural apparition or hallucination is no scientific proof, even when experienced by more than one deluded individual brain. And is this pretension not rather selfish? The belief of Mr. Darwin, thus acquired, would benefit himself and his few friends only, but not mankind at large, and each individual could put forward the claim for an angel to

---

* "Life and Letters of the late Charles Darwin, F.R.S," by his son Francis Darwin. London, 1888.

himself. The testimony of the apparition would be far from satisfactory to all parties; granted the validity of Mr. Darwin's belief in the Angel, would others acquire the faith on his simple assertion? Wallace might perhaps have taken over his belief, but would Huxley have anything to do with the Angel? Herbert Spencer and others could, with equal scientific exigence as Mr. Darwin, insist on their own special angel of light, and each would then have his own revelation to sustain. But why should we now, in believing the apparition, rely more on the testimony of our physical senses,—which are so easily deceived by imagination, hallucination and other abnormal mental conditions,—than the consciousness of our moral senses? Ah!—but "there is the rub;"—Mr. Darwin did not believe in the moral conviction of man; his only conviction was the merely animal origin of man,—without taking into account the moral-mental development in Nature. "Would any one,—he asks,—trust in the convictions of a monkey; is there any conviction in such a mind?"* Well surely there is, so far as regards the monkey existence. For we are all persuaded of the strength and efficiency of animal instinct, which is the conviction of the animal, but, between this and the conviction of the moral-mental organism of man, there is a gulf not yet bridged over by the evolution theory,—no more than the other breaks in the chain of evolution, as described before; this missing link is not yet accounted for by science,—no more than the gap between non-living matter and living organism. Before having drawn a straight line between the mind of the monkey and the human mind, Mr. Darwin might well have patched up these breaks in his theory, in order to allow Common Sense a chance for the comparison; otherwise his question could have no connection whatever with the convictions of the self-conscious human mind, and is thus simply absurd. But the great naturalist was so absorbed in

* "Life and Letters," etc. Letter to Mr. Graham.

the details of the by-paths of Creation, that his mind had no conception of the main track of evolution, which embraces the whole universe, material, mental and moral.

However, let us return to our question:—Is it chance or design which governs the universal process of evolution?

But, what is **Chance?** This question has been treated before, and we have seen that chance without cause cannot be conceivable; **when we think of a** thing as existent, **we think** also of a cause producing the phenomenon; chance, that is non-cause, does not exist,—is unthinkable. If we are to admit the mechanical system of the materialistic cosmic philosophy, it is evident,—as demonstrated before,—that the dinamic theory excludes all idea of chance; no machine is brought and kept in motion by chance. It is thus not chance but absolute affection of matter and energy,—as predetermined by the prevision of the inscrutable Creator,—which issued the rhythmical motions of the homogeneous nebula and thus brought on the cosmic evolution.

This is the only conception that human thought is able to **grasp of the Ultimate Cause** of the mystery of the creative action which took place 'in the beginning.' The facts which our mental **organism, as** enlightened by scientific cosmogony, could conceive, **are** simply that matter, as the groundwork of creation, was primitively of nebula form, that the rhythmical motion of rotation kneaded it into a yielding or plastic condition and that it is finally modelled by a mechanical force.

As now, in all this, there is no chance conceivable, it is consequently all design. That design **determines the modes of** affection in all instances, we see persistently **manifested,**—as explained before,—in the process of evolution. Well does it strengthen our intuitive consciousness of a Divine Creator to contemplate, **free from all** dogmatic prejudices, with unbiased mind and **sound moral** senses, the truths of Nature, as expounded by Organic Evolution, and by the facts of geology in the imperishable rock-records of thousands of **ages.** (Comp. §18, p. 25).

In the minute contrivances of the factors of organic evolution, the variations and adaptations, we contemplate the design of the inscrutable universal persistent energy of the Spirit of Creation, as the Motor of Evolution. This ever present power, balancing energies and motions into obedience to immutable laws, is manifested by the adjustment and harmonious adaptation of matter in organisms, when it displays the growing energy of organic evolution to reach its final object, the Moral-Mental Organism of Man. And all, by that astounding self-adjusting *design*, primordially and potentially enclosed in the globule of matter, manifesting itself in every seed, spore or ovum, that gives origin to the innumerable species,—in the simple cells from which emanate the oak, the dolphin, the eagle, the human being;—life on life, organisms and development, through age on age, moving in stately march from the lower to the higher, upward and upward, through increasing adaptations and adjustments, in the evolution scale of the universe.

But whence, and whither? The answer is: GOD.

Science has removed whole regions and œons of phenomena, from what was considered the supernatural to the natural, and shows further that the evolution-process of Nature accounts for the development of the human mind into that capability of consciousness, called the *moral-mental organism* of man, the highest scale of evolution, for the present, on Earth, where the Soul is manifested by the moral-senses, conscience and sympathy, which combined build up the conviction of Faith,—that the beginning and the end of all things is God.

To the human mind there is no *force* really known but its *free will*, described above (§18, p. 24). It is thus natural that we feel intuitively convinced of a corresponding Supreme Will, as the fountain-head of Energy, capable of giving impulse to all forces in the universe, by putting matter into motion. The congruity of the universe, as science teaches us to conceive it, evidently corresponds with an intelligent Will, which, by its free energy, gave the first impulse, *i.e.*, created Motion,—the primitive Cause of all phenomena, the indestructible energy of which all forces are modifications.

This is the source of our innate consciousness of an Ultimate Causation, settled in an infinite mind, in **a creative will, the Supreme Will of a Supreme Being,—the Personal God.**

CHRIST.

The Goal of Evolution. Evolution is **a fact, but** about its method there are several hypotheses. These,—although being, each by itself, insufficient to explain evolution in all its bearings,—may serve, collectively, as the manifestation in scientific sense, of that potential **energy** in Nature, which we demonstrated above as the Motor of Evolution.

The foremost physical manifestation of the Motor of Evolution takes place through the *Variations*, which are the indicative phenomena of this world-moving power of development, in any direction. These are the chemical variations in matter, organic variations in plants and animals, physiological variations in **species,** and **moral** variations in the development of the human mind. **The** proofs brought forward by the late Charles Darwin in his theory of "Natural Selection" **and by** Mr. Herbert Spencer, in his "Factors of Organic **Evolution,"** and, with regard to inorganic evolution, by Mr. Crookes in his "Genesis of the Elements,"—showing the evolution of matter from protyle,—have not given any *definite* scientific solution, but **are** most valuable, in opening up the ultimate problem as to the cause of *variations*, on the occurrence of which all these theories are based, disclosing the *modus operandi* of the Motor of Evolution.

Viewed from this standpoint, the prominent physical result of evolution, as made perceivable by the evolution-process, is called "natural selection," or (as it is more plainly expressed) "survival of the fittest." This "fittest" is the outcome of a whole congeries of physical causes,—by no means produced by mechanical processes,—and the term "fittest" is simply the generalized expression for the final result of large associations of causes. Of these some are conspicuous, as "heredity," "struggle for existence," etc., while others are utterly unperceivable, and unexplained by empirical science. Among the former the natural activity of causes can sometimes be raised by artificial breeding or training, to procure fancy species,—as in the fancy breedings of pigeons, of the Pekinese "pug-nosed" lap-dogs, the fancy varieties of cattle, horses, blood-hounds, etc.,—of which,—especially of the pigeon-breeding,—the late Mr. Charles Darwin has left such interesting records in his works.

But, as evolution on Earth proceeds into the higher scales of development, the physical causes which produce the phenomena become more complex in their working. Mr. Dallinger, after a clear exposition of the nature of organic variations, proceeds thus: "Variation then is constant and universal; it acts in all directions and in every living thing. That there are factors of evolution not yet discovered is almost inevitable. But having reached this conclusion, we are, at once, compelled to ask:—What is the origin of this unceasing continuity of variation in all living things?—this power to become constantly adapted to change of environment, and, for ever, in the fittest form to survive? The earth, as is well known, is constantly subject to minute as well as to smaller cyclic and great secular changes. Nothing but an ability to become adapted, through all duration, to current and recurrent changes, could have made a continuity of living population of the globe possible. Because we have learned the nature of the law or method by which, throughout all time, these changes have been brought about and because the method *appears* self-acting, like the balance-wheel of a chronometer, must we argue that there is no design, either in the method or its result? That will not satisfy the constant demand of reason. Finding the law, according to which a projectile moves, must not be confounded with the cause of its motion. Natural selection cannot originate anything; variation does not explain itself. Why is it a property of all living things to vary indefinitely, and in all directions? The Darwinian law has no existence without it; but that "law" no more accounts for this tendency than the law of falling bodies explains gravitation, or shows why it acts as it does." *

If science were more generally inquired into, as a moral culture, as well as simply intellectual training of the mind,— *i.e.*, to elevate as well as to teach men,—the poorly instructed would be enlightened with regard to the physical foundation of the christian faith, while, on the other hand, educated men would learn to emancipate themselves from the deceptions of one-sided learning. Chemistry, Botany, Biology and Sociology, all plainly demonstrate the superficiality of the common belief,—prompted by human vanity,—that when we have learned to enumerate "the varied procession of events," by which Nature appears to our physical senses,—we know all about Creation and the Motor of Evolution. Simply recording the course of events in Nature is not tracing them to their sources.

Science is the record of facts of Nature,—*i.e.*, of physical phenomena, as they present themselves, in sequences, to our physical senses. From the regularity of their appearance, we derive the conception of natural laws, but science has no proof of the invariability of these laws; in fact, with regard to the organic world, it has often startling varieties to record. Now, a variation from these laws, in its broadest aspect, never before recorded, is, of course, a *wonderful* event, and is called a *miracle*,—*i.e.*, a variation which the thus far observed and

* W. H. DALLINGER, LL.D., F.R.S. "*The Creation*," oto., pp. 68-71.

recorded course of natural phenomena could not previse in the customary order of Nature. And science, not being initiated into the real nature of matter and force,—not knowing what they really are,—is unable to explain such an unexpected event apparently entirely beyond the nature of matter and force.

Thus physical science is incompetent to lay down the law that the unprevised or the so-called marvelous could *not* happen. Professor Huxley says:—" A miracle in the sense of a sudden and complete change in the customary order of nature is intelligible, can be distinctly conceived, implies no contradiction; and, therefore, according to Hume's own showing, cannot be *proved* false by any demonstrative argument." * Which means that what we call a *miracle*,—*i.e.*, the occurrence of a phenomenon never before observed by human physical senses, in the process of matter and energy,—is not dependent on *science*, in its present state of knowledge, for the criterium of the possibility and truth of the event. Whatever, through the paucity of scientific knowledge, is, at present, unexplainable to physical science, might, with a future development of knowledge, as to the nature of matter and energy, be found simply to be the outcome of very comprehensible attributes of forces, as yet unknown and unrecorded by science.

The constant development of our knowledge of the physical elements,—viz: the chemical forces, electricity, magnetism, etc.—in this century, is daily disclosing and producing phenomena, which would be as many unqualified "miracles" to the erudite sages of antiquity, and thus forthwith condemned as fables by the sceptic. But the *moral* development keeps pace with the *intellectual*, and incontestable is the power of the human Moral Senses in the social evolution-process, in its manifestation of a Moral Element in Nature,—as the active agent in the framing of Civilization. If we strip off the materialistic mask, ascribed to Nature, we find underneath the clear

---
* Huxley's "Hume," p. 133.

manifestation of the Creator's design and the demonstration of Christianity through physical truth. There is no other proof for truth than natural facts; the Divine Author of Nature, as well as the necessity of Christ in the evolution-theory of the human race, is proved by Nature (§26).

Thus the astounding series of *variations*, sprung forward, in physical and moral propensities in the evolution-career of the human moral-mental organism on Earth,—forecasting an ever-increasing scale of developing progress for this organism, and manifesting the Divine design with regard to the human race,—culminated with the advent of Christ on Earth, representing thus, for our imitation, a variety of the human species, in which the moral-mental organism was developed in the highest degree of perfection attainable by humanity, through the Moral Element, on Earth.

This advent manifests the Will of God to impress on mankind the fact of their being connected, through their Moral Senses, with the Eternal Creator. In other words,—the love of God, of the Creator for his creatures, is revealed to mankind through Christ; who, being the link between Divinity and Humanity, is most appropriately explained as the "*Son of God.*"

The history of mankind,—viewed in the light of the natural development of the Moral-Mental organism of man,—proves that the advent of Christ on Earth was a necessary forecasting of the moral condition of that organism in its evolution-process. What could be more natural in the development of the human moral senses than this variation, showing the innate growing power of the human mind in its moral tendency, when moulded by the influence of the Divine Spirit.

The advent of such a moral-mental organism as that of Christ on Earth is the strongest manifestation of the Divine Spirit, which is postulated, in the human moral development theory, as the Moral Element in Nature. It is a natural and necessary event in the evolution-theory to forecast the future state of human beings, by throwing light on the goal to which the Moral Element in Nature is leading. It is a natural and necessary event of evolution, for, if the history of mankind did not already possess this ever living example, the philosophy of evolution, as stated above (§26), if consistent in its search for the goal of the development theory,—for the final link, which unites man, in his highest development, with his Creator,—should postulate such a being as the final link, as the utmost result of evolution on Earth. It is the natural and necessary consequence of evolution;—the potential germ of this event being included, by the primordial Power, in the Energy communicated to the inert nebular mass, which caused the universal motion, by which worlds are whirled into existence.

Thus the moral principle, as laid primordially in the germ, has developed into a natural fact, and the principle of Christianity is revealed to humanity, through Nature.

The Fall of Man and the Redemption through Christ. At the first dawn of reason, the purity of the human soul is conspicuous in the child. Perfectly innocent and pure, the uncorrupted mind of the child, at its first acting on the world's stage, exhibits the natural moral purity of the human race, as it should be, were it not for the temptations of its animal propensities. In the innocent child, of normal type, is clearly observable, spontaneous with reason, the *instinct of the good.* This is the type according to which the race should be,—"of such is the kingdom of Heaven."

But, alas! Soon the gradually awakening animal nature overpowers the nascent moral senses and takes hold on the mind, through *egoism,* from which originate the lie, covetousness, cruelty and all the vicious inclinations, thoughts and actions, characteristics of the rapacious selfish animal nature,—which is the source of evil in the human mind. This deviation from the Divine Spirit is the degeneration from the innate purity with which man comes into the world. This is the *"fall of man,"* from which condition the redemption comes through Christ.

Without the Christian principles, this degeneration of man's moral senses could only partially be checked by Intellect, that is, through the experience of the *utility*, of bridling the animal passions, for mutual safety and decorum. This is the *intellectual reclamation* on the principle of material utility, but it has proved to be wanting in the stability which the moral conception of the good alone can procure. Civilization is not merely a material improvement; where the material element is predominently the civilizing factor, men are merely trained animals. Such materialistic civilization is imperfect and must break down, for its basis is the animal symbol of " Might is Right " in a cultured form. The regeneration of the human race, the *redemption* of the soul from this animal materialism, is Christianity, which, reviving the Moral Element, is fostering the Moral Senses, and thus completing the human moral-mental organism.

From the foregoing it is conclusive that the Moral Element in Nature,—conspicuous in the struggle of the Moral Senses with the animal egoism of the materialistic element (§5),—emphasizes the original endowment of the human race with a natural predisposition for the Good, *i.e.*, with an ability to arrive at a purely moral state through his Moral Senses (§14). Losing this regenerating power by his falling back into the nature of the lower animals, man's "redemption" and "deliverance from evil" is obtained when the Christian Principles get hold of his mind, by developing and strengthening his Moral Senses to combat Evil.

Evil, constantly in strife with the Moral Element in Nature (thus giving the manichean character to Christianity) is the animal egoism of the human mind, when this is lacking the strength of the moral senses. The allegorical representations of "Satan," "Evil Spirits," etc., as exercising evil influences on mankind, find, in the egoistic passions of the animal nature of man, their objective reality, together with the most efficient, ever present and ever active agency to engender evil in the world, as any "satan" ever could conceive for the personification of Evil.

Instead of postulating an outside "Satan," as the cause of human misery, let us look, by the light of our moral senses, within our own mind, and we will trace the "enemy" in the deep recesses of our own impure nature. As we have noted before (pages 27-31) the *origin of evil* is the "rebellion" of the inclinations of man's animal nature against the Divine Spirit of the Moral Element in Nature, caused by a viciously excited imagination, sweeping up the animal propensities and exciting the passions, through evil thoughts in the mind. This poor weak human mind, with its faltering tendency to believe what it desires, and to think only of what it wants to believe, is easily led away by imagination, for "the wish is father to the thought."

Evil is thus engendered in the human mind when man's animal appetites, inflamed by Imagination, are unchecked by the Moral Senses. The heart-bewildering problem of evil finds its solution in the human selfishness predominating over Conscience and Sympathy, which causes the retrogression of man's moral-mental organism. This is the state of *apostasy*, the fall of man from the scale of moral-mental condition into that state of animal materialism,—caused by want of application or through disuse of the moral senses,—in which only the instinctive egoism of the animal nature,—but thousand-fold corrupted by human intelligence and cunning,—governs the will. This condition represents the *fall of man*, the regeneration from which can only be accomplished through the Moral Senses. The *redemption* of the human race is the advent of Christ; which is the forecasting of the *goal of evolution on*

Earth, when the moral senses, having the full sway of the mind, shall have completely subdued the animal nature. By following the principles and example of Christ, every individual is redeemed from sin, by his mind coming completely under the influence of the Moral Element in Nature. Through the whole range of human life, man when having fallen, finds Christ ever ready for his redemption, through his Moral Senses,—which are fostered by Christianity.

When man's moral senses are overpowered by animal passions and rapaciousness,—he having fallen lower than the brute,—the activity of these senses, which cause the natural aversion from acts injurious to others, is stunted and nearly dead. No dread of punishment is able to check the downward career of the criminal, for it is proved that the penalties experienced by the "jail-bird" did not serve to awaken his moral senses (§78, p. 166 *Crime*). It is not because theft is punishable by Criminal Law, that it particularly entails shame and degradation in the eye of society, but because the thief has morally degraded his human intellect and violated his moral training, by falling to the animal nature of rapacity, through his cowardly act. He would go on falling lower and lower, as doomed to destruction, if he be not mercifully reclaimed by Christ. In man's fallen state, it is only the redemption of Christianity, the voice of CHRIST, heard in his inward soul, which can revive his Moral Senses of Conscience and Sympathy, to overrule the rapacious selfish animal nature, and thus to conquer evil.

This is the living natural history of the "fall of man" and the "redemption through Christ."

The human career on Earth exhibits, in the individual, the history of man; how he,—being formed from matter,—evolved, through the Spirit of Creation, from the primordial germ which emanated from the Creator; how he, quickening into organic life, and developing physical and moral senses, appeared in the world, developed as human species, with a pure soul and unpolluted moral senses. His fall is caused by the retrogression of his moral nature, through the ascendency of the material element of the lower animal bias;—his regeneration is his being redeemed through his Moral Senses, as fostered by Christianity.

The principle of Christianity was ever existent in the Moral Element in Nature, working in the world wherever human beings were developed;—but, when "the word became flesh," the principle a fact,—that is, the potential germ developed in the course of evolution into the phenomenon of the advent of Christ on Earth,—then the evolution of the human mind had arrived at that stage of creation, in which a living example of a *perfect* being was necessary, as a *variety* of Nature, to throw light on the goal of moral development,—the destiny of the human race,—and on the way to arrive there. This high-way of human destiny is indicated to our inward consciousness, consolidated by Faith, in the conception of the moral truth: *Through Christ to God.*

THE DIVINE SPIRIT.

The Moral Element in Nature.—If the physical aspect of Nature presents numerous problems to the speculative observer, not the less we find complicated problems to solve, when contemplating Nature from an *ethical* point of view,—that is, from the aspect of the evolution of the social organism,—the sphere in which the Moral Element of Nature is the prominent motor of evolution. Yet, if in the investigation of physical phenomena, Science has its limits drawn by our physical senses,—in the moral sphere of Nature's problems, our Moral Senses procure us states of consciousness far more complete than Science could do with regard to the material aspect of society.

We can elucidate this assertion by resolving, through the test of the Moral Senses, a social problem proposed by Professor Huxley, in his article, (recently appeared in the "Nineteenth Century"*) under the head: "The Struggle for Existence" and which, viewed by the light of the theory of the Moral Senses, is a striking "programme" of the working of the Moral Element, in social conditions where the struggle for material existence is most keenly defying political measures.

Professor Huxley puts his ethical thesis, which is an exposition of the Malthus theory, as follows:—

"The effort of the ethical man to work towards a moral end, by no means abolished, perhaps has hardly modified the deep-seated organic impulses which impel the *natural man* to follow his non-moral course. One of the most essential conditions, if not the chief cause of the struggle for existence, is the tendency to multiply without limit, which man shares with all living things. It is notable that 'increase and multiply' is a commandment traditionally much older than the ten, and that it is perhaps the only one which has been spontaneously and *ex animo* obeyed, by the great majority of the human race. But in civilized society, the inevitable result of such obedience is the re-establishment, in all its intensity, of that struggle for existence,—the war of each against all,—the mitigation or abolition of which was the chief end of social organization."

This is now the old Malthus all over again, and, in the most light-hearted tone, we learn the astounding fact that Society, as an organization of civilization, is a failure. The "chief end of social organization" is defeated by the obedience of the human race to the oldest commandment: 'increase and multiply.'

To argue this, the Professor gives a parable in the Malthusian style.

"It is conceivable, he says, that at some period in history the production of the food should have been exactly sufficient to meet the wants of the population, that the makers of artificial

---
* February, 1888, p. 161 et seq.

commodities should have amounted to just the number supportable by the surplus food of the agriculturists."—(Thus a perfect communistic society, the ideal of the "commune").— "And as there is no harm,"—says the Professor, finishing this picture,—"in adding another monstrous supposition to the foregoing, let it be imagined that every man, woman and child, was perfectly virtuous and aimed at the good of all as the highest personal good."—(Thus complete and perfect altruism.) —"In that happy land the natural (read "material") man would have been finally put down by the ethical man. There would have been no competition, but the industry of each would have been serviceable to all; nobody being vain and nobody avaricious, there would have been no rivalries; the struggle for existence would have been abolished and the millenium would have finally set in." (But, alas! this perfect altruism, this goal of social evolution, has reckoned without Malthus,—and lo!—with the birth of the first baby,—like the day after the perfect division of communistic equality,— altruism is blown into shreds; for the Professor says):—"It is obvious that this state of things could have been permanent only with a stationary population. Add ten fresh mouths; and as, by the supposition, there was only exactly enough before, somebody must go to short rations. This Atlantis society might have been a heaven upon earth, the whole nation might have consisted of just men, needing no repentance and yet somebody must starve. Reckless Istar, non-moral Nature, would have riven the social fabric. I was once talking with a very eminent physician about the *vis medicatrix naturae*. 'Stuff!' said he, 'nine times out of ten nature does not want to cure the man; she wants to put him in his coffin.' And Istar-Nature appears to have equally little sympathy with the ends of society. 'Stuff!' she wants nothing but a fair field and free play for her darling the strongest."[*]

---

[*] Nineteenth Century, February, 1888, p. 166.

Professor Huxley has forgotten the one principal necessary condition to his theorem, viz:—that, in order to complete the hypothesis, his Atlantis-community,—set up to be knocked down by Istar-Nature,—should be entirely separated from all other societies, cut off from the whole civilized world and totally devoid of all outside help and from all sources in the universe. What his "population" is, and how situated as social organism, with regard to its external social life,—*i.e.* in co-existence with other social organisms,—the professor does not tell, and yet this material element is of absolute consequence in the struggle for existence. This is not less the case with the moral element. If silently working Nature would speak out,—alas! how many cases we should know of atrocious blunders of "eminent physicians" she had to patch up with her own design. But, like his friend, the eminent physician, who would not acknowledge the help he had from Nature's process of adjustment (we may hope not at the cost of his patients)—the eminent professor of physical science ignores that moral checks could mitigate the material struggle for existence; he would not comprehend the power of the moral element which he postulated himself in the exceptional virtuous community he depicted; he forgot that this moral power could thus completely subject egoism to altruism, that there could not be any independent individual sufferings; yes,—thus, that nobody would starve alone, but all and every one, and equally,—if need be;—no struggle for individual existence but the moral struggle of each for the welfare of the others; suffering alike, starving equally, and,—if there is no help coming,—then, finally, sinking all together into eternity. Here the backbone of Istar, the egoistic struggle between individuals, is broken. And, though mankind has not yet reached this state of altruistic Christian perfection, by a very long way, yet, while the perfect altruistic society,—as Professor Huxley himself acknowledges,—is thinkable, so it is equally thinkable that the moral element in such society will maintain its influence against all egoistic temptations of the material struggle for existence,—whatever the Malthusian theory may propound.

The inevitable consequence of the growth of Nature, with regard to sentient species, is evil only from the materialistic point of view, and from an inadequate conception of evil. "Non-moral Nature" is a misnomer,—does not exist. In the sphere of the Moral-Mental organism, the physical evil that comes from Nature is a blessing to humanity. As we have explained before (§ 28, p. 34) there are two sorts of evil—viz: the material or physical evil,—the *objective evil*,—which is necessary in the world to stimulate the moral senses, and give impulse to the Good, and the moral evil, which is the *subjective evil*, as being the corruption of the mind. And, as it is evident that, from a moral point of view, the physical evil,—pain and sorrow,—coming from without, serve to improve the mind, by awakening Conscience and Sympathy, so is corruption of the mind,—the moral or subjective evil,—the doom of humanity.

If the brute creation is subject to the brute struggle for existence, marked by events, which, when viewed from our moral standpoint, would appear as cruelty to sentient nature,—this material struggle only exists in a highly moderated form in the sphere of mankind, where the Moral Element is constantly tempering egoism into altruism. We have seen above that Malthus failed by not taking into proper account the conditions of the co-existence of social organisms,—*i.e.* the material support of international social life,—but the fallacy of the Malthusian theory exists also in its contradiction of the operation of the law of evolution,—*i.e.* of the experienced events of the evolution process of Nature, which secures all that lives adjustment to environments; and this is not only true in organic evolution and in all biological conditions, but especially in the moral social organism.

Malthus has not reckoned with the Moral Element in Nature; that his theory is a figment, the history of Civilization teaches in all its stages. Contrary to Professor Huxley's assertion, this history most decidedly proves, that "the efforts of the ethical man" have greatly modified the egoistic struggle for existence and the non-moral conditions of society, through the regenerating influence of the Moral Element in Nature; "the deep-seated organic impulses which impel the *natural man* to follow his non-moral (*i.e. unnatural*) course," have been gradually making place for the reign of the moral senses, Conscience and Sympathy. Everywhere when morality has waned, through the debasing effects of wealth and luxury, devastating wars and other physical *non-moral* checks on over-population,—there,—notwithstanding these checks,—fierce struggle for material existence issued, and this from want of "the efforts of the ethical man." Phoenecia, Greece and Rome threw out their own national colonies, when they were at the height of power and prosperity. At the waning of their civilization, they were overrun by barbaric hordes, whom, in the selfishness and pride of their one-sided civilization, in the palmy days of their prosperity, they had neglected, and allowed to remain in an uncivilized state on their borders; for, when their material prosperity waned with their civilization, they had to give way to the pressure of these neglected barbarians, whom they had no energy left to withstand.

In the ancient world or among savages or less-civilized nations, where the practice of infanticide was and is a regular custom, and the steady occurrence of famine, pestilence and war (all natural products from a soil uncultivated by the moral senses) were and are so many checks on the dreaded over-population, the gross and most brutal struggle for individual existence was and is at its height,—and non-moral Istar reigned and reigns supreme, with the help of this formidable array of emissaries. The danger to a Nation's civilization lies thus not in the unlimited multiplication of individuals, but in the people's actual degradation in the scale of humanity,—*i.e.* the shortcomings in the individual Moral Senses.

If we turn now to the steady growth of civilization, the progress of private and public morality, which entails the respect and care for human life, in the elimination of all that can shorten it, and the integration of all that can tend to secure peace and industry,—and compare then the result of moral civilization with former and present barbarism, we find the incontestable proofs, that where civilization has put a stop to wholesale extermination,—the hoary check on overpopulation,—there the struggle for existence is kept within the limits of the human strife of individual co-existence and is becoming more restricted within the limits of moral competition.

The population of civilized Europe has more than doubled during this century (in Great Britain alone the population has increased, in the decade from 1871 to 1881 by nearly $3\frac{1}{2}$ millions of souls) and yet there has been, during this century, nowhere in Europe, in any country, real want of food, still less a famine,—where the circulation of trade and the traffic of commodities were not obstructed, whether directly through want of means of communication or indirectly as the results of bad legislation. In fact, no famine is recorded, in modern history, that cannot be traced to the stagnation of proper communication, which impeded the practicable supply of foodstuff from neighbouring countries, whether through war or bad government from want of civilization; more conspicuous is this the case in the stagnation of international trade, caused by international jealousy.

The multiplication of human beings, limited only by the progressive moral restraint of civilization, has gone on in Europe for the last centuries, and no Nation has yet been destroyed by overpopulation. Neither has it been proved of any society, that moral restraint has failed to keep within proper bounds the struggle for existence,—which is the normal condition of the co-existence of individuals (§76)—as long as Nations are at peace and international intercourse has fair play, with fair competition of industry, through intelligence and honesty. And, if governments understand the true meaning of state-socialism, with regard to the industrial class of society who perform manual labour, there is no need for communistic driving to interfere with the stability of society. We must here request the attention of our readers to the statements made before, in sections 48 (p. 71), 76 (p. 133) and 78 (p. 142) with regard to the natural agencies, which guard the internal stability of the social organism and promote its development.

ETHICS, ABSOLUTE AND RELATIVE. A man is living under the Moral Law, when all the faculties of his mind act harmoniously together, for then, in the conflict between the moral element of his nature and the evil arising from his animal propensities, his moral senses and his intellect shall act in unison, to hold the lower animal passions and inclinations in subjugation. To avoid his moral senses being conquered by evil, instead of rising above it, he must procure for himself essential moral surroundings,—which he is able to do by virtue of his free will,—*i.e.* he must ever strive after companionship with the virtuous and diligently watch against any contagious contact with vice or the vicious. We have seen how the vine, with its latent instinct, could feel for support in self-preservation; the man with intelligence, free will and design, is surely competent, prudently to use the feeling tendrils of his Moral Senses, as guidance toward sound moral support in his career through life. Like as the physical organism, in the evolution-process, adapts itself to its environment, so in virtuous surroundings, in social life, man's moral senses are fostered and improved, through adaptation to these surroundings (§17).

The necessity of the moral environment, *i.e.* of the moral element in social life, points to the necessity of *public moral education*, equally compulsory on all members of society, for the propagation of virtue, through the fostering of the individual Moral Senses.

As stated before (§ 39, p. 57), social civilization is the outcome of the moral senses of the individual mind; the adaptation of the moral senses for the conception of the good being transferred from the individual to the whole race. If the moral senses are abortive, it is through man's own weakness, or for want of *moral culture* and *religious discipline* of the mind. Moral culture is the work of *moral education* and the discipline of the mind,—as stated before (§ 24)—is formed by the *Christian Religion*, whose teachings of justice and benevolence combined, constitute the fostering of the moral senses. Thus practical morality issues from the Christian Faith.

Ethics are the manifestations of a Moral Element in Nature, or,—as Mathew Arnold puts it,—of "the power which makes for righteousness." The element of all ethical theories is the force, perceptible in the "evolution of conduct," which tends to reach the highest conduct; "that highest conduct,—says Mr. Herbert Spencer,—in which the evolution of conduct terminates, that is, in which the making of all adjustments of acts to ends, subserving complete individual life (together with all those subserving maintenance of offspring and preparation of them for maturity) not only consist with making of like adjustments by others, but furthers it;"—that highest conduct by which egoism goes up into altruism. This manifestation of an active Moral Element in Nature, in the evolution of conduct to its ultimate form, implies the existence of a *natural law of conduct*, which we have called the Moral Law of Nature. This is Absolute Ethics, while Relative Ethics constitute what is called the Spirit of Law (§ 40, p. 59).

The hedonic system of Ethics is based on the false doctrine that happiness, as the highest good, consists in bodily or material gratification. The pleasures which the pursuits of intellectual and aesthetic achievements entail, come from the consciousness of personal efficiency; these pleasures are thus based on imagination, for the actions which brought on the gratification originated from excitement of impending success, as experienced in former similar pursuits. They are the pleasures resulting from an egoistic self-appreciation. It is obvious that these gratifications neither affect our Conscience nor our Sympathy; they are simply pleasures with which the moral senses have no concern, and miss therefore the criterion of ethical experiences, in which the motive of our actions is the natural impulse of the moral senses toward the Good. The natural eagerness of the moral senses to keep the mind to good actions, is the desirableness of the *peace of mind,* which is the result of stability in the equilibrium of the Moral-Mental organism. Hence the inefficiency of the *hedonic* system in ethics, for peace of mind is a mental condition, which is not obtainable through means adjusted to a speculative end. It admits of no *à priori* specification or definition; of no assumption of intensity, duration or certainty, like the physico-sensual pleasures and pains, for it does not owe its existence to the commensurability of these pleasures and pains. Its relative value cannot be gauged by the proximity of a pleasure or a pain, for it does not belong to the egoistic or empirical, nor to the universalistic hedonism,—*i.e.,* in no way is its condition based on the theory **which** *makes happiness the* **end** *of action.* The happiness of self and others is the result of the natural biological and sociological equilibrium, which is maintained by the **stability of the Moral Senses.** This is the effect of the moral **Element in Nature.**

For reason of the frailty of our mental organism,—through whose faculties, the intention of the Soul is brought into action, by the Moral Senses,—a complete code of rules for the guidance of moral personal conduct is, as yet, not realized. The injunctions to perfection, as constantly instilled into our mind, through the persistent action of the Moral Element in

Nature,—being brought to our consciousness, through our moral senses,—are, as stated before (§§ 39 and 40) only *relatively* obeyed by the actual man, under the existing material conditions of society,—ethical requirements being necessarily affiliated upon actual physical particularities. But, as Mr. Herbert Spencer says:—"Though the particular requirements to be fulfilled for perfect individual well-being must vary along with variations in the material conditions of each society, certain general requirements have to be fulfilled by the individuals of all societies." These general requirements are the manifestation of a common ground on which individual Moral Senses agree. This common ground is the domain of *absolute ethics*, where the "requirements to be fulfilled for *perfect individual well-being*" are moulded by the Moral Senses, under the direct influence of the Moral Element in Nature. On the other hand, *relative ethics*, as said above, are formed by those injunctions of the Moral Senses which are only relatively obeyed by man, under actual social conditions.

Hygienic Laws. Conducts, physically considered with regard to self, belong to the requirements of the body, which are comprehended by what is scientifically called hygienic or sanitary laws. These are the rules, indicated by Nature, for the physical preservation of the body, as well as for the conservation of society. Physical purity, personal and public cleanliness are *social duties*, for they form the basis of the sanitary laws of Nature. *Mens sana in corpore sano.* Moreover, civilization is the formulation of conduct as well as the limitation to conduct, in order to maintain the natural ethical relations between self and society. Hence bodily and social cleanliness is an essential mark of civilization.

The Standard of Ethics and the Spirit of Law. We have said before, that Moral Law of Nature is the term for Absolute Ethics and that the term Spirit of Law indicates the condition of Relative Ethics (§40). In support of this definition, we may quote the following passage from Mr. Herbert Spencer's "Data of Ethics," where he says:—"This division of ethics (viz: the set of regulations concerning *justice*) considered under its absolute form, has to define the equitable relations among perfect individuals who limit one another's spheres of action by co-existing, and who achieve their ends by co-operation. It has to do much more than this. Beyond justice between man and man, justice between each man and the aggregate of men has to be dealt with by it. The relations between the individual and the State, considered as representing all individuals, have to be deduced."

These relations between the individual and the State—(which have been dealt with above, under the head *Social Organism*, in sections 43-61)—says Mr. Herbert Spencer,—"having been, in their private and public aspects, considered as maintained under *ideal* conditions and been formulated,—there come to be dealt with the analogous relations under *real* conditions;—absolute justice being the standard, relative justice has to be determined, by considering how near an approach may, under present circumstances, be made to it."

While war continues and injustice is done between States; while militant organization, no less than militant action, is irreconcileable with pure equity,—there is yet the Moral Law of social evolution, the standard of absolute ethics, which is represented, in the development of the moral-mental organism of man, by the Moral Senses. These formulate the requirements to be fulfilled for perfect individual well-being, by impressing on the mind the conception of Justice and Benevolence; thus upholding to our consciousness the vivid ideal of *righteousness*, after which Relative Ethics,—which is correlative to the Spirit of Law,—is moulding practical rules for our guidance. Relative ethics is changing at every state of social evolution,—keeping pace with the correlative civilization,—determining the "range of variation within which it is possible to approach nearer to or to diverge further from the requirements of absolute equity." * This range of variation is represented by what we call the Spirit of Law (§40).

Ethics counterbalancing Evil through the Moral Senses. Ethical science is the specification of the individual conduct of associated human beings, as evolved through the development of the normal mind under the influence of the Moral Senses,— *i.e.* of the mind in permanent consciousness of the spontaneous exercise of its moral faculties of conscience and sympathy. These duly proportioned moral faculties,—while each yielding, when in action, its quantum to form the state of that mental satisfaction, called *peace of mind*,—are consequently so constituted, that defects in any one of these actions bring also their quantum of *mental pain*, caused by the disharmony, then occasioned, in the moral consciousness (§§ 15-24).

By virtue of this constitution of the faculty of the Moral senses, Evil is detected and neutralized in the mind, as these emotions of moral "satisfaction" and "pain" of the morally conscious mind,—*i.e.* of the mind with well developed moral senses,—are the moral guides to conduct, by fitting or not fitting in the conscious adjustment of acts to ends (§§ 30 and 31). It is thus that the motives of actions, that are classed as "moral" and "immoral," are tested, and the mental-process is formed by which the adjustment of acts to ends becomes the subject-matter of ethical judgment, for the detection and discarding of evil from the mind.

This *Test of Good and Evil* consists in the ability of the Moral Senses to combat evil in the mind, through the consciousness of the Good in the Moral Ego, when the struggle between the moral and material elements of the human nature takes place. We had occasion to demonstrate this before when treating of the Moral-Mental Organism of man (§ 5), of the elements of the good (§§ 12-16), Virtue and Evil (§§ 17 and 18),

---

* HERBERT SPENCER. "The Data of Ethics," § 107. *The Scope of Ethics.*

and of the origin of evil and its control (§§ 19-24); to these sections we must here refer our readers.

Egoism and *Altruism*. *Ethical problems.* When viewing self-preservation and self-gratification *(egoism)* in contraposition with the good of others *(altruism)*, several questions arise which may be solved by the test of the Moral Senses, described above. This test is applicable on the principle that good conduct is guided by the perfect harmony of Conscience and Sympathy (§ 14). Conduct thus, which is truly satisfying one of the Moral Senses, is ethically right, as long as it does not excite the other to opposition;—in other words, conduct by which one of these senses is in direct war with the other, stifles the other, and cannot be called ethically right, as it is not complying with the condition of righteousness (§§ 15 and 16).

The ethical problems, which arise from the counterpoise of egoism with altruism, find their solution when tested by the harmony of the Moral Senses, which is the necessary mark of ethical guidance.

Taking the Moral Senses, as above explained, for guidance we arrive at the following Ethical Rules of Conduct, viz:—

I. Even the most natural conduct, as the preservation of life and health, is,—as all conducts of the conscious moral being,—subordinate to this test of the moral senses. For instance: acts committed against others, in *self-defence* are *right*, for they are reconcileable with Conscience, without bringing this in disharmony with Sympathy. On the other hand, they become contrary to sympathy, the moment they over-reach the limits of necessity, and are consequently *wrong*, ethically considered, for then the harmony of the moral senses is broken. Hence all acts in pursuit of *vengeance*,—*i.e.* without the necessary end of self-preservation,—are contrary to the moral sense of sympathy and never leave Conscience satisfied; thus vengeance is immoral, ethically placing the revenger from purely vindictive motive on the same level as the original evil-doer.

II. It is simple justice to self, and in sympathy for those entrusted to our personal care, or dependent, for their support, on our life and work, to do all that is consistent with self-preservation and to avoid what is injurious to life and health. In such cases what is pleasant is not necessarily wrong. But, not right, and often injurious to self, are acts originated from purely selfish motives, without benefit to others,—*i.e.* acts without combining justice to self with sympathy to others,—for such acts, having no counter-check in the mind, degenerate into intemperance. Self-gratification is never enjoyed by the morally developed mind when any conflict between the Moral Senses is the result, for the gratification would be barren of the Good,—and, as we showed before (§23), the genesis of moral consciousness is the essential truth that *outside the good there is no real happiness.*

III. As to the question, how far can self-sacrifice, ethically, be carried out in each case?—the answer is thus:— as long as the sacrifice is entirely that of one's own interest,— *i.e.* not injurious in any way to the interest of others, who have equal or better claim on our service; if carried on further, then, self-sacrifice can become injustice. With other words:— as long as sympathy does not suppress justice, self-sacrifice is virtue.

A mother who starves herself to death, to keep her children alive, and thus renders them helpless orphans;—is she acting rightly? Here motherly love has so overwhelmed her conscience, that this was powerless to protect her self-interest, may be, even for the benefit of others. Ah! Sympathy has many dispensations. When acting against self-interest, Benevolence will often suppress Conscience; which gave occasion to the doctrine that *obligation of justice to self does not exist.* But, though we are not able to condemn sympathy in many instances of self-sacrifice, yet our Conscience is not at fault, when denying the unconditional ethical value of this doctrine..

IV. Other problems, with regard to the test of the Moral Senses on acts of benevolence, are put by Mr. Herbert Spencer in the following words: "How far shall a person who has misbehaved be grieved by showing aversion to him?" "Shall one whose action is to be reprobated have the reprobation expressed to him or shall nothing be said?" "Is it right to annoy by condemning a prejudice, which another displays?"* These problems must be solved by the same arguments which answer the question:—"Whether to avoid inflicting pain, personal feelings should be sacrificed and how far sacrificed?" To this the Test of the Moral Senses answers:—Personal feelings which are matured by Conscience and Sympathy should never be sacrificed, but the impulses, which import to others actions called unjust or actions called unkind, must ever be suppressed. These latter are known by the criterion of the moral senses, as defined above. For instance;—decidedly condemned by the moral senses are those actions, which, though not directly aggressive, are *unjust* indeed, through simply passively maintaining prejudiced opinions or withholding due praise, leaving merit unrewarded; *unkind* indeed, by simply passively maintaining an inequitable claim, a wrong opinion, or sometimes, by refusing a request.

In solving ethical problems, of these classes, in which several meanings are hidden, the Test of the Moral Senses gives the following general moral rules, viz: 1° When Justice requires the infliction of "pain," no more shall be enforced than is necessary to comply with the decrees of Conscience,— *i.e.* without violating the principles of Sympathy, which are warnings against cruelty.—2° Where Conscience is stifled by Sympathy, there the maintaining of any principle, in the desire for another's benefit, is unwarranted.

V. Through the same test we find an answer to the question:—To what extent, under given circumstances, shall

---

* " Data of Ethics" § 110, Chapter XVI. The Scope of Ethics, p. 567.

private welfare be subordinate to public welfare? To this and kindred questions, the answer must be given for every particular circumstance. After having analyzed and subdivided the problem into questions, on each particular topic, which can be responded to by simply "yes" or "no," the moral senses in their necessary harmony,—as depicted above,—form combined the touch-stone of these ayes and noes. By summing up these votes, the balance gives the final verdict on the complicated problem. This verdict is the outcome of justice and benevolence combined.

VI. There is a class of ethical problems so mixed up with emotions of different kinds, that it seems difficult to trace the dictates of the Moral Senses for their solution. Of these we give the following specimen to conclude this series of problems.

A vessel full of passengers is wrecked. Life can be saved only by the boats of the vessel; a struggle for life toward the boats is natural. Fathers think of their families at home, of which they are the only support; on their life the maintenance of many solely depends:—for their families' sake, the struggle for life of these men is more than the selfish impulse of self-preservation. But, hark!—above the tumult of this struggle for the boats, rings the peremptory order: "Women and Children first!" This order is echoed by many voices, demanding that the women and children, before all, be placed safely in the boats. Nobody objects, and if there be any brutish resistance to this demand, it is promptly put down by the majority. Now, why should this be so? Why should by common consent, the women and children be saved before and, may be, at the cost of the lives of these fathers of families, who are anxiously claiming their rescue, not for themselves, but for the poor helpless beings dependent on them for existence and to whom the loss of father or husband may be fatal for ever;—with these useful lives those of the women and children on board must rank lower in comparison:—how is this now to be reconciled, logically with common sense and ethically with the moral senses? The answer is simply this:—It is *justice* to give the weak and helpless the better chance; and does not *benevolence* sanction this act of justice? Here thus Conscience and Sympathy fully agree, which is the cause of the spontaneous sanction of Common Sense.

In these few ethical problems, we have tried to explain the functions of the Moral Senses, as trustworthy guides to the normally developed and morally disciplined mind. But this blissful moral discipline of the human mind is attainable only through earnest effort and diligent training. This moral training of the mind,—essential for the completion of our moral organization,—*i.e.* to make it fit for the impulses of the moral Senses,—is, as we have said before (§24), the province of the Christian Religion;—the religion which, operating, through Divine Love, in the human Moral-Mental Organism, teaches us to adore God through Nature, and shows us, how Eternal Justice is mitigated by Mercy, for the gradual elevation of mankind, through the individual Moral Senses, Conscience and Sympathy.

RELIGION.

The Spiritual World. Nothing exists that is not manifested in Nature. The outward surrounding conditions, called the physical or visible universe is not separated from what is called the spiritual or unseen universe; their union is man, through his moral mental organism. The one is subject to our physical senses, the other is the domain of our internal life of consciousness; the one serves to stimulate the moral senses, by opposing them through the physical element of passions engendered from materialistic egotism,—the other is the source of the Moral Element fostering these senses through Christian Faith.

Spiritual World is simply a name applied to those phenomena, which human intellect is not able to grasp through the physical senses of the mind, but which are the more plainly conceivable through the moral senses, in proportion to the development and strength of these senses. These, in reality, far outgrow the power of the physical senses, in the faculties of discrimination, penetration and sagacity, through the instinctive intuition of consciousness,—the necessary result of the evolved instinct of the moral-mental organism. External influences of perception, sensation and experience are, as said before, stimulants for the moral senses, which are the links between the natural and the so-called supernatural,—between the material element and the moral element in Nature.

In the well-developed mind, consciousness, as generated from instinctive conviction, is far more trustworthy than the conception received from the external influences or sensations, which may result from numerous illusionary, and thus deceitful, surroundings beyond our control. It is no uncommon occurrence, in the civilized world, that thoroughly scientific men, constantly applying the most rigid logical thoughts in the investigation of empirical science, are, at the same time, convinced believers in the Divine mission of Christ as the preparation of the human race for its exalted destination. They can conceive moral facts, through their moral senses, as clearly and completely as they can discern any physical fact with their physical senses;—this proves that the human mind is the living link between the visible world and the unseen universe. We will try to demonstrate this further in the following pages.

Evolution of Religion. The course of the Moral Element in Nature is marked by the religions on Earth. The different Religions,—developed with the evolution of the human mind,—which have left their impressions in the history of mankind, are as many indications of the course the process of development of the moral senses has taken, when carried on by the main current of the Moral Element,—of which the main actions have thus been marked. Though countless eddies, formed by the conditions of societies, may have caused many local counter-currents and whirlpools in the main-stream, yet the head-current goes steadily onward to its destination. In all and every winding, the token is manifest of the creature craving, with outstretched arms, for communion with its Creator.

Religion is thus co-existent with the Moral Senses. It originates, grows, ennobles and transcends with the Moral-Mental Organism of man. Like Ethics in social life, it is, in the individual life, the manifestation of the Moral Element in Nature.

There is an intuitive predisposition of the mind, in all stages of mental development, to presuppose a *moral cause* behind the physically experienced phenomenon. This predisposition is the origin of religion in its most primitive conception. The savage who, falling down a precipice, ascribes the failure of his foothold to the unappeased Spirit, surely does not lack the experience as to the physical cause of the unsafety of the jungle-path; through this he so often crept in the active pursuit of his material life, since the days he began to measure his strength with the lower brutes or with his own fellow-creatures, the enemies of his tribe; but, what his actual mental conception ascribed as the interposition of the revengeful Spirit is not the physical cause of his fall,—which he knows too well, by his own empirical science,—but the *moral cause, i.e.* the temporary distraction of his mind, which caused his foot to take the wrong ledge.

With the development of the Moral-Mental Organism, as stated before (§ 5), the struggle between the animal nature and the moral senses sets in. The animal or material element has its visible basis in physical phenomena, but the moral element must seek for support in a postulated moral cause; the first is supported by material food, strengthening the animal form, while the stimulant of imagination is sweeping up the egoistic passions in their assault on the moral element;—the latter, which is the spiritual element,—*i.e.* the soul,—is kept awake in the mind, through the stimulating effects of the moral senses, conscience and sympathy, from which emanates the faith in a supernatural support. Hence the natural craving or impulse, inherent in every human mind, for something to venerate, for a Supreme Being to whom the soul could elevate itself to arrive at a better and more enduring existence.

This Being to whom the human nature feels an inherent attraction, for support, and this better existence, to which he feels an inherent longing, as a rest from the struggles of life, are naturally depicted to his conception in conformity with the actual state of his mental development, moral and intellectual. For the savage, not arrived at that stage of mental evolution, described above (§ 5) as the Moral-Mental Organism, his God and his Heaven can only be what his lower materialistic conception of the inferior mental condition of the Physico-Mental Organism (§ 4) could allow him to conceive.

The further development of the Moral Senses generates in the mind the consciousness of moral obligations, which leads to the natural conclusion of the existence of a Supreme Power ordaining these obligations. This belief finds expression in various religious *forms* and *dogmas*, which are conditioned by the state of civilization and the freedom and culture of the mind.

The sensual influences of the imagination shaped the formalities and forms of worship of the infant man. And as imagination is apt to upset reason, and is often enticing man to act against his moral senses (§ 22), so the primitive savage religious formalities of the heathen worship,—the product of imagination,—have remained in the religions of some civilized people, long after the developing moral senses have exalted and toned the mind into real faith in the Creator. Such is the power of imagination, that, in spite of the protest of intellect and moral senses against this abuse of the Divine Element of Faith, the habit of idolatry, originated in fetichism,—the crudest forms of religions,—still continues in a refined form and with many apologies, in the Christian Religion, thus constituting an *idolatrous christianity*. As with the *form*, so also with the *dogma*. Ethical conducts are evolved from the impulses of the Moral Senses, while religious dogmas are the consolidation, in some ideal forms, of the moral sentiments originated through these impulses. While ethical science is explaining *how* and *why* certain modes of conduct are naturally beneficial and other naturally detrimental to the moral being,—and thus continually preparing the mind for higher development,—dogmatic religion has already stereotyped the first impulses of Moral Senses, in their infant form, with little chance for their further development through the evolving moral ideas of the human mind.

Following the foregoing propositions to their full consequences, we arrive at a standpoint, from where we can plainly overlook and comprehend the vast field of development, traversed by the evolution of religion, through all the stages of human mental and moral development, until the development of the Christian Faith, the only moral conception which could satisfy the craving of Conscience and Sympathy combined.

It is through Religion that the human mind is to be kept in culture and discipline, in order to foster the moral senses in their struggle with the material animal propensities of the species; but the province of religion is to discipline and strengthen and not to suppress the Moral Senses, by thwarting Common Sense which is the logic of Conscience and Sympathy combined (§ 34).

This is the spirit of Christianity in its natural pure state, as evolved, with the moral organism of man, from the primordial germ placed by the Creator in Nature, and forecasting the highest moral development after the image of Christ. This is the religion, which is not based on belief or imagination, but on the Christian Faith,—(described hereafter)—as being the natural religion of the evolved individual mental organism, stimulating the Moral Senses, through the individual moral responsibility it enjoins.

The individual moral responsibility of the human being to his Creator is the consequence of the Divine impulses, imparted to him through his Moral Senses. This is abundantly demonstrable. As surely as consciousness reveals to me, in the ordinary moral exercise of the mind, *myself* and an objective world *not myself*, so plainly it reveals to my mind, through my Conscience and Sympathy, my objective moral obligations,— and consequently, the conviction of a moral power in Nature and a Supreme Lawgiver. This inspiration of God through our moral senses is the divine revelation of a Moral Element in Nature.

The main branches of Eastern Religion. As we have noted above, the development of Religion is the outcome of the evolution of the human mind, in its course of development into Christianity, by keeping pace with the development of the Moral Senses. Deviations from this main course of the moral-mental development are the Buddhism, Mohammedanism and other Asiatic Religions. These are the eddies and whirlpools in the main current of the Moral Element in Nature, caused by peculiar social conditions, while the overweening Eastern imagination dwarfed the developing moral-mental organism into monstrous eccentricities of asceticism and sensuality.

Mohammedanism sprang out of the revolt of pure intellect against the mechanical religion of the Kaabah,—the old Arabian monotheism, which had lost itself completely in the sensual worship of idols. Mohammed had all the benefit of the oldest history and of logic on his side. To re-establish the old Abrahamic creed historical traditions were in the way, and the criminal quarrels between the Roman and Greek Churches gave him good reason not to trust to the then called Christian Church, with her compromise with the heathen mythology, and image-worship. The God-Father, the God-Son and the worship of the "Queen of Heaven,"—which latter had caused the secession of the *Nestorians* (among whom Mohammed himself had his early religious education)—seemed no logic creed for the new religion;—this being based on strict monotheism with the purification of the worship of the one Almighty God from every tincture of idolatry. "To give God a mother" was in the view of Mohammed the most despisable of all forms of idolatry. The wild Arabian hordes that overran Syria found here a logical support to their fierce fanaticism. Like as Shâkyamuni Gâutama, the founder of Buddhism, had been the leader of the reaction against the caste-theory of Brahmanism, so Mohammed was the mouth-piece of the revolting common-sense against the idolatry of the Kaabah. Both were incarnations of the developing power of the mental evolution-process,—manifestations of the developing moral senses.

Mohammed consolidated his doctrines against the unsympathetic prejudices of the Hebrew tribes,—whose historical traditions were adverse to any amalgamation of their monotheistic creed with that of the kindred but less civilized Arabian tribes,—and, on the other hand, taking advantage of the absurd dogmatic quarrels and corruption among the christians, soon established a powerful overwhelming popular creed. This popularity originated especially with its system of perfect individual equality among all Mussulmans,—*i.e.* all who hold the faith of Islam,—and flourished on the same soil of human enthusiasm as Buddhism, at its height of reaction against the caste-preachings of Brahminism.

Alike Christianity in the West, Buddhism overspread Eastern Asia. About A. D. 65 the first Hindoo Buddhist missionaries arrived in China, and Shâkyamuni's teachings of universal brotherhood supplanted soon, as popular religion, the conditional Ethics of China's greatest philosopher known by foreign historians under the name of *Confucius.*

Confucianism, in fact, is not a religion, but was originally a system of politico-moral philosophy, principally with regard to the public duties of the government toward the people and of the individual with regard to the State. Confucius, born B. C. 551, was a great historical compiler and commentator. His maxim was: "Reading without thought is fruitless, and thought without reading dangerous;"—his genius was thus conditioned by erudition; he was, in his time, the *renaissance* of the old Chinese literature and antiquity;—he modestly said of himself, "I am an editor and not an author." By thus bridling his originative powers he forced his intellect into the furrows of the *doctrinaire.* His political career was not a success; at the age of 55 years he was prime minister of his native State, the little kingdom of Lu,—one of the confederate States then occupying the territories of what is, at present, the Eighteen Provinces of the Chinese Empire,—but, failing in the practical establishment of his theories, modelled on the alleged perfection of the oldest historical government of the State, he gave himself entirely over to the *doctrinaire* statesman's philosophy. His doctrines ever remained political ethics, venerated as sure guides to perfect government, but never practicably followed by those in actual power.

The philosophy of Confucius which is an ethical materialism, serve as a medium of connection between Buddhism and Taoism, forming with these two the conglomeration, called the *San-Kiao,* the "Three Religions," which is at present the popular religion of China,—if ever such a mixture of sceptic philosophy, uniting spiritualism with materialistic idolatry, could be called by this name.

Taoism is called the philosophical system, or religion, founded by *Li-erl,* who lived in the sixth century before

Christ. He was contemporary with Confucius, but senior to him in years and in the philosophical career. Hence Li-erl is also called Laut-sz, the "Old Master," in distinction with his younger rival Confucius. He called his religious system *Tau*, which signifies "Reason," without however the system itself being rational. The Tau philosophy teaches, as attainable to the Taoist, a materialistic corporal immortality in the abodes of the genii. Alchemy, with the pursuits to find the elixir of life, originated from the Taoist belief that the body could, by certain means of discipline, become invulnerable and immortal; thus the philosophy of "Reason" degenerated into a system of magical imposture.*

The leading principle of Taoism, says Doctor Martin, is that every species of matter possesses a soul—a subtile essence endowed with individual conscious life. Freed from this grosser elements, the spiritual element becomes the genii that preside over the various departments of nature. Some wander at will through the realms of space, endowed with a protean facility of transformation—others, more pure and ethereal, rise to the regions of the stars, and take their places in the firmament. Thus the five principal planets are called by the names of the "five elements," from which they are believed to have originated, and over which they are regarded as presiding. The stars are divinities, and their motions control the destinies of men and things—a notion which has done much to inspire the zeal of the Chinese for recording the phenomena of the heavens. A theogony like this is rich in the elements of poetry; and most of the machinery in Chinese works of imagination is, in

---

* W. A. P. MARTIN, D.D., LL.D., President of the Tung-Wen College at Peking. "*The Hanlin Papers*," Edit. 1880. JOSEPH EDKINS, D.D. "*Religion in China.*" IDEM. "*Chinese Buddhism*," London, 1880. ERNEST T. EITEL, Ph. D. *Buddhism: its Historical, Theoretical and Popular Aspects.* Hongkong. 1884. MARCUS DODS, D.D. *Muhammed, Buddha and Christ,* London 1877.

  Further commended works on Oriental Non-Christian Religious Systems are: BEAL's Buddhism in China. DAVID's Budhism. DOUGLAS' Confucianism and Taoism. HARDY's **Manual of Buddhism.** MAURICE, Religions of the World.

fact, derived from this source. The *Liauchai*, for example, a collection of marvellous tales, which, in their general character may be compared to the Metamorphoses of Ovid, is largely founded on the Taoist Mythology. In accordance with the materialistic character of the Taoist sect, nearly all the gods whom the Chinese regard as presiding over their material interests, originated with this school. The god of rain, the god of fire, the god of medicine, the god of agriculture, and the *lares* or kitchen gods, are among the principal of this class. A system which supplies deities answering to the leading wants and desires of mankind cannot be uninfluential; but, in addition to the strong motives that attract worshippers to their temples, the Taoist priesthood possess two independent sources of influence. They hold the monopoly of geomancy, a superstitious art—(the so-called *"fung-shui,"*—literary: "wind" and "water")—which professes to select on scientific principles, those localities that are most propitious for building and burial; and they have succeeded in persuading the people that they alone are able to secure them from annoyance by evil spirits."*

Transcending the conglomeration of the San-Kiao and not belonging to any of the "Three Religions" (all three equally idolatrous) there are luminous traces in the Chinese thoughts, of faith in a Supreme and Almighty God, the ruler of the past, the present and the future. Even the positive philosopher Confucius,—who sneered at the silly ceremonies of idolatrous creeds, and who advised his disciples to "keep the gods at a distance" or to "keep out of their way,"—exhibited this characteristic of the Moral-Mental Organism of man. When he had completed his compilation and commentaries in the laborious work, which is known by the names of *Shu-King* and the "Sacred Books,"— he assembled his disciples on the sacrificial hill; here he erected an altar, and placing on it the edition of this great work, which he had just completed at the age of seventy years,—

---
* Dr. Martin, l. c. page 146.

he fell on his knees and devoutly returned thanks to *Shangti*, the "Supreme Ruler" for having had life and strength granted him to accomplish so vast an enterprise for the future guidance of his countrymen, employing Heaven to grant that the benefit his countrymen may receive from his work might not be small. In a native illustrated biography of Confucius, the sage is represented in this attitude of supplication; a beam of light, like a rainbow, descends on the sacred volumes, while his disciples are standing around him with demonstrative admiration.

These traces of religious veneration of a Supreme Being, under the name of Shangti lay deeper in the heart of the people than a single instance of enthusiastic outburst of Confucius, in the height of his author's pride. The worship of Shangti is based on the popular conviction that, beyond the visible heaven, there exists some unseen Power governing the universe, after certain incomprehensible rules, with a divine will. Shangti is the first of the five objects of veneration,—(the other four are the earth, the emperor, parents, and teachers)—and is worshipped only by the Emperor. The common people worship *T'ien* (which means simply "Heaven") by burning a stick of incense every evening under the open sky, and also at marriage ceremonies; none but the Emperor is worthy of offering at the Altar of *Shangti*. At the South side of the Imperial city, a large marble terrace containing this altar in the open air is built in a simple but imposing style. The worship of Shangti admits of no idols; a tablet inscribed with the characters *Shang-Ti*,—"Supreme Ruler,"—represents the Deity; a bullock is offered, and the Emperor, in person, prostrates himself before the burnt sacrifice.

The conception of a Supreme Ruler of the Universe, equal to the pure Christian conception of God, had thus, of old, generated in the mind of this ancient people; but the idolatry, fostered by the San-Kiao, caused the exalted conception of Shangti to dissolve into the saint-worship of Buddhism, the scepticism of Confucianism and the fetichism of Taoism.

This most illogical conglomeration of thoughts without doctrine, held together by imagination, thus constitutes a living testimony,—as a warning to mankind,—of belief without faith, when the guidance of the developed Moral Senses is wanting.

Ancestral Worship. The politico-ethical doctrines of Confucius were based principally on the demands of Intellect, without due regard to the dictates of the Moral Senses. His teachings are merely regulations for the keeping of discipline and governmental order among the people. The main argument of his philosophy is expediency; virtues are civil duties in social relations; the end is but material well-being. Without a beginning, and void of the pursuits of moral truths—thus of intellect and feeling combined,—the philosophy of Confucius is far inferior to Plato's, while it never reached the generalizing genius of Aristotle. The extent and permanence of the influence of Confucianism as a popular creed in China are due to the conservatism and seclusion of this people. Falling short of the conception of a Supreme Ruler in the Creator, it places paternal rights on the Divine throne, for piety and worship, as a substitute for God. Its doctrines with regard to parental rights far overshoot the mark and have dwarfed the holy feelings of parental responsibility into vile parental egoism and tyranny. Parental rights in China include all, even the life of the child; they are valid, without any mitigation, through the whole lifetime, recognizing no coming of age of the child. The father provides his son with food, clothes, dwelling and a wife, and the son is bound to remit all his earnings into his parents' hands. The child, natural or adopted, is not alone during the whole lifetime of the parents under tutelage of the father, but the exigencies of the parental rights continue after the death of the father, in ruinous obsequies and ancestral worship. Thus the sacred Parental Rights are abused by detracting them from the benefit of the child to serve the ambition of the parents, while the sublime sentiment of filial piety is made the instrument of parental egoism.

A comparative view of Buddhism. The two cardinal principles of Buddhist philosophy, as stated in the Buddhist work, called in Chinese the Kin-kang-king, or "Diamond Classics," are: (1) The miseries of existence with its struggles in the material forms into which the soul is doomed to perpetual transmigration, to live in a sensuous world with its deceptive phenomena. (2) The Nirvâna, a state of material non-existence and unconsciousness of the soul, which constitutes the only way of deliverance from the miseries of existence, caused through the interminable transmigration of the soul; Nirvâna being gained through the unlimited practice of charity and ascetic exercises. It is obvious, that without this postulate of the metempsychosis, there would be no occasion for the Nirvâna. The Buddhist philosophy, thus, first adopts an unavoidable state of relentless misery, and then knows no other way of escape than the total extinction of sentiency and, consequently, spiritual and corporal inconsistency with pain. This is Buddhism as a Moral Philosophy.

The theory of metempsychosis as adopted by Buddhist philosophy is a modification of the pantheistic dogma of Brahmanism that all Nature is animate. The soul which, during its lifetime in corporal form, indulged in selfishness, lusts and passions, will be subject to innumerable births, according to its moral condition. Every breathing being will, after death, be re-born in accordance with the general tendency of its inner life. "The being who is still subject to birth,—says one of the Buddhist writings,*—may at one time sport in the garden of a dêva, and at another be cut in a thousand pieces in hell; at one time he may be Maha Brahma, and at another a degraded outcast," etc. Only those who have succeeded in destroying all thoughts and feeling, by means of ascetic exercises and mental abstraction, are saints and will rest after death, for they are freed from all distinction of name or

HARDY. "Manual of Buddhism," p. 454.

form. "In vain, says Dr. Eitel, we search Buddhist literature for a metaphysical treatment of this deeply interesting problem. In vain we search for a distinct notion of the origin of each individual soul, which the Vedanta philosophy placed in Brahma." *

The fundamental principles, evolved from the two abovementioned root-principles of the Buddhist system, are the so-called "Four Great or Excellent Truths," stated in the "Diamond Classics" as follows:—(1) That in all existence there is sorrow: consequently, existence must be extinguished.—(2) That all existence results from attachment to life, or desire.—(3) That existence may be extinguished by extingushing desire.—(4) That desire may be extinguished by following the path to Nirvâna, which is the peace of individual non-existence,—the goal of evolution for Buddhism.

Let us see now what the "four great truths" of Christianity are, as compared with Buddhism. *

In Christianity, the theory of the Moral Senses, as taught by Nature, finds its conclusion in the following Christian principles, viz:—(1) That in all existence there is sorrow, brought on by Evil, which is physical (incidental) or moral.—(2) That physical or so-called incidental evil is necessary for the stimulation of the Moral Senses, in the struggle between the material and the Moral nature of man, but that moral evil is the corruption of the Moral Senses through Desire.—(3) That sorrow, caused by moral evil, must be avoided by subjugating desire.—(4) That the only bridle to desire is the combined action of the Moral Sense, conforming with the Christian Faith. The Christian Nirvâna represents thus the peace of mind, attainable through the perfect harmony of Conscience and Sympathy, the complete *altruism*, which is the goal of Evolution on Earth (§§ 23—28).

It was the natural revolt against the despotic exclusiveness of the sacerdotal caste-religion of Brahma and the sufferings of

---

* Dr. E. J. EITEL. "Buddhism, its historical, theoretical and popular aspects." Edit. 1885, p. 69 et seq.

fellow-creatures, with this caste-distinction in perpetuity,—which the sacerdotal caste used to confirm their own supremacy,—that occasioned the Buddhist theory of kindred feeling and equality between all fellow-creatures. The leader of this reformatory movement against Brahmanism was Siddartha Gâutama; he was the son of Suddhodana, a rajah of the Shâkya tribe, who reigned in Kapilavastu, a few days' journey North of Benares. The names *Shâky-a-muni* and *Buddha* under which he is known, are titles;—the former means the Muni or Sage of the Shâkya tribe, while Buddha means the "Enlightened."* The legendary accounts of the birth of Siddartha Gâutama and his incarnation as a Buddha are myths of later formation, when the Buddhist philosophy was adopting the form of a popular religion. Hence the striking similarity of many details and incidents of Buddha's life with the life of Christ, as reported by the gospels. Doctor Eitel † gives the following account of this apparent similitude :—" Shâkyamuni Buddha—we are told—came from heaven, was born of a virgin, welcomed by angels, received by an old saint who was endowed with prophetic vision, presented in a temple, baptised with water and afterwards baptised with fire, he astonished the most learned doctors by his understanding and answers, he was led by the spirit into the wilderness, and having been tempted by the devil, he went about preaching and doing wonders. The friend of publicans and sinners, he is transfigured on a mount, descends to hell, ascends up to heaven,—in short, with the single exception of Christ's crucifixion, almost every characteristic incident in Christ's life is also to be found narrated in the Buddhist traditions of the life of Shâkyamuni—Gâutama Buddha. And yet, this Buddha lived and died 275 or even 543 years before Christ! Are we to conclude then, that Christ—as a certain sceptic would make us

---

* The numerous names and titles of the Buddha are elaborately explained in WILSON's Works, Vol. II, pp. 9 and 10; and HARDY's Manual of Buddhism, p. 354.
† l. c. pp. 15 and 29.

believe—went to India, during the eighteen years which intervened between his youth and manhood, and returned, thirty years old, to ape and reproduce the life and doings of Shâkyamuni Buddha? Or are we, who believe in Christ's originality, driven to the miserable subterfuge of assuming—as some Jesuit fathers do—that the devil, foreknowing the several details of the promised Messiah's life, anticipated him and all the details of his life by his own caricature in Shâkyamuni Buddha? Unfortunately for the sceptic who would delight in proving Christ to have been the ape of Buddha, it can be proved, that almost every single tint of this Christian colouring which Buddhist tradition gives to the life of Buddha, is of comparatively modern origin. There is not a single Buddhist manuscript in existence which could vie, in antiquity and undoubted authenticity, with the oldest codices of the gospels. Besides, the most ancient Buddhist classics contain scarcely any details of Buddha's life, and none whatever of those above mentioned peculiarly Christian characteristics. Hardly any of the above given legends, which claim to refer to events that happened many centuries before the beginning of our Christian era, can be proved to have been in circulation earlier than the fifth century after Christ. 'A biography of Buddha,—says Oldenberg,—has not come down to us from ancient times, from the age of the Pâli texts, and, we can safely say, no such biography was in existence then.'" With regard to the source from which those apparently Christian elements flowed into and mingled with Buddhist traditions concerning the life of Buddha, and the circumstances which led thereto,—Doctor Eitel says further:*—"Buddhism was, at an early period, carried to Tibet from Caferistan and Cashmere, where Shivaism and Brahmanism had been for a long time saturating Buddhism to the almost total oblivion of many of its original characteristics. Thus it happened, that Buddhism reached Tibet in an adulterated form, and entering there into an amalgamation with indigenous

---
* l. c. page 29 et seq.

systems of Animism and especially with the necromantic superstitions which have ever been rampant in this country, Tibetan Buddhism departed still farther from the original type of moral asceticism. Nevertheless the spirit of propagandism was astir among the early Buddhists of Tibet as much as among the adherents of Southern Buddhism. Being connected by trade with China, Tibet sent Buddhist emissaries to labour in China even before Buddhism became a recognized power among the Tibetans. The Buddhist Church of Tibet gained its first official recognition during the reign of Lha-lho-lhori (407 A.D.) who claimed to be a lineal descendant of the Shâkya family. About the middle of the fifth century Nestorian missionaries reached Central Asia and made numbers of Buddhist priests of Tibet acquainted with the story of Christ's life and with the ceremonial of the Catholic Church. True to the eclectic instincts of Buddhism, the Tibetan priesthood, then and in subsequent centuries, adopted as many Christian ideas, traditions and ceremonies as they thought compatible with Buddhist orthodoxy. Here we have then the explanation of the above mentioned coincidences in the traditions concerning the life of Buddha with the gospel narratives of Christ's life. Introduced into the Buddhist hagiology of Tibet, these semi-foreign legends speedily found their way into the Buddhist literature of China, and caused generally an adulteration of the original traditions of early Buddhism in Eastern Asia."

Into Japan Buddhism was introduced, via Corea, in the 13th year of the reign of the Japanese Emperor Kin-Mei, Ching-ming, corresponding to 552 A.D. Thus 487 years later than in China, where it was introduced, as said before, about 65 A.D. during the reign of the Chinese Emperor Ming, of the How-Han dynasty.

Buddhism is divided into two broad and general classes, called in China the *Ta-chéng*, Major accomplishment, and *Siao-chéng*, Minor accomplishment. The first comprises the pure philosophical system connected with scientific speculations on the physical system of the universe, based on the stage of development in which natural science existed in India at that time; while the minor part comprehends the dogmatical rituals of the creed, to be followed without any intellectual reasoning or speculation; this includes the paradise with its promises of sensual pleasures and the hell with its eternal tortures.

The original doctrines of Shâkyamuni—Buddha, embodying the essence and substance of Buddhism, were handed down orally, through a series of patriarchs, from generation to generation. It was not until the years 412 to 432 of the Christian era that the whole Buddhist Canon was compiled and fixed in writing.

As it is practically an impossibility that every member of a community should be a priest or professionally a mendicant, Buddhist asceticism had to relax into more practicable and popular means of salvation. And as profound and argumentative philosophical speculations were only attainable by highly educated and developed minds, the common man had to be compensated with the sensual representations of idols and ritualism; while the higher initiated, feeling themselves far above these sensual absurdities, passively suffered their philosophy of Ethics to be transformed into the most idolatrous popular religion and superstition on the face of the earth.

The yearning of the human mind for the halo of lofty spiritual glory, mixed up with the want of weak humanity for something to lean on, in order to reach with some mechanical help this spiritual glory, is amply satisfied in the minor part (the *siao-chêng*,) of Buddhism. Buddhas and Buddhisathwas,—as the principal disciples or apostles of Buddha are called,—are the saviours of the devotees, while monastic institutions combined the charms of holiness,—by which self-denial becomes attractive,—with the ease of a quiet home-life in the convent. This made monastic life a pleasant dream and very desirable for "those whom society can very well spare and is not unwilling to part with." Then there is the doctrine of the *karma*,—which means "act",—and determines the aggregate moral balance-sheet of *good* or *evil* of the life led in each form of the transmigration of the soul. Shâkyamuni Gâutama said, in answer to the Brahman inquiries:—" All sentient beings have their own individual karma, or, the most essential property of all beings is their karma; karma comes by inheritance, not from parentage but from previous births; karma is the cause of all good and evil. . . . It is the difference in the karma that causes the difference in the lot of men, so that some are mean and others are exalted, some are miserable and others happy." Gâutama declared further, that he obtained the Buddhaship "neither by his own inherent power nor by the assistance of the dêvas, but by the meritorious karma of previous births."* Having passed through every form of life, being born as a tree or plant, as a bird, a stag, an elephant, and so on, and having experienced nearly every condition of life, vegetable, animal and human,—he was, after this long long probation, born, at last, into the heaven of the Dêvas, from where Buddhas descend on Earth.

Buddhism, as stated before, is a variation or rather reformation of the old Brahmanical doctrine of the *Véda*,—the oldest code book of Asiatic nations,—the doctrine of emanation, metempsychosis, and final absorption into Brahma. The origin of this dogma is the consciousness of the struggle between the moral and the material elements in Nature,—between the moral senses of man's spiritual nature and his materialistic selfishness, lust and passions, and moreover, the necessity of this struggle to purify and strengthen the soul for communion with its Creator. On this pure conception of the soul, was built the system of the fanciful mysticism of metempsychosis, by Brahmanical priest-craft, which originated the idea of caste, from the priestly craving to identify the Brahman priest-caste more closely with Diety than others. From this tendency originated also the pantheistic conception. Thus it

---
* HARDY. "Manual of Buddhism," p. 445 et seq.

came to pass that a doctrine in its origin full of depth, for soul-elevating religious conceptions, was distorted, through human vanity and selfishness, into a labyrinth of mysticism, which can only afford food for fierce imagination in metaphysical meditations. As the product of Imagination, void of Common Sense, this structure of Metempsychosis affords ample basis for many systems and speculations widely differing in constitution and idiosyncrasy,—from the atheism of D. F. Strausz and the positivism of Comte to the modern Western Buddhism and Spiritualism.*

Of the doctrine of transmigration of the soul in successive degrees of new births on earth, the Caste system is the inevitable consequence. Buddhism, which was meant as a reformation of Brahmanism, abolished Caste, but retained Metempsychosis and its different biological and social conditions of re-births on earth, in distinct gradations, as punishment for sin, and stimulation to virtue. The Buddhist philosophy was thus inconsistent at the outset. If caste distinction held the Hindu people of India in social bondage, at once tyrannical and degrading, Buddhism left them in the far worse moral bondage of inevitable misery on one hand, and, on the other, of sullen despair of the triumph of justice and benevolence in actual life, and of ever escaping the horrifying exactness of this *lex talionis* of the karma, except by physical, intellectual and spiritual suicide. And the means prescribed to arrive at this state of total annihilation of self is the Buddhist morality, "the path to Nirvâna." Can it be wondered at that a religion with such

---

* "Atheistic philosophers, unconsciously attracted by the natural affinity which draws together atheists of all countries and ages, have during the last fifty years almost instinctively gone on sipping at the intoxicating cup of Buddhist philosophy. The Germans Feuerbach, Shopenhauer and von Hartmann, the Frenchman Comte, the American Emerson, with hosts of others, have all imbibed more or less of this sweet poison and taken, as kindly as any Asiatic, to this Buddhist opiate. But most of all that latest product of modern philosophy, the so-called system of positive religion, the school of Comte, with its religion of humanity, is but Buddhism adapted to modern civilization; it is philosophic Buddhism in a slight disguise." Dr. E. J. Eitel. "Buddhism," etc., p. 3.

a system of philosophy has degenerated into the superstitious idolatrous polytheism, of which the Lamas of Tibet and Mongolia give us the living examples? Buddhism, says Doctor Eitel* "acknowledged a design in nature, it recognized immutable laws underlying the endless modifications of organic and inorganic life and attained, even so long as two thousand years ago, to that remarkable **Darwinian** idea of a pre-existing spontaneous tendency to **variation** as the real **cause of the** origin of species—(the Motor of Evolution),—but—like **Darwin** and his school—it **stopped short of pointing out Him**, who originated the first commencement of that so-called **spontaneous** tendency, and who laid into nature the law which regulates the whole process of natural selection, **God, the creator and** sustainer of the universe."

The inexorable fatality of the karma obliterates faith and hope and makes love aimless; striking at the root of the Moral Senses, it makes Conscience useless and dries up the life-sap of Sympathy, all for a barren sophistic nihilism nowhere manifested in Nature. No expiation through repentance, no hope for mercy to the troubled conscience, no Saviour, no merciful Father. Here the mind, carried off on fierce Imagination, leaves Intellect and Feeling behind and wandering from the path of natural Common Sense, misrepresents the destiny of the human race and misses the goal of the Good.

Modern Buddhism and Theosophy. Buddhism we have seen is the most transcendent of mental speculations, with a ready plasticity in its esoteric aspects for any impression of imagination. No wonder then, that it became the favourite field on which many imaginary creeds were cultivated. Its purely idealistic philosophy, without a basis which is manifested in Nature as a reality, is the nursery-bed for metaphysical speculations of every description. Some of these products of the Buddhist doctrine of metempsychosis are called Theosophy,

---
* l. c. p. 66.

Occultism, Modern Buddhism, etc.,—all based on purely abstract mental exercises, and having for their plea the esotericism of Buddhism, which is then represented as having two doctrines, one for the initiated and another for the uninitiated.*

These sorts of experiments,—demonstrating how far the constructive power of imagination can be stretched, to supercede logical common-sense,—are, at present, not within the scope of our inquiries. Nevertheless, in leading the reader over the grounds of various moral-mental investigations,—in our attempt to reach the conclusions of the philosophy of civilization,—we are compelled to point out, by the way, the spurious growths, protruding from mental speculations which have no basis in natural manifestations.

It would be of no avail to enter here into investigations with regard to the different esoteric theories and systems of "modern" Buddhism, called Theosophical Societies; which originated principally in the United States of America, as so many creeds under the auspicious appearance of new religions or religious societies. Their history is so young and their doctrines so entirely transcend the bounds of mental speculation, that it is impossible to guess after which of the manifold versions of the Buddhist Philosophy they will, severally, take shape or dissipate into transanimation.

Not all the Societies which bear the name of Theosophy are Buddhistical, or have any relation to Buddhism. The *Rochester Brotherhood*, for one, is a Christian Society. The members of this Society seem to occupy themselves especially with *Mental Healing* also called "*mind cure*," "*faith cure*," "*Christian science*," etc.

Spiritualism is the doctrine of supernatural communication, whether visible or invisible, with the souls of the dead,

---

* Like the acroamatic traditions of the abstruse Egyptian mythology of Isis and Osiris, doctrines not committed to writing, but to be transmitted through hearing, by the ear of the initiated. Such excrescences existed also on the Aristotle philosophy.

through a *"medium."* Spiritualists are sternly opposed to all schools of "mental-healing" without the help of a Spirit, through the "medium." So also has Spiritualism nothing to do with Buddhism and its transmigration of the soul, for after death the souls of Spiritualists must remain unemployed, to be called upon when required; which could not be, if the soul were eternally incarcerated in one body or the other. Spiritualism and the metempsychosis of the Buddhistic Theosophy are thus in direct contradiction, or rather competition, with each other.

The so-called "Modern Spiritualism" or "Telepathy" is the exaggeratory speculation on the phenomena of sympathetic *"thought-transference,"* which consists in the mental perception by certain individuals, at certain times, of a word or other object kept vividly active in the mind of other person or persons, without any transmission of impression through the recognized channels of sense.* This fact of animal magnetism or rather animal-electricity, by which mind may impress mind, the Spiritualists make use of to exercise their psychomancy and to prove that their divinations by consulting the souls of the dead are natural facts. The complicated physical constitution of the nerve-system, through which mental consciousness is expressed, so sensitive in some individuals, gives often occasion for the influence of animal magnetism, or animal electricity, through which one mind can influence another, even to the complete subjugation of the power of consciousness and individual volition of the influenced mind.

This animal magnetic or electric power, when exercised, is called *hypnotism* or *mesmerism*, and is used by professional spiritists or "spirit-rappers",—who pretend to have direct intercourse with the souls of the deceased,—to dupe their audience at their so-called "spiritual-meetings." Here the magnetic power of an expert spiritist-magnetizer is, in some instances, so strong and efficient that the "subject" is mes-

---

* Report of the London Society for Psychical Research.

merised, as it were, instantaneously, at least without being himself aware that his visionary conception and volition,—though apparently in possession of his normal consciousness and free will,—are under control of the magnetizer. In such an abnormal mental condition,—whether in a trance or apparently awake,—one **sees and conceives whatever** the magnetizer pleases to **present to one's** cognizance. When the mesmerized subject is in a sleep or trance, he or she is called the "medium"; in the waking condition they are simply the dupes of hallucination, through the illusions of that highly sensible perception, which is **occasioned** by the temporary **mental disorder, brought** on by the **disturbed** equilibrium of their own corporal animal-magnetism, **in consequence of the stronger or more efficient** magnetic **power of their operator.** In such mental condition of a waking-dream **the apparition of spirits** seems to be a natural affair.

It is obvious that such straining on the cerebral nervous system must finally lead to idiocy or insanity. Hence the nonsense sometimes uttered by "mediums" in their so-called spiritual revelations from the "other side."*

---

* In a leading Spiritualist periodical ("The Carrier Dove" of San Francisco, August, 1887)—which puts forward, as "Evidence of Spirit Power," a series of common place ghost stories,—appears the following, under the head: "Spirit Authority."—"To what extent ought Spiritualists to accept the statements from 'the other side' as authoritative? When they deal with matters of spirit-life, and the career of the individual after 'death,' a reasonable latitude can be tolerated. They are living that life. Consequently they ought to be the best able to narrate its experiences, facts and general nature. When they deal with matters of practical psychology—from their point of view—regarding mediumship, to wit: we can again accord them a liberal right to speak with authority. When they treat upon the *modus* of the tangible phenomena they produce here, again, we can grant they are better informed than us. When, in a word, they deal with matters that are actually within their ken and practice, we can cordially allow they speak with an authority that outweighs ours."

"The case is different though, when they assume to speak *ex cathedra* upon matters of philosophy, moral religion, or science. We have heard 'controls' give utterance to some very novel and most peculiar ideas in regard to such matters, with the result that the facts of physical science, history and human progress have been so distorted as to be unrecognizable. Re-incarnation, re-embodiment, theosophy, occultism and other more undesirable fungi have grown in our midst until sometimes Spiritualism looks a veritable nondescript in the walks of thought."

When acted upon by imagination, the human mind, in want of moral common-sense, becomes soon unstable, and when to this is added the influence of magnetic agencies, disturbing the corporal magnetic equilibrium, the mind is rendered unfit for healthy subjective conception of its own and the Ego becomes unhinged; in such condition there is no limit to hallucinations of the most obstinate character. On this physiological weakness of the human mind the profession of "spirit-rappers" and "mediums" is constructed. All such cases of spiritualism belong to the department of animal magnetism, if not to that of mental pathology. Many cases, however, may finally find their solution in Police Courts.

Hypnotism in medical treatment had some success, in those cases where the power of volition is physically or morally diverted from executing the conscious will (comp. § 18, p. 23). But even in those cases of pathological paralysis of the physio-

---

"There is no 'authority' where reason is stultified and experience outraged. When the spirit world assumes to teach us regarding the facts of material nature and ignores all our acquisitions, then such teachers themselves need teaching. We do not need to see our beautiful faith become a new form of theocracy and priestcraft. Hence then we should only accord the voice of authority to our unseen visitors when they deal with facts relating to their own lives, or when we find them laboring among us for the interests of truth as seen in our own life's history, scientific achievements, social progress and intellectual advancement."

"At times, when listening to weary platitudes, we are constrained to ask where does the inspiration end, and the mundane thoughts of mediums and sitters come in? We need to know more—thereby rendering less possible the domination of authority in our work and rank." (*"The Carrier Dove."*)

This lecturing of their Spirits by the Spiritualists,—to keep their "beautiful faith" free from "theosophy, occultism and other more undesirable fungi," and their "Spirit Authority" above the imposture of "theocracy and priestcraft,"—is in striking analogy with Confucius' advice to control the Gods by keeping them from too much familiarity. On this Confucian Philosophy is probably based the disciplinary Canon of the San-Kiao, in the Buddhist Church in China, of whipping and scorching the Taoist's God of Rain, when this divinity has been in vain implored to relieve the thirsty soil with a few drops of moisture.

There is nothing new under the sun. If "Modern Spiritualism" would introduce itself into China, in course of time it might,—in spite of the abhorence of its Spirits for regular employment by transmigration,—come to some compromise with Buddhism, in the same way as this has been grafted on to Taoism and Confucianism. It might have a better chance of success here than its rival "Modern Buddhism" in Japan.

logical mechanism through which the volition takes place,
competent medical opinion must sanction the experiment. We
quote the following passage from a letter, written by a
distinguished lady-physician in Paris*, to a friend and relative
suffering from paralysis:—" About hypnotism, let me urge you
most strenuously not to think of it for a moment. If you were
a woman whose illness arose from hysterics, and were half
imagination,—or, if you were an idiot or crazy and would not
eat, etc., I should say, by all means; because you would be in
such a grave state already that there would be no possibility
of making you worse, while there would be a faint chance of
making you better. But for you, a sensible woman, with
control over yourself and enough energy and consciousness to
make you do what is necessary and advisable,—*i.e.* with a
normal volition,—it would be, in my opinion culpable. It is
not at all the same thing as electricity which, in some instances,
is of great service, but that has nothing to do with the mind,
whilst hypnotism has, entirely and exclusively,—and is only to
be employed as mental treatment, of which, thank God, you
are in no need. You must not be surprised at the slowness of
your convalescence. In recovering from all illness, it is the
first stages that are long and tedious. The different organs
have to get back into good order,—bit by bit and layer by
layer, so to speak. Afterwards, when the final stage of getting
up the general strength comes, it is the affair of a week or
two only."

After reading this professional advice, with its lucid stamp
of Common Sense, we cannot help being drawn toward concluding, that, if mental healing through " Christian Science" be
a fact, it must have been arrived at through such sensible
medical prescription, in which sound scientific knowledge is
combined with Christian sympathy.

---
* **Madame** Mary Raveau, *née* Tregaskis, a M.D. of the Paris Medical University. (Rue de la Pompe, Passy-Paris).

The Christian Faith.

Development of the Christian Religion. Religion, as noted before, marks the successive phenomena of the development of the human mind on Earth, for it is the synthetic result of the growth of the moral-mental organism of man. The Motor of Evolution, whose effects we can espy through the whole course of organic evolution, is called, in this sphere of Nature's development, the Moral Element. To the Moral Element in Nature, as we have seen disclosed above (in sections 26–34, pages 31–51), is due the growth of the moral senses, Conscience and Sympathy, and the rules that govern social organisms in the condition of civilization. The history of Religion is the record of the activities of this development of the moral-mental organism on Earth; from which development it is proved that the Christian Religion, is, *naturally*, the *perfect religion*, as being the religion in perfect harmony with the Moral Senses (§§ 24-26).

To arrive at the present stage of moral-mental organism, man had to pass through various stages of mental evolution. So also has religion, to arrive at the present perfect stage of Christianity, gone through different forms, correlative with man's moral-mental development.

Like social life, religion is the natural consequence of the human organism, and thus necessarily develops itself co-existent with the social organism in which it marks the stages of moral progress or retrogression. As such, religion is the test of civilization, and perfect religion is correlative with perfect civilization.

In conformity with the developing mental organism, the Moral Element becomes predominant and forms of religion disclose themselves accordingly. The similarity of religious principles and forms, simultaneously appearing in countries widely separated by climate and locality, as archæological researches have discovered, proves the universality of religion and its growth in conjunction with the human mind, and in proportion with the development of the moral senses. From the Moral Senses originates the feeling of moral obligations with the compulsion to comply with these obligations; from which follow the conception of a Moral Law and the consciousness of a Supreme Maintainer of the Law. This consciousness is the *Religious Faculty* of the human mind, growing and expanding or retrograding conjointly with the Moral Senses. The history of the development of religion among the different races of mankind plainly indicates the mode of this development to be, first intellectual and then moral, through the Moral Senses; and, of these, first conscience and later sympathy to expand. Religion can thus be defined as the moral conception, in which the impulses of the moral senses of the human mind are combined with the highest idea of God.

Physical Mythology,—the worship of the sun, the asters, trees and animals,—was of the time when the phenomena of Nature were less known and thus were contemplated with the awe due to their Creator. Then came the physico-mental or intellectual development, marked, in the Greek and Roman Mythology, by the sensual and poetical, and in the Northern Mythology, by the more vigorous and striking forms, suitable to the adaptations of each climate. Both these forms of religion gradually superseded, at least depleted, the brutish form of human sacrifices, but remained as yet enslaved in the grosser bonds of the lower human passions, prejudice and superstition. But man's mind would go on evolving and developing. Cicero felt already, in his time, the power of mental evolution, when he wrote thus:—" We see that imaginations and mere opinions wear out and disappear. Who now believes in the centaur or chimæra?" . . . . " Time destroys the fabrications of opinion but confirms the decisions of nature. And therefore, both in our own and other countries, the worship of the gods and the sanctities of religions grow daily stronger and purer." (*)

---
* De Nat. Deor., II., 2.

But "time" does not only develop the Intellect. Outgrowing the physical senses, Nature transcends herself in the process of evolution of the moral-mental development of man, disclosing mental faculties of higher order and susceptibility, to meet the exigencies of that higher consciousness which is called Intuition (§§ 8–12), acquired through the highest moral development of intellectual Instinct. These mental faculties of higher development are the moral senses, Conscience and Sympathy. The result of this moral evolution process is the Christian Faith.

Thus the historical forms of religion have marked the traces of this natural development of the human race on Earth, conspicuous in the successive moral conceptions of religious ideas. The objects and forms of the primitive crude fetichism have been superseded and merged into higher mythology, according to the developing conception of right and wrong, but subsequently, the mind, transcending the mystic idealistic vagueness that precedes the dawn of intuitive light, discloses the pure rational Christian Faith, as the fruit of the well-grown Moral-Mental Organism.

This regenerating mental conception is the manifestation of the Moral Element in Nature. As the human mind was gradually developing, the imaginative and mystical mental condition, which superseded the mythological ideas, became more concentrated, and finally condensed into a purer moral element. From this the mystic and imaginative notions,—which consciousness in its developed purer nature is unable to acknowledge,—were, in their turn, gradually expelled, thus making place for the Faith of the developed Moral-Mental Organism. Man's consciousness could then harmonize Christianity with his moral senses and the Christian Faith was established in the human mind as the consolidated conviction of moral truths (§§ 30-32).

This proves the indestructibility and permanence of the Moral Element in Nature, as the Creator's Spirit, permeating all Creation, and finding its focus in every human mind, as so many points of concentration where the struggle between the Moral

Senses and the lower material nature is carried on. The longer the human race exists on Earth the more man's moral senses become developed and sensible to the influence of the Moral Element. As man grew, the mystic imaginative forms of religion,—which have been fostered, for human interest, by irrational dogmas and hollow formalities,—had to make place for genuine Christian Faith, as based on Nature's revelations. In the instances described above of the Eastern religious development, the human mind, in its evolution period, was ready for nobler conceptions and higher characters of religion, but unfortunately human egoism stepped in and deviated the ready intellect, from its natural growth and development, into sensuality and mysticism; thus religious faith became a dwarfed combination of ecstasy and fanatic superstition.

To counteract and remould all deviations from the natural course of religious development, is the mission of Christianity.

Christianity. "Ethics, says Kant, issue inevitably in Religion by naturally leading to the idea of a Sovereign Moral Law-giver, in whose will *that* is the end of creation, which, at the same time, can be and ought to be, man's chief end."* Here the testimony of our Moral Senses gives us the experience of the nature of God's working in our Soul, for Ethics issue in Religion simply because the Religion is in harmony with our Conscience and Sympathy, which are the testimonies of the Moral Law and the originators of Ethics. "The moral law," says Dr. Martineau, "first reaches its integral meaning when seen as impersonated in a Perfect Mind, which communicates it to us and lends its power over our affections, sufficient to draw us into Divine communion."† The conception that the evolution of the human mind culminates in the moral mental organism, clearly harmonizes

---

* "Religion innerhalb der Grenzer der blossen vernuft." Vorrede sur ersten Auflage. Rozenkransz Edition, p. 6.

† " A Study of Religion," II., 29.

with the conception that Christianity is the natural result of evolution on Earth.

When in the human nature, progressive modifications with higher and higher specialization finally attained the present highest special modification in Religion, we find, as the result of the testimony of our whole being, that we have experienced, the Spirit of God, working in us the Christian Faith through our moral senses.

As such the Christian Faith is the highest sentiment of man, a life-giving aspiration to the Soul, native and spontaneous. This conviction, as consolidated from different conceptions of the moral senses, causes the persuasion which exerts an essential spiritual fascination over the morally developed human mind, and renders the sense of Deity not a belief but a conviction of the conscious mind. The trust in Providence becomes then a natural tendency and a necessary factor of evolution, to attain the development of perfection of the Moral-Mental Organism.

This conception of Christianity is in the highest degree conservative for it is the pure primitive revelation of Religion in the human mind, as grown from nature. Rejecting all notions of dogmas, as mere additions and structures, emanating from selfish speculations or ignorance of Nature's laws, the Christian Faith is predominant in the morally developed human mind, not as a question of belief or disbelief in certain dogmas,—as established by the theological art of any clerical institution,—but as a Moral Truth, which strikes the fountain-heads of the innermost consciousness of the Moral Senses, when pure and free from selfishness.

The Dogmatics. We have seen in these pages how Christianity is corroborated by Nature, as explained by science; if such faith can stand the wear and tear of scientific investigation, it is obvious that its metal is sound. This proves that the Author of Nature is the Author of the Christian Religion, and that Revelation is based on the sincerity of Nature.

The gnawing bitterness of the sense of insincerity found in church-dogmatism is fatal to Religion, making Religion useless as a means of disciplining the mind and for the cultivation of the Moral Senses. He who earnestly and with unselfishness follows the scientific investigation of the works of Nature, with genuine common sense, will strengthen his faith, and if the church-dogmatism may lose its hold upon him, the living consciousness of his Creator has not left him, for daily and hourly he receives the Creator's revelation through his moral senses:—that *to love and adhere to the good, and to hate and abstain from sin is a necessity to human organism.*

The dangerous assumption that the criterion of truth is to be found in the doctrines, as created by human speculation in the dark days of the history of the Christian church, had finally degenerated the pure Christian Religion into an institution based on human ambition and vanity, with all the meddling, selfish and vicious working of cunning statescraft, fighting, scheming, bribing and sanctioning murder, like the acute politician, void of justice and mercy, of the Machiavelian school of "the end sanctions the means."

Thus the church had ceased to be the fosterer of the Moral Senses, when the Reformation, born from the unrestrainable power of the developing Moral-Mental Organism, regenerated these church doctrines into *Christianity;* thus saving the teachings of Christ from sharing the fate of Buddhism, by being smothered under the dust of dogmatic formalities and mysticism, or becoming degenerated into Fetichism.

Natural Theology. There is a theological as well as a physical science, but the first must be based on the latter, for the criterion of truth is only to be found in the revelations of Nature. If the Scripture, on which the dogmatic is based, has discrepancies which are irreconcilable with ascertained scientific facts,—and of this the most eminent theologians are convinced,—it is the duty of good faith to find out the means of dealing with these discrepancies, from Nature. Not man's, but God's work shall give the verdict.

When with an unbiased pure mind we get at the consciousness of facts, through the crucial test of Conscience and Sympathy, we shall not fail to find, in the scientific investigation of the development of Nature, startling analogies with the leading features of Scripture-Revelation. But we need not such proofs to rise to the conviction that the spiritual teachings of the Bible can and must be maintained, notwithstanding that some of its scientific or historical statements may be found not to corroborate, in all details, with natural facts. Genuine Common Sense is not chained to the letter;—it is the living logic of the soul, which combines feeling with intellect;—through the letter it arrives at the spirit which it retains. And so with the Bible: the letter is from man, but the spirit of its teachings is of God.

The doctrine that those who believe shall be saved does not exclude investigation, but is a warning against investigation without Common Sense,—*i.e.*, investigation with only the incomplete physical senses of the Physico-Mental Organism (§4) which is the materialistic view, void of that genuine consciousness which is formed and confirmed by the Moral Senses. This is Natural Theology, as corroborated by Nature's teaching: that, *besides the materialistic intellect, the Moral Senses are the necessary elements in the forming of moral Consciousness in the developed human mind.*

When we thus expound the Creator's revelation through Nature by the light of natural Common Sense, imparted to our mind by our Creator, we shall not only find striking analogy with the written revelation in scripture, but we shall also find Christ explained, through our Moral Senses, as developed by the Natural Evolution Process designed by God.

This is Natural Theology, which is the science of finding the basis of Christianity in Creation and tracing Christian Faith to the natural development of the Moral-Mental Organism on

Earth. This will give Theology the claim of real scientific knowledge, and free the Christian Religion from the fatal contending dogmas and creeds, under the pressure of which it is fast losing ground in marching at the head of Civilization.

The Christian Doctrine. The belief in a future state of punishment, or *hell*, is dogmatic and has no more real influence, either in deterring men from vice or in encouraging them to virtue, than the *lex talionis* of criminal jurisprudence. It does not enter into the notions of *real* Faith, for Faith does not stoop to the speculations of any formulated creed for doing good. Faith is not dogmatic, not conditional; it is not called upon to assert or to assume anything, not even the assumption of any form or condition of our existence after death. The Christian Faith is developed in the human mind under complete harmony of the Moral Senses; it is a mental state of *complete trust in the Divine Will*, wherever this may lead our destination (§27). The doctrine of a "future life" is consistent with the Christian Faith; it is a conviction which emanates from Faith but does not constitute Faith.

Dogmatic religions in primitive forms and primitive stages of development, may require the props of descriptive theories of punishment and reward, but Real Christian Faith asks no account of the destiny given by the Creator to His creatures. Endowed with a Soul, emanating from the Divine Essence, the Christian's trust in God, like that of real holy Love, is complete; it asks no preconcerting, it needs no "miracles" for its support. Self-sustaining in its efficiency, it overlooks all, sets aside all, overshadows all, through the all-absorbing irrefragable consciousness of God Himself. It experiences no void in purpose, while following the irremovable impulses, brought to the developing human mind by the advent of Christ, in the leading lights of the Moral Senses.

Such is the action of Christian Faith in the question of the modes of a Future Life as well as in the belief in Miracles.

Miracles are based on Faith; the belief in miracles is consistent with Faith but not essential to it, and examination into their evidence is not derogatory to the divine character of Christianity, as this is upheld by the pure unrelenting Faith in the unchanging character of God the Father.

"If in this life alone we have hope," the egoism of our animal nature would be called common sense and prudence; but, on the other hand, if we have to speculate on the reward of a future life, then Conscience and Sympathy would become sophistical agents, and *virtue* a conventional doctrine, instead of being the reflection of the Divine Spirit in Humanity, created by the pure Christian Faith and loved simply for the love of God.

Christ's teachings had the tendency of bringing a future state before his hearers, as the destiny of the human race. With this object He used to picture the future state to His disciples, in forcibly striking manner; for their better realization He gave them, on the one hand, exalted descriptions of the joys of Heaven, for those to whom spiritual life is prominent, and, on the other hand, awful accounts of the fate of those who persist in remaining in their material-animal nature, and perish as such in corruption and by the fire, to which all matter in corruption is doomed, as the final consummation of the material nature. "Where the worm dieth not and the fire is not quenched" is the allegorical description of *hell*; while, on the other hand, we can *feel* better than comprehend the "peace of God that passeth all understanding" of *heaven*.

St. Paul says: "there is a natural body and there is a spiritual body." * The distinction between the future destination of the spiritual or moral nature, on the one hand, and the end of the material condition of existence, on the other, is the logical and natural consequence of the difference between these

---
* 1 Cor. XV. 35.

two elements of Nature. This every human mind with developed moral senses is conscious of. There can be no doubt, that Christ's verbal utterings,—which were always formed after striking earthly images, in order to convey tangible ideas to the common understanding of the mass, (which could not otherwise have grasped His ideas)—took also, in the representation of the ideas of "heaven" and "hell," the allegorical form, corroborating with the existence of a physical body and a spiritual body.

Christ, while on Earth, took all the occasions possible to raise the dormant Moral Senses of the human race, the development of which was his mission on Earth. At one time the most awful representation of the unrelenting Justice of the Creator served to impress a vivid conception of right and wrong, while on other occasion, unconditional Mercy was held up by the promise of Salvation through Faith.

This is the Faith in the Creator,—the FATHER OF MANKIND,—from whom,—for the manifestation of God to man,—emanated the incarnation of His Divine Essence,—called the SON,—whose first advent on Earth took place in the form of a variation of the human species, as a living example and forecast of a higher destination, in order to show to mankind the goal to which the evolution of the human moral-mental organism is leading to; and of whom, the CHRIST, a second advent must be expected, when this goal is reached, and this for the *final* consummation of the destiny of Creation. The medium through which the development and perfecting of the human race is to be sustained in the human soul, until this Second Advent is consummated, is the Moral Element in Nature, called the HOLY SPIRIT,—which pervades the moral-mental organism of man;—this is the medium of the Divine light in the human mind, for the development of the Moral Senses, through whose impulses man is guided by his moral senses, towards the Good,—and which will carry him safely to his destination, if he sincerely adheres to the Good.

Hence the Christian Faith involves the idea of the "Father", the "Son" and the "Holy Ghost", adopted as the Christian Creed. The conception of God, of Christ and of the Moral Element in Nature (the "Holy Spirit") is thus, as demonstrated above (p. 213 et seq. and p. 222 et seq.), deducible from the scientific principles, which confirm the teaching of Religion. Through these scientific analogies the mysterious Apostolic creed of the Trinity is rendered thinkable in its principles. Much evil has been wrought by the heaping of theological constructions on these simple moral truths, rendering them unthinkable mysteries, which, instead of elevating the Moral Senses, sound as absurdities to Common Sense.

The duty of every Christian is the propagation of Christianity in Civilization. This renders it our duty to search after physical demonstrations of religious principles. The doctrine that Christianity contains mysteries insolvable by human common sense is simply degrading the pure Christian Faith into Fetichism. The Christian Faith is not based on conventional dogmatism, but on the inward conviction of a morally and intellectually developed mind. What does not recommend itself to Conscience and Sympathy is not the Christianity as taught by Christ. Who can sustain that what is apparently mysterious must not be submitted to reason? Mystery is the enemy of Faith. If God has spoken, the explanation of His word could not be more surely looked for than in His own work in Nature.*

It is not a sensible or logic conclusion that a morally developed mind must be doomed to scepticism or atheism be-

---

* "It was assuredly no system or theory, most assuredly no exhibition of thaumaturgic power which attracted men to Jesus Christ, but the irresistable influence of soul upon soul. To those who forsook all and took up their cross and followed Him, He exhibited no set of doctrines, no code of laws, but Himself, as being, in every deed, that truth, which **is the supreme desire of the Soul**. The gospel which St. Paul,—in an undoubtedly genuine letter,—declares himself to have delivered to the disciples at Corinth, was no catalogue of dogmas, but the manifestation of a Person, who claimed for Himself the heart of man, to reign there as in His proper throne."—W. S. LILLY. "Chapters in European History," Vol. I., p. 55.

cause it can free itself from the bondage of conventional religious dogmas, emanating from Religious Institutions that are kept together by superstition, based on human vanity and the assumptions of Egoism.

The caged bird of God's Nature, who escaped the trammels of the gilded wires, is not an outcast in his natural freedom. Unless his wings have been clipped and his sight blinded by his cruel custodians, he really regains the existence the Creator has designed for His creatures. The mystic element in religion is not the anchor of Faith, no more than the dogmatics called "Catholicism." The distinction between Faith and Superstition is that the one is based on the conviction that God is manifested in Nature, while the other leaves Nature and science for the easier acquired support in human selfishness and imagination. All what is really from God is simple truth, comprehensible to his creatures for so far as meant for their guidance, and although the finite human reason is not able, by far, to grasp the Almighty Design, man's Moral Senses constitute his common sense,—which is Reason and Feeling combined,—into the touchstone to discern dogmatics from *real* Divine Revelation.

Man's Place in Nature.

Man's place in Nature,—as indicated by the evolution process on Earth,—asserts that the Christian Duties of Society form the test of Civilization. This thesis shall be treated at length, in the Fourth Chapter, which concludes this essay. For the illucidation of the coming conclusion, however, I must first bring under the observation of the reader the constructive elements of my thesis. These are the Principles of the Christian Faith which guide our path in the imitation of Christ.

Here we enter the holy ground open to all God's creatures, where Christian Churches of all denominations find their common source, and thus a common basis of reconciliation.

A man who has no Faith in the Creator has missed his place in Nature. His mind is poor indeed. Although he might excel in science, literature, art, politics, trade and a thousand other things, yet, with all that, he has not reached his place in Nature, for his mind has not reached the normal state of development in Nature,—*i.e.* the moral-mental organism.

> "Unless above himself
> He can erect himself,
> How poor a thing is man!"

In proportion to the development of man's moral-mental organism he elevates himself above the mere selfish ends of his animal nature. His conception becomes clear, his vision far reaching, when not obstructed by narrow selfish ends; and the progress of science, which, to the mere materialistic, and thus incomplete consciousness of the atheist, appears fatal to Christianity, is to him the progressing revelation of the Creator; for to him,—more than to the prejudiced atheistic mind,—nothing is beyond the jurisdiction of Truth.

The discovery of truth, in all its aspects, is the privilege of Science,—but of the complete Science as based on genuine consciousness, such as is only possessed by normal, pure and unprejudiced minds, unbiased by *à priori* conclusions.

Intellect, cultivated through a selfish life of materialistic details, fosters conceit and self-assertion and is fatal to genuine Common Sense. Thus it is, that Intellect can degenerate the noblest mind, when this is wrapped up in prepossessions and prejudices, and leads it,—conscious or unconscious,—to blind self-laudation. This intellectual condition often renders a man,—who, in a normally developed state of mind, would have been generous and impartial,—so bigoted with his hobby, that it becomes impossible for him to act fairly in matters of sentiment antagonistic to his settled opinions. The fact is, that the mind especially given to materialism is unable to conceive or follow pure abstract thoughts which may elevate him above physical details, and make generalization of thought possible. The result is, that the man, thus suppressing Feeling,—the not less essential element of Common Sense than Intellect,—is not likely to follow the Good, where Intellect must submit to the Moral Senses in the guidance of humanity. He is apt ever to remain an intellectual species of being, falling short of the highest phase of mental development, and, as such, a man who has missed his place in Nature in behalf of Civilization.

Like the prejudiced and conceited "literati" and savants of the half-civilized Eastern Nations, so those "civilized" scientists, who have lost themselves in the by-paths of Creation, wandering from the main tract, are void of the mental power and aptitude to elevate their train of thought to the full consciousness inherent to the Moral-Mental Organism. With this species of organism, as with all classes of phenomena in Nature, individual modification is connected with systems of correlative modifications of type, as formed by environment,—*i.e.*, with regard to the human mind,—by education.

Hence the existence of *moral* as well as *intellectual incapacity* of certain individual minds. The moral incapacity of the mind,—*i.e.*, that with regard to religious conception,—presents itself under the passive aspect of *moral doubt* (§ 25),—which is sometimes called "agnosticism,"—or as positive *atheism*. Agnosticism or moral doubt is passive, taking a negative position with regard to the Creator, Atheism is the positive denial of the existence of a Creator of the Universe; it is aggressive in all its forms, but absolutely unable to give any proof for its assertion that there is no God. Agnosticism is the common manifestation of the unthinking mind, although it is generally affected with a presumption of deep intelligence. Atheism is more the result of one-sided mental development,—*i.e.*, of a mind in which the moral development does not keep pace with the intellectual. Agnosticism does not deny that behind phenomena there may be something of which we know and can know nothing. It believes in a Motor of Evolution, for phenomena and their relations seem to imply as much. Atheism, the grossest of superstitions, positively ignores all such things, for it originates from a combination of prejudices,—the wild oats of a badly cultivated one-sided common-sense, *i.e.*, of intellect without feeling (§ 26).

The Imitation of Christ. From the evolution process of Nature we learn that "variability" which is not an improvement of type dies out, while improvement in the species is forecasted by variabilities after which new types of a higher order are moulded. These latter are the variabilities called the "links of evolution," and, having a manifest end, they evolve with special design.

In Christ the human race behold,—as it were,—the "variability" after which to mould his moral organism. Man's material nature is, so to say, complete, but the moral element is still developing in his mind after the nature of Christ, the highest moral "variability" produced by the Moral Element on Earth. In Christ we behold the union between the absolute and the relative, between abstract being and the sensible world. The person of Christ, in whom we see the forecasting of the Creator's communion with His creatures, was to the earliest Christians the direct source whence they derived their rule of life in its highest and lowest details. And as it was in the first age of Christianity, so has it been throughout the ages since. "Amidst all mutations of the social order, in all diversities of physical environment, through all our political and intellectual revolutions, the life lived, 'in loveliness of perfect deeds,' has been the supreme standard and the great exemplar of the foremost races of the world: the imitation of Christ has been a never-failing fount of all that has been noblest in individual action, all that has been most precious in moral civilization. Of His fulness have eighteen centuries received, each finding in Him the ideal to satisfy their different aspirations: the character answering to their loftiest conceptions: the perfect and all-sufficient standard of right thought and right doing."* And after eighteen centuries, as foremost factor of Moral Civilization, Christianity,—when carefully preserved in its original grand simplicity,—is the only Religion which, through the moral-mental organism, can harmonize intellect with the higher spiritual aspirations of the human race.

Faith in the Creator leads necessarily to Christ. The moral sense of Sympathy reflects the Moral Element of Nature in human minds, and **Faith is** the manifestation of the persistency of this moral energy. The craving of sympathy to exhibit our love for our Creator, through our actions, induces to Divine Worship, and Christ taught us the most exalted form of worship to glorify God, in the simplest but all-embracing Prayer to "Our Father in Heaven."

The development of the Moral Senses caused the revival of the Abrahamic or Hanyfite faith among the Arabic idolaters of the Kaabah. This faith was originally brought forward in all its purity, by Mohammed and the hanyfs, but, from seeking after the "form of worship the most pleasing to God," the faith finally degenerated into the convenient form of *pleasing God without curbing the indulgence in human lusts.*

This is the form of worship that fired the enthusiasm of the sensitive but sensual and warlike Arabians:—indulgence both in this world and the next, and how to please themselves by pleasing God.

This religious policy, however, was not established without some struggle of the Moral Element against the animal egoism of man. The zealous but honest hanyf Zaid, when perplexed through opinions about rites and the "ritual language" in which to adore God,—but, above all, vehemently repudiating all forms of idolatrous worship,—cried out in despair: "O

---

* W. S. LILLY. "What is left of Christianity." Nineteenth Century, August, 1888, p. 294.

God, if I knew what form of worship is the most pleasing to Thee, so would I serve Thee, but I know not!" But his more astute brother-hanyf Mohammed left the doubt, and took the practical measures of leading the mass to success, by means of the most powerful persuasive forces, viz., human enthusiasm fed by the hope of the most desirable delights of the sensual imagination.*

Such spoil Christianity cannot promise. Was it then to be wondered at that the triumph of Islam was the doom of Christianity in Arabia. And, may be, this has saved it also from totally degenerating, among races not yet properly developed in moral-mental organism to receive the highest form of religion.

Mohammed was well aware that perfection was not attainable through directing the hopes of his people to a material paradise. When in the full glory of the success of his teachings, he, beholding the exiled Zaid dying on the hill Hira, with

---

* Reward to the faithful is upheld by the promise of the Mohammedan Paradise, described in the Koran as follows:—"These are they who shall be brought nigh to God, in gardens of delight; a crowd from the ancients and few from later generations. On inwrought couches reclining on them face to face: immortal youths go round about to them with goblets and ewers and a cup from a fountain; their brows ache not from it, nor fails the sense: and with such fruits as they shall make choice of, and with flesh of such birds as they shall long for; and theirs shall be the Houris with large dark eyes like close-kept pearls, a recompense for their labours past. No vain discourse shall they hear therein, nor charge of sin, but only the cry, Peace! Peace! And the People of the right hand,—how happy the people of the right hand! amid thornless lote-trees and bananas clad with flowers, and extended shade and flowing waters and abundant fruits, unfailing and unforbidden and lofty couches. Verily of a rare creation have we created the Houris, and we have made them ever virgins, dear to their spouses, of equal age with them, for the people of the right hand, a crowd from the ancients and a crowd from later generations." THE KORAN. SURA LVI, 10.

The grand cause of the success of Islam was the use of the sword combined with the promise of Paradise. "Paradise is under the shadow of the Sword" is their battle-cry. Khaled's address to his troops, before battle, was: "Paradise is before you, the devil and hell behind. Fight bravely and you will secure the one; fly and you will fall into the other." Khaled's youthful cousin, at the battle of Emesa, cried out, "I see the black-eyed Houris of Paradise. One of them, if seen on earth would make mankind die of love. They are smiling to us. One of them waves a handkerchief of green silk and holds a cup of precious stones. She beckons me. Come hither quickly, she cries, my well-beloved." (Irving. "Successors of Mahomet," p. 67.) In truth could Khaled write to the Persian King:—"I will come upon you with men who love death as much as you love life."

only his honest simple Faith and full unconditional trust in the Creator, the successful prophet appeased his conscience, by canonizing the rejected hanyf with the formal allocution:—" I will pray for him; at the resurrection he too will gather a Church around him."*

Mohammedanism, at its best aspect, is but Piety without Faith.

Although Faith always includes Piety, yet there can be Piety without real Faith. Piety, born from credulity and superstition, abstains from searching the truth from fear of doubt, but Faith excludes doubt while it includes Piety. Piety without Faith is simply a training of the mind by smothering intellect and thus fostering credulity, while Faith is the instinctive consciousness of Spiritual Truth, which outlives the searching lights of Intellect and Science.

The relation which the Christian Faith impresses on our mind, as existing between God and man, is established through the Soul, as particle of the Spirit of the Creator infused in His creature. As such emanating from the Spirit of Creation, the Soul imparts to the human being the germ of moral development (§14). Intellect finds out the cells which build up our bodily tissue from the first to the last,—from birth to death and decomposition,—through the persistency of force. Science discovered the development of the evolution process through the differentiation of these tissues, while the unseen vital activity of this persistency in differentiation is manifested by these things to be seen. This "knowledge of the things we see" brings us, through the manifestations of Nature, to the knowledge of the mystery of existence,—*i.e.*, of the origin of the things manifested in Nature. These cells and tissues as well as the whole universe,—the "All,"—could not exist,— not even as atheistic meaningless forms of matter,—but for the

---

* MAJOR OSBORN. "Islam under the Arabs," p. 34 et seq. SPRENGER. Das Leben und die Lehre des Moh." Vol. I., p. 45 and 81.

unseen force which keeps them in the universal evolution-process. Human physiology points to an unknown force, which science postulates under the name of "vibrations of nerve-cells and brain-molecules;" the sequence of these vibrations we call Mental Evolution and the constructive energy, which is manifested through this order in the succession of vibrations, is the Soul (§ 10).

This mental evolution-process irresistably raises in our mind the idea of a purpose or plan of the Creator with regard to the development of the human being. This idea becomes a conviction through the consciousness we experience by the working of our moral senses, and this conviction developes into Faith.

The Christian Religion is the expression of Faith, as fostered by the Moral Senses, and thus the natural growth from the Moral-Mental Organism of Man. It originates in the natural development of the human mind under the intuition of the Soul, which emanates from the Creator. Through the Soul God has spoken to man and is ever speaking to each individual. Thus the natural origin of religion is affirmed by our moral senses, and of these the goal of development is shown to us in Christ.

CHAPTER IV.

THE TEST OF CIVILIZATION.

§81. Man's place in Nature. The Moral-Mental Organism.—§82. Biological and Future State.—§83. Man's Duty toward Civilization. Measure of Ethical Conduct. Virtue in Civilization. Social Happiness in Civilization. Family Life, Industry and Property in Civilization.—§84. Christianity the Test of Civilization. Christian Missions. CONCLUSION.

§81.—*Man's place in Nature. The Moral-Mental Organism.* Man is conspicuously the principal object of Creation on Earth. As far as human knowledge goes, there is no higher finished product of evolution in Nature than the Moral-Mental Organism, which is the human mind in the state of moral and intellectual development.

The consequence of mankind on Earth is not to be measured or dependent from the rank and apparent influence which astronomy assigns to our Globe. Physical Science has dispelled the dread of barbaric clerical ages, that the rank which the Earth occupies in the Universe would be the measure of God's interest in mankind. Galileo, Giordano Bruno, and other martyrs of scientific truth, were accused of imposture, heresy, blasphemy and atheism, because they sought Divine revelation in the Creator's work; but their successors on the same path have revealed the truth that Nature's qualification of small and great does not coincide with human opinion. "If the Earth were only one of the smaller planets revolving round the Sun,—an insignificant body in the solar-system, she would disappear entirely in the immensity of heaven, in which this system, vast as it may appear to us, is nothing but an insensible point,—of what consequence could man then be?"—This was the question anxiously put to Science, and although Science caused the alarm, it is yet her light which guides us to Nature's revelation:—that *we are not to mete out qualifications to phenomena in the measure they appear to our physical senses, for in Nature's appreciation nothing is "big" and nothing is "small."* The Universe consists but of minute interactions of the minutest material atoms, guided by the smallest measurable forces; and although both atom and force may be imperceptibly small to human physical senses, yet they are the creative structures to development, the vastness of which is even more incomprehensible than the minuteness of the atoms. The imperceptible germ is pregnant with the vastest scheme of the world's development.

What then if to human shortsightedness the Earth appears physically an insensible point in the Universe? And if this apparently insignificant dust-mote in the space is just the better constructed to cultivate life than many other of the largest bodies of our solar-system,—why should not this physical energy called Life,—and this moral element called Soul,—of which, combined, we witness the most marvellous development worked out in the process of evolution,—be of absolutely the greatest consequences in creation, as the germs destined to develop the spiritual as well as the material element in the Universe and which, as said before (§ 5) are combined in the Moral-Mental organism of man. If the human being,—yes, the whole race,—were, in comparison to the Universe but an ephemerical atom, again, biology teaches how the minutest atoms form the groundwork of life; the germs of the loftiest of creation are perfectly imperceptible to human senses in their origin, while their power in development is immeasurably vast.

This shows us the consequence of the moral-mental organism,—
i.e., of Man,—on Earth.

§82—*Biological and Future State.* The judge "who neither feared God nor regarded man,"—because he had neither Conscience nor Sympathy,—is the infidel who is only compelled to do his duty from selfish calculations:—"this widow troubleth me; I will avenge her, lest by her continual coming she weary me":—such is the motive for action of egoism void of moral senses.

It is this egoism,—in perpetual strife with the moral element in Nature,—that made the dogmatic description of "heaven" and "hell" necessary, to impress the religious idea of a future state where the good, that sacrifices itself, shall find its reward and egoism its punishment. Such was the condition of human nature, at the time of the first advent of Christ, that it could not then grasp the real purity and fulness of the moral element in Christianity.

When contemplating the process of evolution on Earth it is rational to believe in the *principle of continuity of life*, which alone can answer to the demands of Nature for an infinite series of development, which begins and ends in the Unseen Universe. We are driven by the speculations of Cosmic Philosophy, to acknowledge the existence of this Unseen Universe, from whence the intelligent forces of Nature manifest themselves in the present physical Universe,—and thus, by analogy, to conclude that the Unseen Universe is the seat of Life and Energy,—but we are not justified by *scientific speculation* in assuming that we can ever attain to empirical knowledge of this so-called Spiritual World. As we do not know what *life* is, the less can we bring *death* under experimental investigation. Bishop Butler says with truth, that: "if there is an idea that death will be the destruction of living powers, that idea must arise either from the reason of the thing or the analogy of nature. But it does not arise from the reason of the thing; for we do not know *what* death is. Again we do not know on what the existence of our living powers depends. Neither does it arise from the analogy of nature, for death removes all sensible proof, and precludes us, consequently, from tracing out any analogy which would warrant us in inferring their destruction."

We may compose a nicely balanced verbal definition of death,—as philosophical, as logic as the definition of life,—but there ends our speculation, which, from the reason of the thing, is undemonstrable through empirical science, for man after death has passed beyond the sphere of human inquiry. Thus human knowledge is not in position, at present, to assert or deny the continuation of the soul, in any form, after death. But as we are, on the other hand, as said above, compelled, by scientific analogy and the speculations of cosmic philosophy to conclude that the unseen source of Creation is full of life and intelligence, the non-existence of this presumed spiritual world must first be proved, before it could be logically concluded, from the analogy of nature, that spiritual life in some form after death is impossible, and that the existence of the individual soul is but the work of imagination. All human nature corroborates this spiritual life. For the same reason, we acknowledge God. Apart from all dogmatic religious revelation, and taking the world and the human mind as we find them,—in the present state of evolution on Earth,—and proceeding on the scientific data of evolution and the historical data of civilization,—the conclusion which these seem to render inevitable is that the moral faculties of the mind compel us to acknowledge a Supreme Spiritual Power, a Paramount Power, which influences the human mind as it underlies all phenomena in the physical world, in one word, to acknowledge God.

From the above stated propositions, we draw the following conclusions:—Faith in the Creator,—like our Moral Senses,—is the instinct of the Soul, which serves the double purpose of revealing God to man, and raising man towards God. Where the invariability of the laws of the outer works of Creation is insufficient to manifest the whole perfection of the Creator, there the inward consciousness, emanating from the Soul, supplies the want, through the conviction of Faith and the light of the Moral Senses. We need not *asume* the existence of God, we are compelled, by the Moral Senses of our mind, to be *convinced* of the existence of the Creator, and of the working of His Spirit in us, and, as we vainly endeavour to grasp His magnitude, He appears to us both infinite and eternal. Thus enters into our consciousness the idea of immortality of the Soul, as having emanated from the Spirit of the infinite and eternal Creator.

There is a conviction in man, that though he be a developed product of evolution, he is still a *rational being;* not a mere portion of matter fortuitously developed through blind mechanical forces, but endowed with self-consciousness, intelligence and a Free Will. This rational conviction is the manifestation of an intelligent world—energy. If there were no Divine design in Creation, man, instead of being all this, would be a blank negation of the evolution-theory, and the human race would stand apart from Nature—(which, without design, would be irrational and blind)—as a separate and special creature which had no connection with the irrational universe in which he lives.

The principle of *Continuity of Energy* in the Universe, which is derived from our present experiences of physical and moral evolution on Earth, furnishes us with the assumption of a *Continuity of Evolution*, and is the scientific ground on which man can become convinced, that the present state on Earth is not the consummation of his destination (§27).

§83.—*Man's Duty toward Civilization. Measure of Ethical Conduct.* Ethics, as described before (pp. 229—234), deals with the most highly evolved (moral) conduct in the most highly developed being; it thus includes all conduct which furthers or hinders, in either direct or indirect way, the conduct of others, and to which the qualification of justice and benevolence can be applied; in other words, all conduct dictated by the moral senses. The welfare of self is not included in Ethics, in so far as the conduct concerns pleasure or pain, caused by material means of individual self-indulgence, but the moral welfare of self, the *moral pleasure* caused by *peace of mind*, is directly promoted by actions in conformity with the moral senses. Hence the furthering of the welfare of others, in conformity with justice and benevolence, gives the pleasure of peace and harmony to the morally developed mind, while the hindering of the welfare of others, in opposition to the moral senses, causes pain,—the affliction of a disturbed conscience.

This rather elaborate definition of Ethics is stated here, in order to guide us in the further demonstration that practical Ethics is the mark of Civilization, and that man's duties toward civilization,—*i.e.*, as civilized member of society,—must bear the mark of morality.

The mental process by which acts are adjusted to ends in the highly developed mental organism of man can be traced up from the different stages of evolution of the animal world. Where the development of the mind is low and simple, the mental process consists of the simple guiding of immediate acts, by immediate stimuli to immediate ends. But with the development of intelligence and the growing of the moral senses, the ideality of the motives grows also, and the ends to which the acts are adjusted cease to be exclusively immediate, but form a complex impulse of the soul. When men live exclusively the life of the physical senses, their moral senses become degenerated, and overpowered by animal passions. Such individuals can, scientifically speaking, be contrasted with those in whose minds the moral senses are in full development, at the same ratio as the lower animal stands to individuals whose minds have not developed above the physico-mental state of organism (§4). The animal prompted by hunger has no other motive than to satisfy the instinctive animal necessity; while the thief, who, led by the imagination of material profit, instigated by cupidity, deprive others of their property or rights for his own benefit, is below all comparison with the lower animal pouncing on its prey. On the other hand, the intuitional restraint of the conscientious man, whose mind is under habitual control of conscience and sympathy, acts righteously, simply because it is in conformity with his nature to do so. It is not the intellectual notion of legal punishment, dealt out by Criminal Law, which shall bridle the rapacity of the one or is the cause that the other remains honest. Only the well developed Moral Senses can overrule the rapacious selfishness of the animal nature of man, causing the egoistic idea of material "pleasure" and "pain" to give way to the altruistic notion of honesty. Conscience claims justice for the person owing the rights or property, while Sympathy keeps alive the picture of the pain which the loss is apt to entail on the deprived owner.

This action of the Moral Senses, from which emanates the natural aversion to all conduct injurious to others, does not originate from the so-called "inherited effect of experience," but direct from the intuitional power of the Moral Element in Nature on the developed Moral-Mental Organism. This is the power by which the fallen and degenerated human being is reclaimed through the Christian Faith.

The degree of infamy, attached to bad conduct with regard to man's duty to Society, is not measured, on the Scale of Civilization, by the amount of legal penalty of Criminal Law, but is determined by the degree of lower animal propensity which the deed exhibits, in other words, the fall of man on the scale of creation is the cause of the moral horror which crime entails (§78, p. 165 et seq).

Virtue in Civilization. We have defined the Good as the perfect harmony of the developed moral senses—Conscience and Sympathy (§14). Consistent with this definition, we call good or bad conduct that which produces the pleasure of the peace of mind, or which causes the tortures of an accusing conscience. Here is meant by "pleasure" and "pain" the mental gratification and dissatisfaction, *i.e.*, the affections which concern man's own feeling, and which depend from the state of development of the individual moral-mental organism. These naturally differ from the sensual pleasure and pain which effect the physico-mental organism of the material man.

If we call "*good,*" as Mr. Herbert Spencer puts it in his Data of Ethics, each act so adjusted to its end as to further self-preservation and that surplus of enjoyment which makes self-preservation desirable;"—if we call "*good,*" "every kind of conduct which aids the lives of others, and does this under the belief that life brings more happiness than misery,"—then it is obvious that we do not consider what is here called "good" as the result of *moral motives*, but simply as the result of means by which pleasurable ends can be obtained. Logically we could then call intrinsically or morally good any proximate cause of any agent conducive, immediately or remotely, to any sensual enjoyment, as good music, a good wine, a good appetite, etc. The good will then be of a merely objective nature, and, if so, each act so adjusted as to get the desired end,—*i.e.* that it brings happiness to others,—should be *per se* good. That this theory must land us in the magic circle of "the end sanctions the means" is obvious. If the good is objective only, it would become conditioned by personal taste, and the merit of good conduct would be the conditioned pleasurable. In the highest state of civilization the highest evolved conduct could then only be called good incidentally, for the *objective result* of a good action (which is beyond the control of the actor) would then be the criterion of the deed and not the *motive of action,* which alone, in fact, is the result of the "evolution of conduct."

Such is the consequence of the "ultimate derivation of right and wrong from pleasure and pain;" this shifting basis of Materialistic Ethics, which, in vain, looks for corroboration in the Free Will of man. But human Free Will, we know (§18, p. 25), ceases to be free the moment the deed is done; the result of the voluntary act comes immediately with the execution of the free will in the order of the sequences of Nature, and thus we can never know, with certainty, the *result* of our action. Our guides are our Moral Senses which form the *motive, i.e.* the test of the right or wrong of *moral actions* (§18). The character of the agent and the quality of the deed always partake of the nature of the *motive*. For this alone conduct is responsible; the results, being beyond our control, are incidental in their effects.

Mr. Herbert Spencer* says: "Suppose that gashes and bruises caused agreeable sensations and brought in their train increased power of doing work and receiving enjoyment: should we regard assault in the same manner as at present?" . . . "Or, again, suppose that the picking of a man's pocket excited in him joyful emotions by brightening his prospects; would theft be continued among crimes, as in existing law-books and moral-codes?", etc. But such *reductio ad absurdum* proves no more, with regard to motives of moral actions, than an actual economical problem could be solved by an answer on the question: "Suppose that men walked on their hands instead of, as now, on their feet, would the shape of our walking-boots be the same as at present?"

It is obvious that the measures taken to meet actual social and biological wants must be adjusted to the wants conformably as these develop. No man will deny that the act we *know* directly to benefit or to injure another is correspondently called

---
* "Data of Ethics." §11.

a good or bad act, for it is again the *motive* of pleasing or injuring a **fellow-creature** that qualifies the act, and every one knows by experience that what we call the badness of an action is not ascribed to it solely for the reason that it entails pain immediately or remotely, not more than acts which are pleasure-giving can always be called good. Although the results of well-meant motives may sometimes be **mere failures,** with regard to the amount of pleasure intended, yet we could never bring our moral-senses to class any act of **instructing** the ignorant in **religion, ministering to the sick,** caring for orphans, doing justice to **good behaviour,** or combating intemperance and immorality, as useless, because some necessary pain must be inflicted.

When cultivating charity and other effects of the Christian Faith, the result might not always answer to the motives that prompted the acts, but, as said before, the test of good and bad conduct is not to be looked for in the results. The test is the harmony of the Moral Senses. This test forms the standard of civilization,—"the ideal goal of the natural evolution of conduct,"—*i.e.* that practical form which society assumes at the **highest stage of** the evolution of the human mind, when the *good* is presented to the normal conscious mind as **a state** of perfect harmony **between** well-developed Conscience and Sympathy, the only **criterion for** *good conduct.*

Our reasoning power **as well** as our judgment might fail, with regard to the final result of our conduct on self and others; **this is** the natural consequence of the frailty of the human organism, with which mental faculties keep equal pace, but this does not and cannot dispense a rational **man,** endowed with a sound mind, **from** the natural obligation (when not prevented by forces beyond his control) to act as, in his Christian Faith, he sincerely believes to be right.

The good is not definable only **by** what benefit an object of good actions might acquire in **a** material or physical sense, for the good,—like the Moral Element in Nature, of which it is the manifestation,—is a universal element of civilization, which embraces the subject as well as the object. In this light only **Virtue** is conducive to general welfare. The subject acts in conformity with the impulses of the individual conscience and sympathy; his conduct originates in sincerity of purpose,— which is purity of mind free from undue bias of interest and speculative motives,—and the end of the motive is defined by the actual standard of civilization as moulded by the Christian Faith.

It is not with the most intelligent or the best adjustment of acts to ends, neither in any skilful organization of the power of human vanity, selfishness and superstition, in church or state, that we must look for the criterion of virtue,—not more than in acts most conducive to material happiness or most pleasure giving in its total effect on self or others or both. Perfection of the moral-mental organism of man must be looked for in the purity of the motives under which he acts, in complete harmony with *truth* and *benevolence*, *i.e.* with conscience and sympathy. Unless it is asserted that virtue is inconsistent with pain or sorrow on self,—as in all degrees of self-sacrifice,—or on others, incidentally, it is an error to define good conduct as the adjustment of acts to ends to secure the most pleasure-giving in its total effects on self or others or both. Happiness is surely to be found in Virtue, but Virtue cannot be tested by pleasurable feelings. Happiness can be defined in terms of Virtue, for to be in harmony with one's moral senses gives the feeling of happiness, called peace of mind, but to define Virtue in the terms of happiness is to apprise conduct by its result and deify the infernal maxim that the end sanctions the means. The idea of happiness cannot be separated from that of the good, for happiness which is not based on virtue fails to satisfy the human mind, even in the first stage of its moral-mental development.

Social Happiness in Civilization. That virtue is primordial and independent from mere pleasure-giving effects is no reason why there should not be any correspondence between virtuous conduct and conduct that is pleasure-giving in its total effects on self or others or both. The motive of action, in all instances, is the promotion of happiness in Civilization.

Happiness, as we have seen before (§17), is the experience of the emotion caused by a combination of physical, mental and moral conditions, all in perfect harmony. **As such,** happiness does not comprehend only the pleasurable feelings, accompanying actions that **constitute** mere living and enjoying of the animal *physical life*,—nor only this, **combined** with the **mental state** which **the life of** external perception yields through the physical senses, and which combination constitutes **material** happiness;—and even this material life, improved by the modes of consciousness accompanying **mental** capacity, which is called knowledge, can only constitute *rational life*,—i.e. the intellectual happiness. But when the physical and the rational forms of life, being combined, are enhanced by the harmony of the Moral Senses, happiness will be experienced by the *civilized man*, in the complete activity of his intellectual and moral **nature, as** the *unrestrained energy of knowledge* **and** *goodness*. And so, as **we** have seen before, there **is no** happiness outside **the Good and the** Good is Peace of Mind,—that **is,** the conviction of Duties well performed.

Duty is thus the compact **of** harmony established between the Moral Senses and the Intellectual Will, under the guarantee **of Faith** in a Supreme **Judge.** Without Faith in **a** Supreme Ruler, the contract cannot be enforced and Duty becomes then a convenience of Intellect, as often as this can bully Conscience and Sympathy **into** silence. Thus the basis of peremptory absolute duty is Faith, forming the connection between Ethics and Christianity.

As such, the objective result **of** good conduct,—*i.e.* of conduct in harmony with the Moral Senses,—does not concern individuals only, as particular objects of ends of motives, but is generally beneficial to the whole social organism, by forming the Spirit of Law of the civilized society. The outcome of the Spirit of Law, thus formed by the Moral Senses, is, as described above (§§29, 33 and 40), the framing of those ethico-legal rules for the guidance of the social organism, enumerated before (§§43-61), called Laws.

The progressive development of the ethico-legal rules of society, shows that Civilization,—which is the work of the Moral Senses,—is appropriately defined as the actual sociological condition in the process of forming the subjective conception of the Good into objective practical Good (see §§41 and 42).

Family Life, Industry and Property in Civilization. The people who, in the struggle for existence, effectually employ the most efficient material agencies on intellectual method, are said to be progressing in material welfare, but the nation who apply this welfare to carry into higher perfection the relations between man and man for the amelioration of the social state on moral principles,—*i.e.* to attain a moral end,—is acknowledged as progressing in civilization. This progress is mainly attained through the agency of *Family Life*, constituting the centres of social life, from which the germs of Civilization go forth into the Social Organism.

Social Happiness is the test of the civilization that is based on Christian principles, and Family Life is the focus of social happiness. With family life is intimately connected *Industry*, and with industry, *Property*.

Property is thus a factor of Civilization as well as Industry is.

Family relation is the link between egoism and altruism in society. As long as family life predominates and legal property is respected in a society, its stability is guaranteed.

Property is the result of *Labour*; if you attack property you demoralize labour. It is the basis of family life, when combined with the rights of will and bequest and inheritance.

Property is the safety-valve of society. Where **the struggle** for material existence and the fierce competition in labour, between all and every member of the society, had to go on perpetually unmitigated; where no one has saved enough to be able to retire from the field of daily competition, in order to make room for succeeding generations, **there** the struggle, through the ever oversupply of labour, must perpetually increase in intensity finally **to** end in the brutish strife of barbarism.

This salving capacity of Property modifies the struggle for **existence.** As such Property is **a factor** in the evolution-process of the social organism, provided the conditions **between** labour and property,—the latter under the name of *capital*,— be regulated on sound ethico-political bases, as treated before, in the sections dealing with the co-existence of individuals, in internal social life (§§76–79).

§84.—*Christianity the Test of Civilization.* Civilization, **we have** seen, is the state of process in the attempt to bring the subjective Good,—engendered in the individual mind through the moral senses,—into objective form, for the maintenance and practical **guidance of Society.** Hence Christianity whose laws of Justice **and Benevolence,** in harmony combined, constitute the natural form of objective Good, is the **natural standard by** which Civilization is to be gauged all over the **Earth.**

In the preceding pages, we have noted **the** principal forms **of** Religions which, as creeds **or** philosophy, or both, have, **for** many centuries, before and after Christ, governed the human **mind** on Earth. These are the Buddhism, Taoism and Confucianism,—as the peculiar religious conglomeration of China,—and the Mohammedanism of the Arabic tribes. It is for our present argument not necessary to enter into any investigation of their several schools and branches; the retardment of civilization which these have caused on Earth, is conspicuously marked in the History of the Eastern Nations.

Buddhism, old and evanescent, gradually makes place for the Christian Creed, so necessary for the completion of Civilization on Earth. Nations on the determined road to genuine development, tend instinctively toward Christianity, for the ennoblement of feeling and action. The Buddhist Nirvana, with its purposeless negative conclusion, is no stimulant to social perfection, and, without being aware of the change, the people are slowly but surely drifting away from abstract philosophy and mysterious creeds toward the search of a practical Religion, in conformity with the natural drift of the developing Moral-Mental Organism.

Confucius, Buddha and the old philosophy of Greece and **Rome are all** pointing toward Christianity. From them we learn, how social errors and blemishes,—which paltry prepossession of the mind, preconceived ideas and systems based on imagination are fostering in religion,—can dwarf the human **Moral Senses for** centuries, but, at last, to regenerate through Christianity. With Christianity the human mind enters into that higher state of **development of** the Moral-Mental Organism, **in** which freedom of examination becomes possible through Conscience and Sympathy,—*i.e.*, through Reason and Feeling **combined, which** is the intuition of the Soul.

We have seen, by facts as stated **above,** that Religion, **like Social Life, is the** natural consequence of human organism and, as such, necessarily develops itself in conformity with the moral-mental activities of man in social co-existence. The Theological (the *School*), the Political (Aristotle, Confucius, Hobbes), the Emperical Utilitarian (J. S. Mill), the Expediency-Morality **and** the Rational-Utilitarian (Mr. Herbert Spencer), Buddhism, and Mohammedanism ; all these theories are marked by the Moral Senses, in this aspect, viz: that their characteristics are based either on the entire ignoring of the evolution of the Moral Senses as the motor of human conduct, **(Aristotle), or** by asserting this **natural** causation of moral actions, by implication (Buddha) or only partially asserted by induction (Mohammed). Christianity, on the other hand,—as above described being based on Biology,—comprehends the only religious theory which is based on the complete natural **relation** that exists between the evolution of the Moral-Senses and human conduct, as emanating from rational and moral beings. This shows that *Christianity is the Natural Religion of the developed Moral-Mental Organism on Earth.* **This natural** relationship **accounts for the** degeneration of **the people whose** actions are contrary to the principles of Christianity and for the progress in civilization of those whose Spirit of Law is based on Christianity.

Hence Christianity that fosters the moral senses is naturally the objective form of the Good and the natural standard of Civilization.

The race among which intellect and sympathy, reason and feeling are equally balanced in the well developed individual mind, is really the predominant race on Earth, and could be called the Aristocracy of Nature. Below the normal standard of civilization are those nations among whom the moral-mental organisms, **and** consequently the moral senses, Conscience and Sympathy, are **wanting in** sufficient development to be **equal** to the task of forming, **combined,** the moral agency of society. Selfishness and rapacity,—*i.e.*, the lower **animal** propensities which hold sway over the scantily developed moral-mental organism,—leave their stamp on all **actions which mark the** social life of these organisms.

Nations among whom the predominant idiosyncracy of the race consists therein, that they possess the most luminous intellect, often show the most pitiable lack of Sympathy; and without the softening dews of Sympathy the soil of human actions remains barren of moral fruit, and the light of intellect becomes the scorching sun on the desert-sands of materialism. Such nations are exclusive and one-sided, and hardly admissible to the higher calls of civilization. The state of moral inadequacy of having only the physical and intellectual faculties developed is manifested in their hollow forms of etiquette,—only a sham of civilization,—and in their conceited one-sided selfish culture, the erudition of which has no practical utility. Luxurious abodes for the self-glorification of despotic rulers,—while works for public utility and roads for the most necessary communications are neglected,—are the marks of semi-civilization.

On the other hand, while good roads, railways, canals, passenger-steamers, hotels and postal-establishments are undoubtedly tokens of material progress,—if they should stand alone, unaccompanied by Institutions with *moral ends*, and recourse for the poor and sick, they would fail to convey the idea of progress in civilization.

Again, religious institutions may erect gorgeous edifices in the forms of temples, cathedrals, chapels and monasteries; but these alone are no proofs of civilization;—they are no signs of advancing moral development, when they look down, in gloomy solitary grandeur, on the desolate roads of town and country, wasted land, or a demoralized population.

Only when practical application of the physical and intellectual faculties is combined with public benevolence, toleration, suppression of vice and propagation of morality, the progress in Christian civilization is recognizable in the Moral-Mental development.

While all non-christian Nations have, long since, passed the culminating point of the highest perfection they were able to attain, Christianity is yet ever progressing. The Christian Religion differs from all other religions which, in the history of mankind, have marked the course of the moral development of the race. It is not limited, like the Jewish theocracy, to certain tribes; nor bound to any special, social or economical condition or form of government, like Mohammedanism,—

propagated by fire and sword and sustained by fanatical hatred and envy toward other creeds. The Christian Religion, abrogating the old theocratic distinction between Jew and Greek,—circumcision and uncircumcision,—and, resting on no national or theocratic basis, but purely upon free individual conviction,—as being the natural religion,—makes the most powerful appeal to the moral senses, to elevate the creature toward its Creator.

The Moral Senses point to altruism, and altruism is the goal of Christianity. And, though the struggle be hard and continuous with the lower propensities of the material animal nature, yet the moral-mental organism, in order to comply with the evolution process, *shall* reach the goal when upheld by the powerful support of the Christian Faith.

Individuality is the strength of Christianity. While other creeds have moved the mass with sweeping fanatism that brought whole tribes into fierce activity, with religion and their God for war cries, to be smothered in blood, or, while stereotyped dogmas, built on sickly imagination, have ended with a stunt in the moral-mental growth, Christianity is developing and growing with the human organism; working and growing and being perpetuated by ever recurring conversions; winning its souls one by one but growing surely and steadily, working the moral-mental organism to its destination. In strengthening the human mind against any impure contingency that might enslave the moral-senses, it works unrelentingly to the perfection of the race. Christianity, this universal religion of mankind, is based on the natural evolution-process of the Moral-Mental Organism of Man, and thus constitutes the natural Test of Civilization.

Goethe said that the true standpoint to be taken in all criticism,—thus also in the criticism of civilization,—is not to deviate from the whole, the good and the beautiful.

"Im Ganzen, Guten, Schönen,
resolut zu loben."

We may all resolve to live in the "whole," the "good." and the "beautiful;"—but, where is the good and what is the beautiful and can we ever grasp the whole? Goethe gave a good prescription,—but where are we to look for the ingredients? Such is poetry!

But there is a sure guide in Nature, and the present dissertation is an attempt to bring this to light in Christianity, which is the harmony of our inward nature with the rest of Creation. Here we find the standpoint for an enlightened view of Civilization. Our moral senses, Conscience and Sympathy, strengthened by the Christian Faith, will ever be the sure guiding lights to our life's destination.

> The Good man, through all the dark drifts of life,
> Is ever conscious of the right course in strife.
> Two Moral Senses, the Creator's gifts through your Soul,
> Give you Conscience and Sympathy, guides to the goal.
> When your Conscience is clear, your Sympathy bright,
> It is Justice that leads with Mercy in sight;
> Two headlights, lit by Faith that in Christ finds support:
> Keep the two lights in one, and Heaven is your Port.

Christian Missions and Civilizing Agents. Moral Courage is the safeguard and the vindicator of Virtue; it is the courage called *true courage* which sternly and unflinchingly upholds virtue under any disfavouring circumstances; it is the courage of the Christian Missionary in non-Christian lands.

It is through the agency of Christian Missions that the Christian duty to Civilization, in the propagation of Christianity, is to be fulfilled. This duty devolves on every civilized Christian, and ranks first among acts of Charity.

Charity has its qualifications as all human actions. Those who are unable to contribute personal labour find a substitute for their labour in money gifts. Yet there are, both men and women, in Christian Civilization, who give their labour as well as their money, by following up their gifts with painstaking husbandry in all charitable work, as to secure the appropriate fruit to the bountiful sowing. Well directed charity in Christian Mission-Work can be practiced without extravagant demands on **the citizen's person** or his purse.*

Besides the Christian duty toward Civilization, there are two main arguments of necessity for the propagation of Christian Civilization through **Mission** Work,—the one of political and the other of moral **nature.**

The Christian Mission field is extensive. **The uncivilized** non-christian nations of the Earth far exceed in quantity **the** morally civilized portion of the human race. Christian **Civilization is thus continually** placed in jeopardy of being destroyed **by the** brute force of material humanity. The **arduous** propagation of Christian civilization **is thus** not alone a **task of** Christian duty, but also a necessity **of social** self-preservation. Civilization, continually **assailed,** internally as well as from

---

* Charitable Institutions working on this line in China are all worthy of observation. There are several established and working through Western money and Western labour, independent of the real Religious Christian missionaries.

Of **four** distinct categories of Charity, I can mention here working **Institutions** of the class indicated—viz: (1.) The *"Children's Home,"* established in 1887 in Shanghai, by public subscription, under the presidency of CORNELIUS THORNE, Esq., and managed by Ladies. (2.) The *"Ladies Benevolent Society of Shanghai"* with which the best names of the foreign communities **in China are** connected. (3.) The *Society for the Diffusion of Christian and General Knowledge among the Chinese*, of which Sir ROBERT HART, G.C.M.G. is the President, and **the Rev.** ALEXANDER WILLIAMSON, LL.D. the Hon. Secretary; an institution which speaks for itself and well worthy of the support it enjoys in China **and** in Western civilized countries. Through this Society is published—besides many other educational Chinese works,—a monthly paper in Chinese Vernacular, the *Wan-Kwoh-Kung-Pao* ("Review of the Times") edited by Rev. Dr. ALLEN of Shanghai. The cheapness of this paper (one silver dollar per annum) and the highly interesting and instructive articles from able contributors, would make the *Wan-Kwoh-Kung-Pao* an efficient agent of civilization in China, as soon as a wider circulation could be secured. Among this class of agencies for the propagation of Civilization through Popular Education, must be reckoned the various ably conducted *Mission Presses in China, Japan, India, etc.* From the old establishment of the American Presbyterian Mission Press, at Shanghai, under the able management of Rev. GEO. F. FITCH, are constantly issuing forth series of religious and educational Chinese Publications of eminent sinologues. (4.) The "*White Shield Union*," an association for defending and promoting Social Purity, originated by Mrs. LOUISA H. GULICK, of the "American Bible Society's Agency" at Shanghai. Mrs. Gulick, strong with noble Christian energy, is the Hon. Secretary of the "White Shield Union."

without, requires strong and intelligent supporters. This is the *political argument* for the propagation of civilization through Christian Missions in non-christian lands.

The short-sightedness of ignoring this argument was the cause that many progressing conditions of ancient civilization have been rudely thrust back by invading hordes of savages, and History shows that this was the result of the overbearing pride and selfishness, with which civilized nations kept the despised barbarians from any participation in their one-sided civilization. The barbarians were regarded by their more fortunate but selfish neighbours as beings, with whom civilization had no concern; as weeds and wild-oats, not worthy of more notice than that of carefully keeping them out of the fields of higher culture. Void of sympathy, these civilized people of former ages were, with all their highly intelligent culture, narrow-minded and blind through egoism. Their Civilization was no Christian Civilization, and thus void of the life-inspiring impulse toward altruism.

When treating above the social co-existence of individuals, in the co-ordination of Labour and Capital, we have seen (in §78, page 148) for what reason the labourer's wages cannot be regulated by market-quotation, as being dependent on the standard of living, in conformity with the actual conditions of civilization. The labourer's wage must keep equal pace with the state of civilization under which he lives. To introduce into the civilized community masses of uncivilized labourers to compete with the civilized labouring class of a Christian Society, is detrimental to the standard of Christian Civilization. Every member of such society has the moral right to oppose this deterioration of the moral standard of their community and to keep out the degrading element.

Now, all this is conscientiously true, but yet, it seems we are not quite satisfied with this thesis as it stands. Put it to the test of the Moral Senses, and we find that, though it be fairly sanctioned by Conscience, yet Sympathy does not harmonize with the act of excluding fellow-creatures from our shores. Sympathy peremptorily claims an equivalent, and this consists therein that serious efforts should be made to civilize those whose lower state of civilization makes them, as yet, unfit to be taken up *unconditionally* in a civilized community. This is the *moral argument* for Christian Missions.

State-interference with regard to Slave-trade and Coolie-traffic, in behalf of Civilization. We have seen now that, besides the Christian duty to propagate Christian Civilization, there exist two main sociological arguments for Christian Missions in non-Christian lands:—the first, the political argument of self-preservation, *i.e.*, the propagation of Christian Civilization, to ward off the danger of civilized nations being swamped by uncivilized tribes; the second is the moral argument just described. Thus the lessons of History teach us that the material and moral progress of civilized States depend upon the cultivation of Intellect combined with the fostering of the Moral Senses and show the modes by which Christian Civilization must be brought home to non-Christian nations.

There is however another aspect in the intercourse between Christian and non-Christian nations, viz: that which places *Civilized Governments* in the light of propagators of Christian Civilization. Such is the case when, in the great problem of Civilization, State-interference becomes a duty imposed on civilized Governments, by the claims of right and humanity, by Conscience and Sympathy equally peremptory.

The *African Slave-trade* and the *Asiatic Coolie-traffic*, both stand as yet in dusky array against Civilization, as an aspect of gloomy accusation against civilized Governments.

While the Arabian Slave-dhows are being hunted down, their living cargo set free and the vessels destroyed,—and thus the slave-trade crushed out under the avenging heel of Civilization,—what are civilized Governments doing against crowded coolie-steamers, carrying their consignments to the great coolie-emporiums, which in reality are not better than slave-markets?

While Malay and African slave-hunters are caught by foreign vessels and slung up in their own territorial waters, what are civilized Governments doing to crush out the *imperium in imperio*, established in their colonies, by vicious Asiatic coolie-dealers whose trade is not allowed in their own "uncivilized" countries?

This coolie-trade has created its *coolie-market*, whither the coolies are shipped from their native country, as chattel consigned to the monopolizing coolie-dealers, who, through a monstrous scheme of bribery on all sides, prevarications and perversion of truth, have secured to themselves this lucrative trade in human beings. At this coolie-market, the human chattel is dealt out in lots to be delivered to the highest bidders for plantation and mining-work in other countries.

With the coolie-dealer, as the owner of the coolie, the *labour-contract*,—for one to three years' service of the coolie on the foreign estate or mining enterprise,—is made, and to the coolie-dealer the coolie returns after the expiration of his contract. His savings are soon spent in the coolie-brokers' opium-kits and gambling-houses, and he is again at the tender mercies of this dealer in human labour. *

---

* The present enlightened **Government of China** in their noble effort to protect their subjects from greedy **labour speculators** have forbidden the engagement, in China, of Chinese **labourers under contract.** Unfortunately this has led to the much to **be regretted** result of delivering the poor labour-seeking emigrants to the **mercy of the** coolie-markets **in** foreign countries. To check the mischief of **these foreign** Coolie-markets, it would be advisable for the Imperial Government **to organize** *Official Labourers-Depôts* in **their** own Treaty-Ports, under direct **supervision** and control **of** Imperial Chinese Customs-Officials. Here *labour-contracts* should be made by the *bonâ-fide* Employer, **or his** acknowledged **Agent**, *direct with each individual labourer*, and signed **or** stamped in the presence of said Chinese employés. In the labour-contract **should** be mentioned the real name of the plantation or mine, where **the coolie** has to work, and the conditions of *time, wages* and *passage*, to **and back**, under which the labourer is engaged for the foreign country. **A** moderate charge, to **be** paid by the employers to the Imperial Customs Administration, would cover the extra expenses **en**tailed by this service with regard to the Official Labourers-Depôts.

And to think that all these abuses could soon be put a stop to,* if civilized Governments would only come to some mutual understanding about the Coolie-traffic like it has been done with the Slave-trade.

If the coolies, before **leaving their native places,** could make the labour-contract,—under supervision **of their** own native authorities,—direct with their *bonâ-fide* employers, **and clearly** mentioning the place **where they have to go to, the nature of the work, the wages, and other usual terms of a labour-contract; with the condition of passage direct to the** country where they **have to work,** and, **after** expiration of their contract, passage back, direct to their homes,—where their earnings shall **be paid** out to them,—then, through these simply logical proceedings, **the** poor labourer would be kept out of the clusters of the coolie-dealers of the foreign land, he would remain the owner of his own labour and **enjoy all the** benefit it brings home to him. **Then, also, as** the labourers are leaving, in separate batches to the different countries, where they are to be employed in agricultural or mining labour, there would be **no** more danger **to be** feared from crowded coolie-vessels, carrying their **miserably** confused **living freight to the** coolie-market.

The African **Slave-markets are** dispelled **at the point of the** bayonet, but what **are civilized** Governments **doing against this** violation of civilization **by the coolie-markets on their own** territories?

Non-Christian Nationalities of the **lowest types of morality** cunningly seek out the shelter of Christian **Civilization,—profiting by the immunity** from bamboo-lash **and executioner's axe,—to carry on** their wily **crafts** and trade **in human beings,—thus** "turning the grace of God into lasciviousness."

Are the sacred privileges of civilization thus to protect vile Asiatic cupidity, like the skin of the slaughtered sheep the greedy wolf? **What are** civilized Governments doing by **such** unconditional admittance to the freedom of Civilization of all the gallows-birds of their uncivilized neighbours? Why allow the infamous coolie-market to disgrace your civilized colonies?—But, alas! the Revenue!—the emoluments of greedy officials.—You may as well plead with the opium-millionaire for the closing of the opium-dens!

But all these are temporary evils which will vanish before the advancing Christian Civilization. Slave-trade and Coolie-traffic with slave-markets and coolie-markets are simply incidents of the actual uncivilized condition of the great mass of non-Christian populations as yet to be worked upon by Civilization.

In this subjugation of civilization by the selfish rapacity of the lower human nature, we see a new proof that no civilization can exist which is not based on Christianity.

Christian Mission-work among Eastern Nations. Civilization, as we see, is thus only attainable through Christianity, but not by the special creed of any denomination. Civilization wants Christianity, no Church-Polity. Idolatrous Christianity is but Buddhism or Taoism in a new garb; you might make many converts, for the sake of the newness of the thing, but Eastern Intellect has long since outgrown images and dogmatics. It scoffs at the superstitions of Buddhism and Taoism, shall it have faith in new mechanical means of sanctification?

When contemplating the history of these ancient religions, we learn how dogmas and church-rites, acting on the physical senses and bare imagination, are deadening to the moral senses and fatal to genuine Faith, and how they have failed, by inforcing church-polity and mechanical means of salvation, to establish the Religion of the Soul.

When, on the other hand, we think of the many elaborate creeds and formularies which the different Christian denominations hold out to the non-Christian Eastern Nations, can we hope to impose all or any of them on their mature Intellect? *

---

* Rev. ALEXANDER WILLIAMSON, D.D. LL.D., at the Chefoo Association, on 3rd September 1888, read a paper on "*Missionary Organization in China,*" containing a most zealous appeal to unity in spirit in the Christian Mission-

The crust of ancient philosophy,—hardened by ages of materialistic teachings,—has sealed the well of the Moral Senses with the rationalism of pure Intellect, and this can only be pierced by the steel of scientific logic. Science is the only power that can wrestle with the refractory intellect of these one-sided Mental-Organisms. Here we must arrive at the heart through the mind. Sympathy must be roused through Intellect, to arrive at the conviction of Faith.

Prove to them that physical science is but the interpretation of Nature as God's work; that Christianity is explained through the revelations of Nature. Show them Christ through this sound intellectual culture, and their Faith based on conviction shall soar far above Eastern philosophy and Western dogmatism.

Teach them the natural religion of Christ,—which is the only conclusion human common-sense will arrive at, when carefully studying the Moral-Mental evolution-process on Earth,—and their souls shall work with their minds. The Mind, being thus morally as well as intellectually developed, shall then conceive, through the developed Moral Senses, the conviction of the Christian Faith.

---

work in China. The Rev. gentleman, in this elaborate lecture,—in which intellect and feeling were combined to impress on mind and soul,—urged on his brother-missionaries to lay aside the varied creeds and formularies of the different Christian denominations, working in the mission-field in China, in order to arrive at the one object of the entire missionary body, namely:—"the enlightenment of the nation; the strengthening of the nation; the elevation of the nation into the clear atmosphere of Divine truth and a purer civilization;"—in one word,—the well-being and highest interest of China. "In this case,"—says the Reverend Doctor,—"we must first of all win the respect and goodwill of the people, command the assent of their intellect, and secure the affection of their hearts. We must instil our faith, allow it time to work its own way, nourish and guide it as well as we can, and wait patiently the development of the new character and the renewal of the body co-operate which it will ultimately effect." (From "*The Chinese Recorder*" of January 1889.

CONCLUSION.

In the foregoing pages we have tried to explain that the norm of civilization, as based on human nature, is constituted by the intuition of the moral senses, Conscience and Sympathy. This is disclosed through the study of the development and activities of the human mind, which we called the *evolution of the moral-mental organism* (§5). The phenomena of consciousness of the mind, apart from any direct conception brought on from without, we called Intuition (§10), and found this connected with the development of the moral-mental organism. The existence of Conscience and Sympathy, which we designated as the moral senses (§15) of the developed moral-mental organism, needs no demonstration. Common consciousness corroborates these facts; every sound mind is fully cognizant of justice and benevolence, as experiences which are involved in the very exercise of his natural faculties.

On above stated facts is based the *theory of the moral senses*, as expounded in the present study.

The object of this theory is the convergency into one focus of the physical, the intellectual and the moral activities of the moral-mental organism, in order to organize a system by which the divergencies of human sentiency can be gauged with relation to the social organism (as shown with some ethical problems on page 235 *et seq.*).

It is a self-evident truth that not only men of different races, but also different men of the same race and even the same men at different periods of life, have different conceptions of the principles on which their standard of happiness is based; hence the common notion of the relativity of happiness. This is the natural consequence of the divergency of sentiency in different stages of civilization and correlative mental condition. But as we have seen, from the study of mental evolution, there is a physical, a physiological,—*i.e.* instinctive and intellectual,—and a moral sentiency in the developed moral-mental organism. Also that there is a natural relationship between these different classes of human sentiency, for the higher emotion can completely neutralize the lower feeling. Thus physical pleasure or pain can be subdued by instinctive emotions, while intellect is subordinate to the moral senses:—the moral exigencies of Conscience and Sympathy overrule all.

The "dictates of absolute equity,"—of which Mr. Herbert Spencer speaks in his *Data of Ethics**,—are not thinkable without the idea of the subjugation of physical or intellectual selfishness, by the intuition of the moral senses.

From the foregoing theses is conclusive that the moral senses,—as described in this work,—are the moral factors of social evolution.

The Christian Faith, we have seen, is the outcome of the moral senses as the manifestation of the Moral Element in Nature (§§32 and 40). And so is the Spirit of Law (§33) which in political sphere is the sociological exponent of the Common Sense of Society, as formed by intellect and feeling combined (§34).

Thus the theory of the Moral Senses shows the natural causes of man's social changes, while Sociology tries to find the purpose of these changes with the object of judicious organization of society. This is done through the Spirit of Law, which, as the social moral sense, is the *moral momentum* of the mass of individual minds composing the society, when this is stimulated by the prominent great minds of the society, as noted before.

Bringing now into condensed form what is expounded in this study with regard to the evolution of the social organism, we find that Civilization is dependent on three factors of social

---

* §107. "The Scope of Ethics."

activity. These are the three characteristic faculties of the human race; when equally developed they constitute civilization, viz: (1) Man's Intellectual Faculties, *i.e.* his subjective conception of physical truths (§30), which form the basis of Science, Art, Industry, Trade,—in one word, the general intellectual activities in social existence; (2) the activities of the Moral Senses, which constitute the consciousness of moral truths forming the basis of Law *(jus)* (§§33 and 40), and (3) the Spirit of Law, which,—being, as the Common Sense of the Social Organism, the result of *reason* and *feeling* combined, partakes of both the other factors of social development (§§33 and 34).

The Spirit of Law, forming the practical activities of the morally as well as the materially developed social organism, regulates the laws of the society. Society being an aggregate of human beings, the social organism naturally evolves analogically with the biological organism.

Social organism and biological organism are thus interdependent. In this study evolution is asserted in all branches of Creation, in Moral as well as Physical Nature. Evolution is the universal law of Creation,—*i.e.* as Mr. Herbert Spencer says: Everywhere there is expansion and concentration: advances from the homogeneous to the heterogenous, *from the less to the more determined*. This is like in the evolution of the individual; while, on the other hand, there is a process of differentiation of simplicity to complexity, for the preservation and expansion of the individual, which can as well be applied to the evolution of society.

The motor of evolution in the development of the moral-mental organism of man, and thus equally in the development of social organism, is called the Moral Element in Nature as described in this study (§§32 and 39). This motor of evolution is the agency in forming great men, or rather, *great minds*, as well as the generation in which these great minds leave their impressions.

With regard to the influence of individual great minds in history, the same philosopher says :—" Before the great man can remake his society, his **society must make** him, so that all these changes of which he is the proximate initiator, have their chief causes in the generations he descends from.". But what developed the "generation" itself? Mr. Spencer's sentence continued we get the answer :—" If there is to be anything like a real explanation of these changes, it must be sought in these aggregates of conditions of which both he and they have arisen." Now these aggregates of conditions form collectively a motor of evolution, a power in the mental evolution-process of man which is called in this study the Moral Element of Nature. This force is manifested in the evolution of the moral-mental organism and its varieties. The varieties of the moral-mental evolution on Earth are called *prominent minds*. They are signs of the age and exponents of the Spirit of Law. They are the indicators that changes are being produced in the Spirit of Law of the Society, whether as advance or as retrogression of the Moral Senses in the struggle of these senses against the animal propensities of man.

Beneficial "variations" in the moral-mental evolution, from a sociological aspect, are those prominent minds which indicate an advancing Spirit of Law. These are naturally called *great minds*.

The great minds influence the mass of society and stamp their characteristics on the age, while instigating thinking minds, of their own and many subsequent generations, to further mental and moral development of society toward civilization in its broadest definition, viz : that of transforming the subjective conception of the Good into objective practical Good (§§29 and 41).

The Theory of the Moral Senses in History and Statesmanship. The Theory of the Moral Senses has relation to the events brought on by human actions through the moral instinct of the human mind in all spheres of life. It thus compasses the simplest moral action of the individual, while the greatest historical events of human accomplishment are tested by it. Wherever individual actions are the constructive features of events, it shows how History is formed by the fluctuating development or degeneration of the Moral Senses of the human mind, while the so-called historical characters are the "variations" of the upward or downward growth of the human species; it shows that the great events of History are the results of these Variations. It shows how the development of the moral-mental organism has so characteristically marked the epochs of history in conformity with the stages of this development, that everything that followed on an epoch seems to be of different nature than what went before. The difference thus generated gave rise to the division of History into *ancient*, *mediæval* and *modern*. Through the theory of the moral senses History is represented in its individuality as well as in its social aspects, for it proves the moral responsibility of human *free will*.

Solon and Lycurgus, and so many philosophical law-givers after them, have been aiming at the construction of a standard code of political laws, not on the natural growth of the social organism, but as things ought to be according to some abstract notions of a state of their own imagination. On the other hand, our present *laisser-faire*, easy-going modern statesmanship, instinctively feeling that there is a power in the process of social evolution, which does not follow an artificial legislation,—and caught by the current of reaction which set in after the ages of absolute despotism, in church and state,—gave up all observation and study of real sociological facts. From magic and witchcraft and miracles of the Church developed Rationalism. All attempts to become thoroughly acquainted with the cause and working of the social evolution,—as based on the moral physiology of the individuals composing the society,—is abandoned by modern statesmanship. Modern Statesmen, falling into the same mistake as the philosophical statesmanship of the ancient, in creating ideal social laws without sound natural basis, declare *laisser-faire* the law of Society,—probably as being the most convenient system for the present generation of leading minds. But this is the ostrich-policy of hiding the head to ignore inevitable facts. Not being able to conjure the development of popular liberty through the absolute power of direct imperative authority, they gave up all hope of leading the source from which sprung the powerful motives of social conditions, and left *laisser-faire* lord of the social conditions. It is as absurd to frame ideal politics which have not their basis in the condition of development of the human mind as to formulate any conclusion in physical science without empirical investigation into the laws of the experiment. The rule to arrive at what *ought to be* is to take due notice of what *actually is*, testing this at the Moral Senses,—*i.e.*, at the exponent of what men, in social life, naturally do and think and feel, as the result of motives which arise out of the universal instinct of the human race.

Justice and Benevolence in practical life is Truth and Love combined.

Moral actions of the Government of the State are to be gauged by the standard of the Good (§19). Morality is known in the State where virtue and goodness are kept in countenance by the Government. Where modest worth is encouraged, the advocate of truth respected and the counselor of peace listened to, for the reconciliation of the hearts of men, and especially of good men, there Civilization is recognized in the outward actions of the State.

In this Study we have examined the laws of the social and biological evolution of the human race, with the view to arrive at a standard of principal data with which the requirements of any social condition can be gauged and tested. With this we may also be able to draw comparisons between the histories of Nations, for the discrimination between the causes of human happiness and misery on Earth.

In drawing a parallel between Eastern, the oldest, and Western, the modern form of human thoughts, we mean, by

Eastern, the North-African, the Asiatic and other non-Christian nations, and by Western, the Christian nations of Europe, and America, and their Colonies. As to Central Africa, there the **ovum** of civilization has scarcely entered the very first stage of incubation; there exists as yet no body of civilization to apply any measure of comparison on.

The Eastern and Western Civilization, as thus understood,—are the two main courses which the evolution-process of the moral-mental organism has taken on Earth, forming the two great branches of civilization, viz: the non-Christian and the Christian.

The glaring contrast between the Western Civilization in its unrelenting activity and the stagnation in development of the social organisms of Eastern Nations is a matter of intense interest to science, and the doctrine of the universality of the Christian standard of civilization is greatly enhanced when instituting a comparison between Eastern and Western progress.

The relation in which the Western Civilization stands to the Eastern is that of a new generation to the old exhausted parent-stock; civilization having travelled from East to West.

The difference in Eastern and Western mental progress is conspicuous in the development of their respective philosophies. This difference is felt through the whole range of thoughts.

Philosophy has, as such, no other basis than natural science, with other words, its starting point must be the "law" of nature. The philosophy which does not answer to this condition, although it might be singularly beautiful and apparently logical, is simply a product of imagination, with no depth or root. Its conclusion cannot be reliable as it has no beginning and no foundation of its own. Hence no system of philosophy can be based on religion, although the outcome may finally merge into religion (§26).

Since the Greek philosophy—which from its origin kept itself essentially distinct from Greek mythology—began to flourish, Western philosophy was kept free and independent of dogmatics and followed the rules of Intellect alone. Thus it gradually developed with the human mind, partaking in the evolution of the moral-mental organism, and forecasting the mental development; so that, when the Moral Senses were proved distinctively to consist of Sympathy as well as Conscience,—and *Feeling* took its share in the construction of human thought,—the logic of Western Philosophy had already become Common Sense, *i. e.* **Feeling** and Intellect combined (§34). The Asiatic or Eastern philosophies, on the other **hand, did not assume form and body** except on the basis of Religion. **They never severed** themselves from their religions, **and had thus no** power for the free development of the minds of Eastern Nations. The Hindu-Brahminism and the Asiatic Buddhism are systems of philosophy based on **systems** of theology and have to stand or fall with these religions.

Hence the difference in mental development between the **Eastern and** Western **nations.**

As in philosophy, the teacher of the mind, we find **the** same disparity, with regard to the records of History, in Eastern **and Western** literature. History in Western civilization **is** always philosophical, **as** not being only true records of the "*what*" but, **at the same time,** a thorough exposition **of the** "*how*" and "*why*" **of the** changes in events, indicating thus the different stages of social evolution with the corresponding Spirit of Law. We have in **it, as it** were, the spontaneous utterance of human life, from generation to generation, in conformity as the **ever** recurring changes in the activities of social life **represent** themselves to reason and **feeling, combined, in the** ever developing human mind.

In **the Eastern** literature, **on the** other hand, we find **History in its** lowest form, never going closely or deeply **enough to admit of** philosophical speculations. It does not **elevate itself above** the simplest narrative of **the** minutest events. Connecting no principles and relative to no cause or effects, such history simply gives the expositions, from which the state of development of the human mind and the Spirit of Law of the generation are left to be concluded at option. There are no reasons given for the selection of facts, no manifest desire to get below the surface of the facts, to find some broader causes than mere individual volition in the determination of the causes of events. Of such absolute form of mind appear the historians among the Eastern Nations, in their "dry-as-dust" records without any political speculations, giving evidence of minds not sufficiently developed to trace and handle the principles which underlie human affairs.

The dependence of enormous populations on a central autocratic and sometimes despotic government, the concentration of populations in vast cities, the existence of a large influential literary class, with its characteristics of book-erudition and hair-splitting critical genius, can fairly account for the antiquity and authenticity of Eastern historical records, in all matters regarding royal genealogies, registration of military expeditions and treaties, lists of tributes and other chronicles of bare facts; but, on the other hand, the absence of civil and political life and the utter want of independence of judgment, which are the unavoidable consequences of such forms of social organisms and their governments, are conditions from which no philosophical treatment of history can be expected to originate. This makes the history of these ancient Nations,—however trustworthy in details,—unqualified to rise above the lower stages of mere historical records and to be of much practical use to the modern philosophy of civilization.

The history of the Hebrew Nation, however, stands apart, being, in all respects, superior to any of the Asiatic people of that period; their national and religious exclusiveness, as compared with other ancient people, and the pronounced religious character of "the chosen people,"—which the Jewish historians chiefly aimed to exhibit,—make their Scripture history of a form that cannot be compared with histories of other nations. In whatever light the facts of the Hebrew history might be contemplated, it cannot be denied that the deep philosophical sense with which it is permeated, bears lucid evidences of the developing moral-mental organism of mankind, as preparing the way for that most prominent "variation" of this human organism, which the Earth beheld in the advent of Christ (§80, pages 213 et seq.) We cannot help contemplating as something more than mere history the records of a vast scheme of mental-evolution, which culminated into the Christian Faith.

The comparison between Eastern and Western civilization brings us to the contemplation of Political party-activities. These partake, naturally, of the respective idiosyncrasies we have seen exhibited in philosophy and history. Where history is void of speculation there can scarcely exist any political disquisition.

Despotism and anarchy, as said before (§57), are the two extreme poles of an organized society. Between these two deadpoints of society,—the extreme of social authority and the extreme of individual independence,—lie all political speculations. Where extreme social authority predominates, there the man as an individual does not exist; he is merged in the community, which is the only unit,—whether this community be represented by a single man,—as in the absolute autocratic government,—or by the tyranny of municipal laws that leave no individual freedom of action in politics, and lead to the ideal State of the Communist. In both extremes there exists unmitigated despotism; at this point *les extrèmes se touchent.* On the other hand, where anarchy prevails, there the social faculties are dislocated and the social organism is in decomposition.

These two principles of social existence, viz: the principle of *authority* and the principle of *liberty*,—*i. e.* Order and Freedom,—form combined the political discipline of the normal social organism. Order and Freedom are thus as indispensable to civilized human society as Conscience, the sense of strict justice, and Sympathy, the sense of liberal humanity, which form, combined, the morally developed human minds that constitute the civilized Christian state.

These two political principles exist in the civilized individual minds composing the society, but not in the same degree or **in** perfect harmony in every individual **mind.** In some the principle of social authority is the predominant one, while others are chiefly inclined to the principle of individual independence; hence arise the two main political parties in the State, viz: the so-called conservative, and the liberal party. Each party exists fairly on a principle of truth, but not of the whole truth, upholding only a part of the true **principles on** which society is maintainable,—being only *one* of the two elements of social life while, for the proper iquilibrium of the state, *both* are indispensable. Thus, if the **one** succeeds in excluding the other, the state is necessarily driven to despotism or to anarchy, which means that, in either case, society will come to a state of dissolution. Thus it is that partly by counteracting each other and partly by co-operating with each other the stability of the State can be secured.

On these two main stems of political life **are** grafted the many minor branches of sociological, **economical** and politico-religious digressions.

The Moral Element in **Nature is** *the Motor of Civilization.* History records the material struggle for existence of the human **race in** different forms. On the one hand we find striking attempts of man to raise himself above the position of the animal appetites of the "Hobbesian war of each against all;" on the other, frightful failures in this struggle. And yet, from the first dawn of history it is proved that man had intuitive conception **of** a higher destiny than the wolf, the hyena or the mammoth among which he lived. As to prehistoric man, the imperfect relics of rock-records give no evidence whatever to base any conclusion on, with regard to the origin of the link between man and brute. As stated before (§80, p. 194), the link is entirely missing; there is a gulf not yet bridged over by science or history. The ethical germ implanted in this particular species of Nature is manifested, as *fact*, through his continuous struggle to attain to better material and intellectual development, not only, but **to arrive also at higher moral attainments**, in **higher conditions** of thought and conduct. **This ethical germ is slowly** yet surely developing **into the higher type to which** the human species **alone is destined to arrive**. This ethical germ, whose **existence is thus proved**, is the manifestation of the human Soul, a particle of the Spirit of Creation (§2), discernable **in all** pursuits of man, as the preordained principle of development. It is the level of the Motor of Evolution (§39) of the individual moral-mental **organism and** of the social organism.

In the most exalted moral strife like in the plainest pursuits of human conduct, in industry, in art and science, this **ethical level is** perceptible. If naturalists would only join hands **with** moralists, the investigation of the course of evolution in the moral-mental sphere would **become a** practical science. If eminent naturalists would only lay aside, for a moment, their jocular-flippant way of explaining the origin and growth of the human species, and, **when** free from these fashionable modern free-thinker's affectations, if they would also cast off the prejudices of atheism, science would wring from Nature convincing revelations with regard to the Moral Element,—the undeniable power we plainly conceive is underlying human actions. And by diligently recording the peculiar ethical habits of the species called man, with the care naturalists usually bestow on the observation of the instinctive habits **of plants and** insects, they **would** find the human soul more clearly demonstrated in the human instinct than any tendency in the cross-breeding of pigeons, the habits of dogs or variations in orchids, to which minute observations such giant patience and perseverance are applied by eminent naturalists, for the immortalization of their own name.

If Naturalists would give but a tenth part of this patience to the careful observation of the development of the *soul* in the infant, during the first decade of its life, they would learn the origin of the Moral Senses from the unsophisticated *truth*, unselfishness and sympathy, so naturally and spontaneously elicited by the innocent child.

The Moral Element, by manifesting itself in all human actions, indicates the way to solve the social questions, with regard to the struggle for existence between the moral and material nature of man.

Let us take, for instance, the material condition of Great Britain at a certain time. In 1881 the population of Great Britain was 35,241,482, exceeding the number in 1871 by 3,396,103, giving an average increase yearly of 339,610 souls.* This frightful increase of claimants to the world's granaries seems appalling and it looks like the coming of Malthus' merciless prophecy. And yet, has any wholesale starvation brought down to its so-called economical level the population of this country,—of which it is moreover asserted that the produce of the soil falls short by nearly one half of the real quantum-sufficit—?—No, notwithstanding its fierce struggle for existence, this population has gone on steadily progressing, under the greatest Malthusian disadvantage, viz: that of some seventy years peace, without pestilence or even an epidemic worth speaking of to lighten the burden of this struggle a while. No catastrophe has befallen this ever-energetic race. "Shopkeepers" or not, their unflagging industry and energy have kept this people ever in the vanguard of material progress and

---

* I take the figures from Professor Huxley's article "The Struggle for Existence," quoted on page 223.

moral civilization. Compare now this Nation with any other in the world, which had all the material help for the keeping down of the population to the economical level,—in the shape of famine through bad government, pestilence and war,—and we will have not to strain our imagination to conclude, that the living proof of the fallacy of the Malthusian doctrine is the British Nation.

And how came this to be?

In the first place, through the condition of internal and external peace, which is the main object of social organization; secondly, free scope for fair competition, hand in hand with security in the enjoyment of all the fruits of honest industry; thirdly, in the measures to mitigate, as much as possible, the burden of internecine material struggle for existence, through the application of State-actions, based on intellect and moral principles combined, as described above (§§76-79),—*i. e.* by improving the productive power of the labouring class, through technical education, and maintaining the social stability by labour-legislation.

When the labouring-class is convinced that the laws are made with strict observance of Justice and Benevolence, they will not incur the perils of the consequences of anarchy, by revolting and upsetting their only guarantee to progress, which consists of good legislation. Unavoidable bitter times of low wages, stagnation in trade and other unforeseen calamities, will be borne patiently by the majority,—if the Moral Senses keep their sway and confidence in the Laws keeps discipline. But when, with unavoidable material misery is joined the want of moral senses, and the lower appetites get free scope, then the animal struggle for material existence of the brutish type sets in. Starvation, disease, physical pains and moral degradation all combine to sink the standard of civilization to its lowest stage.

Such a society is sick, dangerously ill, but it is not necessarily a hopeless case; it depends solely upon the way of treatment of the complaint to effect a radical cure, or to render the disease a chronic one by applying the dangerous opiates of the demagogue,—*i. e.* by flattering the masses with vain promises of reconstructing the social organism. The radical cure is the moral and intellectual treatment, not the anarchical.

"Intelligence, knowledge and skill,"—so truly says Professor Huxley, *—" are undoubtedly conditions of success; but of what avail are they likely to be unless they are backed up by honesty, energy, goodwill and all the physical and moral faculties that go to the making of manhood and unless they are stimulated by hope of such reward as men may fairly look to? Any full and permanent development of the productive power of an industrial population then, must be compatible with and indeed based upon a social organization which will secure a fair amount of physical and moral welfare to that population; which will make for good and not for evil."

This opinion of the great naturalist shows that on crucial social questions Science and Ethics go hand in hand. This is conspicuous with regard to Political Economy, where Ethics must necessarily coöperate to arrive at lasting results.

"Society,"—says Professor Huxley further,—" differs from Nature in having a definite moral object; whence it comes about that the course shaped by the ethical man,—the member of society or citizen,—necessarily runs counter to that which the non-ethical man,—the primitive savage, or man as a mere member of the animal kingdom,—tends to adopt. The latter fights out the struggle for existence to the bitter end, like any other animal; the former devotes his best energies to the object of setting limits to the struggle." †

---

* After the divergences with Professor Huxley, which we ventured to set forth on pages 223 *et seq.*,—we are happy to be able to quote here, from the same article "The Struggle for Existence," passages which fully agree with the theory we have tried to propound in this essay.

† Prof. Huxley. "The Struggle for Existence," *Nineteenth Century*, February 1888, p. 165.

Thus,—as stated at the beginning of this section,—*the Moral Element in Nature is the Motor of Civilization*, for it is the ethical notion of men,—more and more consistent,—which must become the governing principle of society, in order that the ethical man might succeed in setting limits to the animal struggle for existence. This, the course of the social evolution-process indicates it should be. The history of civilization,—that is of Society,—is the record of the attempts which the human race has made to follow the Moral Element in Nature, as governing principle of society:—"for society not only has a moral end but, in its perfection, social life is embodied morality."* (Comp. §79).

Christianity is the Test of Civilization. The Ego of consciousness of the human mind, the centre of the moral senses and the will, is what we called the Soul,—manifesting the Moral Element in Nature (§§11 and 12). The loyalty of the human Soul to the Almighty Creator is firmly rooted and might be appealed to with confidence, even under circumstances apparently the most unfavourable. Enthusiastic and rapturous devotion abounds in every period of life in the minds endowed with Moral Senses; and this in the face of all the derision of old and modern wits and vulgar scepticism, who imagine they possess, through their limited physical senses and conditioned intellect, an open-sesamé into the secret apartments of the human moral-mental organism. There is the vulgar sceptic, who finds it easier to doubt than to examine his own inward consciousness, endeavouring to assume the credit of being an *esprit fort*,—in spite of his own moral senses, which invariably points to a Power beyond the limited scope of selfish comprehension.

The animal nature of man when not rigorously kept in check by the Moral Senses, will always secure success to the

---
* l. c. p. 166.

logic which supplies its **appetites**; the worm **bred** from decay must feed on decay.

Writers like David Friedrich Strausz, c. s. are communistic agitators against the property of Faith. They trust on the force of their **logic** as the communist on dynamite. Void of faith, as fostered by moral senses, they are in desperate conflict against the peace of mind of their neighbours, whose spiritual property they envy. Being incapable of acquiring these blessings for themselves,—like the fierce communist,—they try to pull down the stand to which they cannot elevate themselves.

Strausz in his atheistic "confession" on what he calls "The Old Faith and The New," represents Nature as an accidental self-developing and self-rectifying fatalistic infinite mass of worlds which he calls the ALL. "Infinite" but yet the "All." "The All being the All, nothing can exist outside of it; it seems even to exclude the idea of a void beyond." "In the investigation regarding our relations to religion we finally arrived at the idea of the cosmos." *

Strausz must have got his "All" from the Buddhist view of the universe. "Buddhism," says Doctor Eitel, "knows no creative prime agent, no supramundane or ante-mundane principle, no pre-existing spirit, no primitive matter. But Buddhism does not say that our world is without beginning or without end. For the universe, in which we live, is but one of an endless number of world systems. Every one of these innumerable co-existing worlds has individually a beginning and comes to an end, but only to be reconstructed again, in order to be destroyed again in endless succession. What is eternal therefore and absolutely without beginning is not any individual world or any universe, but the mere law of evolution, the mere idea of constant rotation through formation, destruction and reconstruction, or rather the polar force of evolution

---

* "*The Old Faith and The New.*" Edit. 1874. Vol. I, pages 169 and 171.

and involution. To the question, how the very first universe was **originally** brought into existence, and whence that eternal law of ceaseless reproduction came, Buddhism honestly confesses **to have no** reply. When this very query was put before Buddha, he remained silent, and after some pressure explained, that none but a Buddha might comprehend this problem, that the solution of it was absolutely **beyond the understanding of** the finite mind." *

This would have probably also been the manner in which **Strausz** would have answered if this question had been put to him, with regard to his positive "All," comprehending *all* and yet being infinite. All working **subjectively** but without purpose cause or effect and yet by the process **of** evolution. And out of this aimless universal-absolute anarchy he contrives to evolve,—without the least scientific basis to build on,—man, in its highest civilized state with a most decided teleological tendency to patriotic national particularization, to combat socialism by the theory of natural anarchy, to uphold capital punishment, to worship military glory in **the power to be, in** the **adoration of** social order and discipline, the mainstay **of** which he **has** just been blowing up by his anarchical annihilation of God and religion. Rejecting Feeling, he yet appeals to the Aesthetic faculty **of the** mind,—calling up the ghosts of Lessing, Goethe and Shiller, **of** Mozart, **Bach and** Gluck; Handel's oratorios and **Haydn's** "Creation," to allure, **with** Sirenian songs, the Religious Faith of his countrymen to the destructive cliffs of an atheism of the most **merciless type.**

But this appeal to the Aesthetic nature of man **betrays** again the weakness of atheistic arguments. As we have seen before (§§39 and 79, page 183,) the influence of the Moral Element in Nature,—as indicated by the ennoblement of the mind,—can be traced in art, poetry, music, literature, in fact

---

* "*Buddhism: its Historical, Theoretical and Popular Aspects.*" Hongkong 1884, page 64.

in all concerns of life in which the mind has actually a share, and which are moulded by the inspiration of the Good; the aesthetic quality of man is the mental faculty to conceive the *good* and the *beautiful* combined, and to reproduce the subjective conception thereof into objective products of the *Arts*,—in plaster or paint, in poetry or music. The power which the fine arts, poetry and music exhibit, in the impulses given to the development of culture is due to the Moral Senses. But should poetry and music instruct and elevate intellect and heart, then there must be a shifting and choosing among the mass of works of poets and composers, and what could guide judgment and taste in this discrimination but the Moral Senses?

And mark, these form the basis of the Christian Faith!

The egoism and conceit of the atheist cannot conceive prayer except as the result of a wish, and as a request to the Almighty, for wordly boon. The origin of religion is not, as Strausz conceived it, merely the outcome of wish or desire in the human mind,—or, in other words, the speculative formality of egoism,—for the man who possesses real Christian Faith, as depicted in these pages, has the least to desire and it is yet he who feels his soul the most readily attracted to communion with his Creator through prayer. Herein lies the misconception of atheism. That desire is not the origin of religion neither the basis of prayer, Strausz could not comprehend. His book ("The Old Faith and The New") he said was a "confession and not an historical dissertation; it had no concern, therefore, with the question as to what had been the effects of Christianity on mankind, (that is as motor of civilization)—whatever its effects have been and these, at any rate, will continue to exist—but only with the question whether persons holding certain opinions could still continue members of its church?"*
His work, which is neither scientific, philosophical, or historical,

---
* "The Old Faith and The New." Edit. 1874. Postscript p. 257.

is thus merely the subjective utterance of an intractable theologian, who, disgusted with the dogmatics of his church is building up a worshipful object of his own creation.

Desire is not the origin of prayer; it is the consciousness of our utter dependency on the Creator which makes the Soul cling to its fountain-head, and prayer is the means of strengthening its vital element which is the source of the Moral Senses. Where prayer is neglected there the moral senses are deprived of their natural stimulant and the mind misses the discipline necessary for its moral development.

Materialistic scientists and atheistic philosophers generally pride themselves on rigidly abstaining from all logomachy, or the treatment of any subject for mere exercitation. Minute accuracy of observation based on purely intellectual distinctions form the dignity of their logic; no persuasion by appealing to any such means as feeling, sympathy or intuition; their common sense is rigorously defined within these purely empiric limits.

How painfully it must then effect the *bonâ fide* intellect to find sometimes the foremost among its apostles stooping to claim alliance,—not from the unknown and scientifically undemonstrated moral element, Oh no!—but from base common-place *jeux de mots*, the charlatanism of the vendor of quack-medicines, labelled with big words to dazzle the prigs. Humour is certainly a most desirable quality in the literary man whose calling it is to amuse as well as to instruct his fellow-creatures. Like genius itself,—which, by the way, has a humour of its own, but quite distinct from joking,—it sharpens the intellect. The drawback however is that the humorist, whether he be a lecturing professor of biology, or a Mark Twain in profession, is necessarily always bound to amuse his readers,—and more particularly his hearers, for the humorist's favourite pose is the platform;—the consequence is obvious that the humorist is apt to draw largely on his imagination in his flippant humorous style, for a man cannot always talk sober common sense when he is bound to amuse his "appreciating audience."

I have always cherished profound respect for the positive scientist, that unchallenged and incorruptible expositor of evidences at the bar of Nature;—rightly spurning the siren allurements of fine rhetorics, as superfluous to demonstrate truth, he persistently avoids every tincture of that polemic bias, which is the characteristic of the newspaper controversial style,—his style being as free from all artificial means of persuasion as the sober facts of Nature from any needless colouring to court acceptance from the unbiased mind. Trembling we often come to him, for the final verdict between our intellect and our feeling. With him we might expect that the single-minded normal human intellect would be able to understand the interpretations of the Great Book of Revelation, without having to swallow the unpalatable dust of scholastic fabrication, preparatory to artificial intellect. Here we could shake off all prejudices fostered by imagination. But Alas! How often, when we expected simple language with genuine common sense, we met but with an appeal to our aesthetic appreciation of rhetoric sport. With sore disappointment and disgust we find then that the judge, while spurning the wig of scholastic pedantry, has donned the jester's cap.

Pure Nature shrinks with shame when her sublime nakedness is being awkwardly abused by apologetic coverings of purple rags; but what must be her indignation when she finds her impeccable harmonious forms carelessly discussed, with sportive jokes, by humorous scientists, for the amusement of a public that adores such style? Unworthy apostles, abusing her secrets for their own glorification, are polluting the waters of the fountain-head of knowledge, whence her faithful children, nursed with her own genuine common sense, must imbibe the divinity of her origin. But Nature will ever avenge herself;—when courted from mere selfish motives, she hardens into barren intellect, but when sought for holy love, her **gifts are the fertile blossoms of Conscience and Sympathy.**

Drawing to a close, we briefly sum up **our conclusions.**

The great principle which has guided us throughout this study, is the principle of continuity in **the Evolution-Process of** Nature. We have seen the product of evolution to be the Moral-Mental Organism of Man, the **highest stage of creation** at present on Earth. From the nebular beginning, through all stages of creation, we have seen manifested the persistent Cosmic Energy, with its various transformations of force, which we called the Motor of Evolution in physical development, the Moral Element in the development of the moral-mental organism, and the Spirit of Creation in all. We have seen that the necessary goal of evolution in the moral-mental development is the proof of the advent of Christ, and that the Moral Element in Nature,—manifested by this development of the moral-mental organisms, indued with the moral senses Conscience and Sympathy,—is the living **principle of Christianity.** As such Christianity is the natural test of Civilization. The achievements of human thoughts, called civilization,—depicted in these pages, in rough but I trust clear outlines,—lead to this conclusion.

Whatever may befall the theories put forward in this philosophy,—if all be swept away or **utterly demolished by criticism,**—one fact cannot be suppressed: it is the **living consciousness of Justice and Benevolence.** Our Moral Senses no one can deny, and whatever critics may choose to do with the arguments of this Philosophy of Civilization, it is beyond human power to smother Conscience and Sympathy. Both, ever-active monitors of duty, will search out the religion that fosters the Moral Senses of the morally developed human mind, and will find, in the annihilation of selfishness, the Christian Faith which **leads through** Christ to God.

THE PHILOSOPHY OF CIVILIZATION,
A Sociological Study.

TABLE OF CONTENTS.

Introduction - - - - *Pages* i–xx.

CHAPTER I.
The Moral Law of Nature.

		Pages
§1.	The Universal Law of Nature. - - -	1
§2.	The Spirit of Creation.—Its agency the motor of evolution.—Is the manifestation of the soul - - - - - - - -	2
§3.	Hypotheses in general - - - -	3
§4.	Hypothetical demonstration of the Universal Law of Nature, in its course of Evolution. The Stages of Creation on Earth. The Physico-Mental Organism - - -	6
§5.	The Moral-Mental Organism of Man.—Consciousness of the Good.—The struggle for existence between the moral and the material element in the human mental organism - - - - - -	8
§6.	Origin of Species - - - - -	10
§7.	The Links of Evolution - - - -	10
§8.	The impossibility of demonstrating the primary motor of evolution - - -	11

		Pages
§ 9.	Intellect	13
§10.	Hypothesis regarding Intuition.—Feeling. Spiritual Feeling. Inspiration	13
§11.	The Soul	14
§12.	The Ego of Consciousness	15
§13.	The Conception of Primary Truths	16
§14.	The Good	17
§15.	The Moral Senses, Conscience and Sympathy. Righteousness	18
§16.	Evolution of the Moral Senses	19
§17.	Virtue. Happiness	20
§18.	Moral Actions. Free Will. Volition. Motive	21
§19.	The Standard of the Good	26
§20.	Origin of Evil and its control	27
§21.	Imagination. Love. Friendship	28
§22.	Imagination. Vice	29
§23.	Attention on the Good controls Evil in the Mind. *There exists no happiness outside the Good*	29
§24.	Religion the Moral discipline	30
§25.	Moral Doubt	31
§26.	Christianity	31
§27.	The Creator	34
§28.	The Occasions of stumbling. *The two sorts of Evil*	34

CHAPTER II.

The Institutes of Law.

§29.	The human mind. Development of Law (*Jus, Droit, Recht.*)	36
§30.	Moral Truths and Physical Truths	37
§31.	Conscience.—The Law of Conscience	40

		Pages
§32.	The Moral Law of Nature manifested in History, is the origin of International Law. Grotius	43
§33.	The Popular Consciousness, the concentrated *sensorium* of the social organism, is called *Spirit of Law*, "*Spirit of the Age*," (*Zeitgeist*). The Ego of the social organism. The National Spirit of Law. State-Education. Public opinion. Public Press	47
§34.	*Common Sense*	50
§35.	The Scholastic Philosophy and Positivism	51
§36.	The International Spirit of Law	52
§37.	International Law is the manifestation of the influence of the Moral Element in Nature, in Civilization	53
§38.	The Philosophy of Law and the Historical School	54
§39.	The Moral Element in Nature is the Motor of Civilization, *i. e.* of Material as well as Moral progress. The Aesthetic. *Moral progress comes through the individual to the Race*	57
§40.	The subjective and the objective form of Law. (*Jus, Droit, Recht.*)	59

CHAPTER III.

The Data of Civilization.

I.—*What is Civilization?*

§41.	Definition of Civilization	63
§42.	The Standard of Civilization. The *Theory of the Moral Senses*	65

II.—The Social Organism. States.

		Pages
§43.	The social nature of man is the origin of States	67
§44.	*Natural* and *Political Nationality*	68
§45.	Conditions for the political individuality of States as persons of International Law.	68
§46.	Law governing States in their outward relations. *International Law*	70
§47.	States, as incorporate persons of International Law, have the same moral obligations as man, but modified by special prerogatives	70
§48.	The social organism is based on biological organism	71
§49.	The Physiology of the State	74
§50.	The physical and moral faculties of the State are corresponding with those of the human body	76
§51.	The *Natural-Constitutional form* of State-Organization is that of the Civilized State	78
§52.	The natural evolution of the social organism is opposed to Anarchy	79
§53.	*The Government of the Natural-Constitutional State*	80
§54.	The *People*. Forming the people into *good citizens*	82
§55.	The *Representatives of the People*. Qualifications	84
§56.	Public opinion *versus* the Representative Body	85
§57.	*Political Parties*. State-policy. Authority *versus* Liberty	86
§58.	The *Right of Veto*	87

		Pages
§59.	The necessity of an *hereditary head of the State* is the result of the Natural-Constitutional form of State	88
§60.	The *Constitution*	90
§61.	The two Branches of Legislation	91

III.—The co-existence of Social Organisms.
External Social Life. International Law.

		Pages
§62.	International Rights and Duties of States	92
§63.	International Morality	94
§64.	*International Jurisprudence*	96
§65.	The moral principles of International intercourse	102
§66.	Interdependence of States	105
§67.	Right of Negotiation and Treaty	107
§68.	Moral Causes of the imperfect observance of Treaties. The durability of International treaties is dependent upon the International Spirit of Law	108
§69.	Material Causes of the imperfect observance of Treaties	108
§70.	The *Laws of Peace*	115
§71.	Intermediate state between Peace and War. The Confirmation of International facts, with regard to truth, is a moral duty of Civilized Governments	117
§72.	The *Law of War (Jus belli)*	120
§73.	The principles of the Law of War considered in the light of Civilization. *Effect of war on private individuals and private property. Enemy Character. Enemy's private property on the high seas*	122

		Pages.
§74.	Means of peaceable settlement of International Disputes. *Application of the Laws of Peace*	129
§75.	Measures *via amicabili* and *via facta*	131

IV.—Internal Social Life. Co-existence of Individuals.

§76.	The natural agency of Internal Social Development	133
§77.	State-action is Justice combined with Benevolence	137
„	Controversy between Mr. Herbert Spencer and Mr. *de Laveleye*	137
„	*State or Scientific Socialism.*	141
§78.	Socialism *versus* Communism	142
„	Political Liberty	144
„	Equality	146
„	The Co-ordination of Labour and Capital	147
„	The Income-Tax. Legal Interest	149
„	Labour Legislation	149
„	Moral Measures. Material and Economical Measures	151
„	Poverty *versus* Political Economy. *Labour, Intellect and Capital, the three factors of material progress*	153
„	Co-operation	155
„	Free-trade *versus* Protection. International Competition	155
„	Laws	159
„	Public Law. National Jurisdiction	160
„	Law of Persons. Private Law. Civil Law. Private International Law. Law of Con-	

		Pages.
	tracts. Political Rights *(jus civitatis)*. Civil Rights *(jus civile)*	161
§78.	Jurisdiction of Criminal Law	163
,,	Exterritoriality and Concurrent Jurisdiction	165
,,	The Theory of Criminal Law	165
,,	*Capital Punishment*	166
,,	Codification. Codes of Criminal Law	169
,,	The Trial by Jury. The " *habeas corpus* "	173

V.—The Intellectual and Moral Activities of Individual Co-existence.

§79.	The *material element* of Civilization. Science. Industry. Trade	179
,,	Factory Labour	180
,,	The Fine Arts. Aesthetics	183
§80.	The *moral element* of Civilization. The Spirit of Creation. Scientific manifestation of the Creator's work	185
,,	Motor of Evolution	195
,,	Science versus Theism	196
,,	Design	200
,,	The Ultimate Cause. The Personal God	208
,,	Christ. The Goal of Evolution	213
,,	The Fall of Man and the Redemption through Christ	218
,,	The Divine Spirit. The Moral Element in Nature	222
,,	*Professor Huxley's* ethical thesis of the " non-moral " Nature	223
,,	Ethics, Absolute and Relative	229
,,	Hygienic Laws	232

TABLE OF CONTENTS.

		Pages.
§80.	The Standard of Ethics and the Spirit of Law	232
,,	Ethics counterbalancing evil through the Moral Senses	234
,,	The test of Good and Evil	234
,,	Egoism and Altruism. Ethical problems	235
,,	RELIGION	239
,,	Evolution of Religion	240
,,	The main branches of Eastern Riligion	244
,,	Mohammedanism	244
,,	Confucianism. *San Kiao*	246
,,	Taoism. Buddhism	246
,,	Shanti	248
,,	Ancestral Worship	250
,,	A Comparative view of Buddhism	251
,,	*Fundamental Principles of Buddhism and Christianity compared*	252
,,	Modern Buddhism and Theosophy	259
,,	*Spiritualism. Thought-transference*	260
,,	Hypnotism or mesmerism	261
,,	*Hypnotism in medical treatment*	263
,,	THE CHRISTIAN FAITH. Development of the Christian Religion. The Religious Faculty	265
,,	Christianity	268
,,	The Dogmatics	269
,,	Natural Theology	270
,,	The Christian Doctrine	272
,,	Man's place in Nature,—as indicated by the evolution-process on Earth,—asserts that the Christian duties of society form the test of Civilization	276

		Pages.
§80.	Agnosticism and Atheism	277
,,	The Imitation of Christ	279
,,	Faith in the Creator necessarily leads to Christ. The Abrahamic or Hanyfite faith. Piety and Faith. The Christian Faith expresses the relation between God and man	280

CHAPTER IV.
THE TEST OF CIVILIZATION.

§81.	MAN'S PLACE IN NATURE. The Moral-Mental Organism	284
§82.	Biological and Future State	286
§83.	Man's Duty toward Civilization. Measure of Ethical conduct. Virtue and Social Happiness in Civilization. Family Life. Industry. Property	288
§84.	Christianity the Natural Religion	297
,,	Christian Missions and Civilizing Agents	302

CONCLUSION.

The *Theory of the Moral Senses* applied to History and Statesmanship	310
The Moral Element the Motor of Civilization	320
Christianity is the Test of Civilization	325

ERRATA

WHICH MIGHT BE CORRECTED WITH THE PEN.

On page 14, line 10, from below, stands: *unknownable*, read: *unseen*.

„ „ 14, the footnote on this page belongs to page 15, as *first* footnote.

„ „ 15, line 19, from above, stand: *Thus the Soul is represented through Intuition by the Moral Element*, read: *Thus the Soul represents, through Intuition, the Moral Element*.

„ „ 22, on lines 2 and 7 from above, stands: *centers*, read: *centres*.

„ „ 41, line 10, from above, stands: *dispense*, read: *release*.

„ „ 43, „ 11 „ „ „ *Bentley*, read: *Berkeley*.

„ „ 44, „ 2 „ „ „ *particular*, read: *particularly*.

„ „ 55, line 10, from above, read: *development*.

„ „ 62, „ 18 „ „ stands: *Representive*, read: *Representative*.

„ „ 62, line 20, from above, stands: *Monarchial*, read: *Monarchical*.

„ „ 62, line 22, from above, stands: *Legislation*, read: *Legislature*.

„ „ 72, the footnote on this page belongs to page 71, as *second* footnote.

„ „ 74, line 3, from below, stands: *section*, read: *sections*.

„ „ 88 „ 12, „ below, „ *maitre*, read: *naitre*.

„ „ 89 „ 8, „ above, „ *li*, read: *il*.

„ „ 89, lines 8, 9 and 10 from above, read: *toujours*.

„ „ 100, in the first footnote stands: *Blemtschli*, read: *Bluntschli*.

ERRATA.

On page 101, in the first footnote **read**: se détent.
 ,,   ,,   114, line 17, from above, **read**: practical.
 ,,   ,,   116, in the footnote, **read**: les conflicts.
 ,,   ,,   116 ,,   ,,   ,,   **read**: Diplomatie.
 ,,   ,,   165, line 16, from above, **stands**: *their* immediate, **read**: *his* immediate.
 ,,   ,,   174, line 21, from above, **read**: administer justice.
 ,,   ,,   180, ,, 6, ,, below, **stands**: *industry*, **read**: *industries*.
 ,,   ,,   193, line 2, from below, **read**: homogeneous.
 ,,   ,,   194, ,, 10, ,, above, **read**: concomitants.
 ,,   ,,   194, ,, 19, ,, ,, **read**: congruity of the cosmos.
 ,,   ,,   197, on the last line, **stands**: *suborganic*, **read**: *superorganic*.
 ,,   ,,   208, line 3, from below, **read**: olfactory.
 ,,   ,,   211, ,, 12, ,, above, ,, dynamic.
 ,,   ,,   212, ,, 19, ,, ,, ,, æons.
 ,,   ,,   215, ,, 12, ,, below, ,, recording.
 ,,   ,,   216, ,, 7, ,, above, ,, marvellous.
 ,,   ,,   224, ,, 4, ,, below, ,, coffin.
 ,,   ,,   259, ,, 2, ,, above, **stands**: *monotheism*, **read**: *polytheism*.
 ,,   ,,   261, line 18, from above, **read**: psychomancy.
 ,,   ,,   272, ,, 7, ,, below, **read**: irrefragable.
 ,,   ,,   297, ,, 17, ,, above, **stands**: *Christianity the Test of Civilization*, **read**: **Christianity the** *Natural Religion*.

On page VII of the *Introductory Notes*, **line 16 from below, stands**:—"This law represents the conditions under which the intellectual and moral development of human beings exist in their relations," etc . . . . *Please read thus*:— This **law** *represents the conditions of the intellectual and moral development of human beings in their relations*, etc.

www.ingramcontent.com/pod-product-compliance
Lightning Source LLC
Chambersburg PA
CBHW032045220426
43664CB00008B/863